D1131350

TRAGEDY IN THREE VOICES

Tragedy in
Three Voices

The Rattenbury Murder

by

**The Rt Hon Sir Michael Havers, QC
Peter Shankland and Anthony Barrett**

WILLIAM KIMBER · LONDON

First published in 1980 by
WILLIAM KIMBER & CO. LIMITED
Godolphin House, 22a Queen Anne's Gate,
London, SW1H 9AE

ISBN 0 7183 0147 1

Typeset by Watford Typesetters Limited
and printed and bound in Great Britain by
The Garden City Press Limited,
Letchworth, Hertfordshire, SG6 1JS

Contents

List of Illustrations

Acknowledgements

We wish to thank Mrs Rattenbury's friends and family, particularly her two sons, Christopher Compton Pakenham and John Rattenbury, for kindly making their correspondence and their recollections available to us; also Mrs Daphne Kingham for important information, Simona Pakenham for recollections of her father, Mrs Katherine Bentley Beauman, H. R. H. Dolling and Judith Rattenbury. Mr Keith Miller Jones, though he was very ill at the time, talked to us about Alma Rattenbury. He has since died and we wish to express our sympathy to Mrs Betty Miller Jones who has been very kind and helpful. The late Mr Frank Rattenbury talked to us freely about his father.

Many others have given us their willing assistance which we greatly appreciate; Miss Alison Duke, Mrs Antonia Landstein, Mr Gerard Wyllis, Mr Ruston of H. G. Cummin Ltd, Mr Derek Mosedale, Miss Dorothy Riggs, Mrs Sanson, Mrs Edna Ritchie of Toronto, Mr Stephen Warren and Miss Helen Paterson of the Toronto Symphony Orchestra, Miss Poole of the National Portrait Gallery, Miss Mary Dennys, Principal of Havegal College, and Miss Joan O'Connor; C. H. D. Everett, MA, JP, Headmaster of Tonbridge School, Mr D. Browne, Director-General of the Commonwealth War Graves Commission, Major C. L. St. H. Pelham-Burn, Royal Military Academy, Sandhurst, Lt Colonel F. A. D. Betts, Coldstream Guards, Major E. L. Kirby, Royal Welch Fusiliers.

The librarians, as usual, have been unfailingly obliging – Miss Jaquelin Kavenagh, BBC Archives Centre, Mr T. C. Charman of the Imperial War Museum, Mr David Doughan, assistant at the Fawcett Library, Mr R. Gillespie of the Mitchell Library, Miss Bailey of the London Library, Miss Barbara Browne of the *New York Times*, Miss Judith Thomson, Department of Vital Statistics, Victoria BC, Miss Helen Bickel, Royal Conservatory of Music, University of Toronto, Miss Jennifer H. Heron, Archivist Assistant Government of Yukon, and the staffs of the British Library Newspaper Library, the Vancouver Public Library and the University of British Columbia Library.

We acknowledge with thanks permission from the following to quote from published sources: Mr J. D. Casswell, QC and Messrs George G. Harrap & Co. Ltd., Miss Simona Pakenham, Messrs William Hodge & Co. Ltd., the Hutchinson Publishing Group, Messrs Adam and Charles Black, Messrs Curtis Brown Ltd., Messrs Jarrolds Publishers (London) Ltd., Robson Books Ltd., EMI Music Publishing Ltd., Syndication International Ltd., News Group Newspapers Ltd., Associated Newspapers Group Ltd., and the editors of *The Times*, the *New York Times, Newsweek*, the *Bournemouth Evening Echo* and *Times Herald* Newspapers, Poole.

CHAPTER ONE

Murder

When Alma married the distinguished architect Francis Rattenbury, she appeared to be perfectly happy though she was looked upon by local society as an adventuress : he was fifty-seven and rich whereas she was in her thirties and poor. Envy no doubt inspired many of the unfavourable comments that were made about her at the time, for she had brilliant qualities and in any social gathering was likely to be the centre of attraction. Besides being a talented musician she was, by all accounts, a beautiful woman with a magnetic personality.

Of Rattenbury's feelings about her, his surviving letters leave no room for doubt : he believed there was no one like her, and that he was extremely fortunate. In spite of his worldly success and apparent popularity he had been a lonely and disappointed man whose first marriage had been a failure. Announcing his second marriage, to Alma in 1925, he told his sister : 'I have a wonderfully happy home – bright, joyous and full of fun all the time . . . [She is] a very interesting – most lovable – human soul. . .'. He goes on to say that he cannot imagine life without her, that everyone loves her, men and women, old and young, and all animals, birds and even insects – 'the butterflies eat out of her hands. . .'.

A year or two after their marriage, Rattenbury retired and they rented the Villa Madeira, a pleasant little 'bijou' residence in a pine-scented avenue in Bournemouth. Here they lived quite happily for several years with their small son John : Alma had a son by a previous marriage, Christopher, who was at boarding school not far away, near Christchurch, and came to them for his holidays. By 1935 they had settled down to an ordinary humdrum way of life. Rattenbury, with nothing to do but worry about the depreciation of his securities, tried ineffectually to raise money to finance a block of flats; and it became a habit with him to consume, every evening, a considerable quantity of whisky. He and Alma had not lived together as man and wife since the birth of their son, but as Alma was to an extraordinary degree without resentment in her character, and as it was her way to mother everyone, they remained on terms of affectionate friendship. Alma still had her music. She was becoming quite well known as a composer of popular songs, a number of which had been published and recorded: she longed to be famous so that her children, whom she adored, would be proud of her.

Saturday, 23rd March, was a day like all the other days. With the chauffeur-handyman driving the car, she picked up John at his school and they spent the afternoon watching Christopher playing football. She spent the evening, as she spent most evenings, playing cards with her husband who was in one of his frequent bouts of depression. On Sunday he was worse and insisted on reading aloud to her from a novel about suicide. In the evening they played cards as usual. By 9.30 p.m. Alma was ready to turn in. She let her little dog out into the garden by the French windows and closed them – Dinah would not stay out if they were left open. She kissed Rattenbury goodnight as usual, then went upstairs to her room with a magazine, leaving him in the drawing-room, browsing over his book: he was sitting by the fire with his back to the French windows. Above the mantelpiece hung a cavalry sabre Alma had inherited, a short sword and a heavy antique pistol.

Irene Riggs was employed as companion-help at the Villa Madeira. She had the afternoon off, so she went to visit her parents in Holdenhurst Road. She was supposed to be in by 10 p.m., but it was already a quarter past when she got back. The front door key was hanging in its usual place, concealed by a shrub. She let herself in, and returned it to its hook. There was no light on in the hall. She went upstairs to her room, then decided she would like something to eat, so she came down again to go to the kitchen: on the way she paused with an uncomfortable feeling that all was not well. She heard heavy breathing. She listened, but could not tell where the sound was coming from. Finally she plucked up courage to knock on the door of her employer's bedroom – it was on the ground floor. Getting no reply, she opened it and switched on the light. The room was empty. Telling herself she was being foolish, that her fears were groundless, he must have fallen asleep in the drawing-room, she turned and went upstairs again, without going to the kitchen. She was no longer hungry.

A few minutes later she again left her room to go along to the lavatory: there was a man in pyjamas on the landing, leaning over the bannisters at the top of the stairs. It was George Stoner, the chauffeur-handyman who lived in. He was the only other servant.

She asked him, 'What is the matter?'

'Nothing,' he said, 'I was looking to see if the lights were out.'

She thought nothing more of it, and went to bed. There was no one else in the house except Mr and Mrs Rattenbury and their little son John, aged six, who slept in his mother's room on the first floor above the drawing-room.

After about ten minutes, Alma Rattenbury joined her for a chat and to exchange the gossip of the day as she usually did, for they were on terms of friendship rather than of mistress and servant. She told Irene that she and her husband were going to Bridport next day – about forty miles west of Bournemouth – because Rattenbury, or 'Ratz' as they called him affectionately, was in one of his moods and needed a change : they would spend the night with his friend Mr Jenks at Dean Park. It was not yet certain whether he or Stoner would drive the car. Irene thought Alma was quite cheerful and looking forward to the trip.

When she was alone again she settled down to sleep, and was just dozing off when she heard someone rushing downstairs, and then Alma shouting hysterically, 'Irene!' She jumped out of bed and ran down to the drawing-room where there was a light on : there she saw Mr Rattenbury leaning back in his favourite armchair as if he was asleep, but his left eye was black, his hair was matted with blood, and there was a pool of blood beside him on the carpet. Alma, in her bare feet and pyjamas, was shaking him and chafing his hands to make him come to, and trying to push his false teeth in which had come out, so that he could speak to them.

When she saw Irene she shouted, 'Someone has hurt Ratz! Telephone the doctor!'

While Irene was doing so – the telephone was in the downstairs bedroom – Alma ran to the bathroom, brought a towel and wrapped it round Rattenbury's head; then she seized a bottle of whisky and poured herself a stiff drink. It made her sick, but she took another.

Irene fetched a bowl and cloth, and bathed his damaged eye, then they tried to lift him, but he was too heavy so they both at once called Stoner to come and help; he came down at once, dressed now in shirt and trousers, and between them they managed to get Rattenbury to his room and onto the bed. While they were trying to undress him, Alma told Stoner to take the car to the doctor's house and hurry him up. She was talking all the time :

'Poor Ratz! Hurry up! Can't somebody do something? . . .'

Suddenly she remembered the child, and afraid he would be

frightened by the sight of the blood, she tried ineffectually to mop it up. Irene got a bucket and floor-cloth, and wiped the carpet; they took his jacket and waistcoat, and the cretonne cover of the chair to the bathroom where Irene tried to clean them. The blood-sodden collar she threw into the dustbin outside.

When Dr O'Donnell arrived at about 11.15, tall, grave and efficient, the front door was open. He walked right in and along the corridor to where Rattenbury lay unconscious, partly dressed, with a blood-stained towel round his head : Alma was beside him with a glass of whisky in her hand, still clad only in pyjamas with bare feet.

'What's happened?' he asked her.

She could only reply, 'Look at he blood! Somebody's finished him!'

O'Donnell removed the towel, took one look at the wound, then telephoned a surgeon, Mr Rooke, who lived not far away, told him he was sending a taxi for him, and would he come at once please. In the drawing-room Alma tried to show him a book her husband had been reading that evening about suicide, but he wouldn't look at it. She put it back on the piano.

Mr Rooke got to the villa at about midnight. He saw at once that Rattenbury was seriously injured, but he found it impossible to make a proper examination of the wound because of the matted blood, and because Alma, with her well-meaning efforts to help, was in his way : she was trying to remove some more of his clothes, calling for scissors to cut away his shirt, and making remarks which appeared to Mr Rooke to be utterly incoherent.

'If you want to kill him,' he told her, 'you're going the best way about it.'

He phoned for an ambulance and made arrangements for the operating theatre to be got ready at the Strathallen Nursing Home which was immediately opposite his own house in Wharncliffe Road. Then he left in the taxi to prepare his instruments. Dr O'Donnell followed with Rattenbury in the ambulance, telling Stoner to bring the car and wait for him outside the nursing home.

On the operating table, when the hair had been shaved away, they could see there were three wounds on the left side of the head at the back, obviously caused not by accident but by external violence. O'Donnell informed the police.

Meanwhile Alma had been drinking steadily. At about 2 a.m. the front door bell rang : she ran to open it. On the doorstep stood Police Constable Bagwell. He was in uniform. She brought him in to the drawing-room, talking all the time excitedly, while Irene followed her about, trying to calm her. Bagwell followed too, trying to make her understand that he had just come from the nursing home and he wanted particulars of how her husband had come by his injuries.

Occasionally an idea or a sentence penetrated the confusion of her mind, and whenever anything she said appeared to make sense, he solemnly wrote it down in his notebook : she was babbling about having played cards that evening with her husband, and going to bed early, and hearing a yell, and finding him in his armchair and the doctor had taken him away . . . And all the time she was behaving as if she wanted to focus all the policeman's attention on herself. She kept filling up her glass, she played records full blast, she laughed hysterically, she danced, she tried to kiss Bagwell – who beat a hasty retreat in search of reinforcements.

Alma tried to follow him, but Irene locked all the doors, then pushed her down onto a chair in the dining-room and sat on her. Soon Bagwell returned accompanied by the policeman on the beat who didn't enter but stood in the doorway. A few minutes later, Inspector Mills arrived with two or three other policemen and took charge. He too announced :

'I have just come from the Strathallen Nursing Home where your husband has been taken seriously injured. Can you give me any particulars as to how it happened?' And he too pieced together from her rambling talk what he took to be her account of the affair.

Then, with Bagwell, he searched the premises, noting the bloodstains on the chair and on the carpet, finding Rattenbury's jacket and waist-coat newly washed in the bathroom, and the cretonne chair cover in the bath, and retrieving the blood-soaked collar from the dustbin. Then he left the villa with the other officers.

Bagwell was again alone with the two women. Alma suddenly announced, 'I know who did it!' Out came the notebook, and he cautioned her that she was not bound to say anything, but if she did it could be used as evidence. She went on undeterred : 'I did it with a mallet.'

In the course of the next hour or so, he was able to note down a few more phrases to add to this bald statement. She said Ratz had frequently talked about suicide, that he had lived too long. Asked what had become of the mallet, she seemed not to know, and answered, 'It is hidden,' and added, 'It is urine on the chair.' Then she changed her story and said it was her lover who had done it. She offered Bagwell ten pounds and then said, 'No, I won't bribe you.'

At 3.30 a.m. Inspector Mills came back and told her Rattenbury was in a critical condition. 'Will this be against me?' she asked. It sounded like a confession, so he too cautioned her, and she went on talking, using whatever concentration she could muster to convince him that she had done it. Sometimes it was possible to understand what she said, and sometimes it wasn't She went on about Rattenbury threatening to commit suicide, that he had given her the book, that he said, 'Dear. Dear.'

Questioned about the mallet she still couldn't, or wouldn't, tell where it was, but promised to tell them in the morning. 'Have you told the Coroner?' she asked, which seemed nonsense. She babbled on, insisting that she had done it but had made a proper muddle of it, that she thought she was strong enough, and so on. It took the inspector perhaps half an hour to get as far as this.

At about four o'clock Dr O'Donnell came back and found him still questioning her : there were four police officers in the house and she was staggering about amongst them from one room to another talking excitedly. The radio-gramophone was playing 'Dark-Haired Marie'. He caught her in the passage and tried to explain to her the condition of her husband, but she couldn't take it in. To stop the exhibition she was making of herself, he took her arm, helped her upstairs to her room and gave her an injection of half a grain of morphia. The indefatigable Bagwell followed them up, and searched under the bed.

The doctor came down and told the inspector what he had done. Then he went into the kitchen to talk to Irene about her, and to Stoner who had driven him back from the nursing home. Five minutes later he found that Alma had come down again and that the inspector was questioning her in the drawing-room, asking her, 'Do you suspect anybody?'

She answered, 'Yes, I think his son did it.'

'What age is he?'

'Thirty-six.'

'And where is he?'

She said she didn't know.

Here Dr O'Donnell intervened and told the inspector she was not in a condition to make a statement as she was full of whisky and he had given her half a grain of morphia. To get her upstairs again to bed she had to be supported on one side by Stoner and on the other by a policeman. The doctor waited until he was quite sure the drug had taken effect and she was asleep, and then he went home.

He had no sooner left the villa than Detective-Inspector Carter appeared on the scene in plain clothes, with two other detectives. He went up to Alma's room and saw that no information could be got from her in her drugged sleep. He studied her statements compiled by his colleagues, and determined to arrest her. Meanwhile, assisted by Bagwell, he searched the rest of the house and the grounds, and went through the papers in Rattenbury's desk from which he learned his full names and that he was an architect. Several times he asked Irene if her mistress was awake yet as he was anxious to get her up. As a matter of routine he questioned Stoner who said he had gone to bed early and been called down by the women to come and help. He had found Mr Rattenbury injured and Mrs Rattenbury crying and screaming.

At about 6 a.m., when she'd had less than two hours' sleep, Alma's eyelids fluttered open. Irene was in the room and also the three detectives. Carter told her to get up. She muttered a few words that none of them could understand, but it was apparent that all she wanted to do was to go to sleep again. Carter sent one of his men to telephone for a police-matron, and asked Irene to make some coffee. When it arrived, Alma was propped up to drink it. She felt sick and could not hold the cup properly or drink out of it without assistance.

Irene protested, 'The lady can't get up with three men in her room. Give her a chance!'

So they went out, except Carter who wouldn't let her out of his sight until the police-matron arrived at 7 a.m. and helped Alma downstairs to the bathroom. Meanwhile Bagwell had made an interesting discovery in the garden – a heavy mallet with blood and hairs on it, hidden behind a trellis. He handed it over to his chief, and then went off duty.

When Alma was fully dressed, Carter came into her room, told her he was a police officer, cautioned her, and charged her that she did, 'by wounding, do grievous bodily harm to one Francis Mawson Rattenbury in an attempt to murder him on Sunday, 24th March 1935.'

She made a statement in reply which he wrote down as she made it : 'About 9 p.m. on Sunday, 24th March, 1935, I was playing cards with my husband when he dared me to kill him as he wanted to die. I picked up the mallet. He then said, "You have not the guts to do it." I then hit him with the mallet. I hid the mallet outside the house. I would have shot him if I had had a gun.' She asked to see what he had written. He handed her his notebook. She read her statement aloud, and signed it 'Alma Rattenbury.'

Before they took her away, she found an opportunity to whisper to Irene, 'Tell Stoner he must give me the mallet,' forgetting that he could

hardly bring it to her at the police station, but her thoughts were still
unco-ordinated. In the hall on the way out, escorted by Carter and the
police-matron, as they passed Irene and Stoner, she said to them, 'Don't
make fools of yourselves.' Stoner replied, equally non-committally,
'You have got yourself into this mess by talking too much.' Getting into
the police car she looked back at her home and saw her little boy
standing in the doorway, white-faced and uncomprehending.

At Bournemouth Police Station, Alma was again warned and charged
with attempted murder. She replied, 'That's right. I did it deliberately,
and I'd do it again.'

Irene had telephoned her solicitor, Mr Lewis Manning, but he hadn't
arrived yet. At eleven o'clock she was brought before the Magistrates'
Court. Here, on Mr Manning's advice, she pleaded not guilty. Carter
asked for the case to be remanded until 2nd April, and this was done.

Mr Manning and Irene Riggs then saw her briefly at the police
station. At about 12.30 Dr O'Donnell was allowed to see her. He was
shocked at her condition; she was unable to stand without swaying, and
had to be held up as she came into the room by a police-matron on one
side and Detective-Inspector Carter on the other. Her eyes were
contracted as a result of the morphia given her the previous evening,
and she tried repeatedly to vomit. They talked for about twenty
minutes: she was particularly anxious about what arrangements would
be made for her children's schooling, and the doctor promised to do
all he could. Shortly after this interview she was sent to the Royal
Holloway Prison for Women, in London.

That afternoon the first headlines appeared: AN EAST CLIFF
SENSATION. WOMAN IN THE DOCK. ATTEMPTED MURDER CHARGE.
REMANDED FOR EIGHT DAYS.

> The charge read out to her was that, 'On 24th March you wounded or
> caused grievous bodily harm to Mawson Francis Rattenbury with intent
> to murder him.'
> The accused woman, who appeared dazed, was dressed in a fur coat
> and a dark brown costume with lace collar, and a hat of similar colour.
> She was accommodated with a seat during the three minutes the
> proceedings lasted. (*Bournemouth Daily Echo, 25th March 1935*)

CHAPTER TWO

The Prodigy

An air of mystery surrounds the circumstances of Alma Rattenbury's birth. Throughout her varied career, no one really knew her age – and it didn't matter. She was one of those women with more than a touch of the eternal feminine who affect profoundly everyone they meet, men particularly, and it made no difference whether she was five or ten years older than she appeared to be. A recent attempt to discover the date of her birth met with no success: the Department of Vital Statistics – the Somerset House of British Columbia – refused to supply a copy of her birth certificate without the consent of one of her parents (who at the time of the request had both been dead for many years). A further attempt was made, and this time a genealogist at the Department made a thorough search of the records for fifteen years each side of the supposed date of her birth, and nothing was found. The logical conclusion is, therefore, that her birth was not recorded.

It seems to be fairly well established that she was the daughter of a mining prospector, a German immigrant, named Wolfe, who wandered in the north-central Canadian Rockies and Alaska in search of gold. His wife accompanied him, sharing the hard conditions of his life: she was English, and on her mother's side belonged to the Gloucester-shire family that produced the famous cricketer, W. G. Grace. When her daughter was born in 1898, or it might have been 1895 or 1896, she returned to civilisation and settled in Victoria, the capital of British Columbia. She and her two sisters, according to family tradition, were reputed to be the best-looking women on the Pacific Coast of Canada: they were the daughters of an animal trainer who had nine children. He kept them all in order with his whip.

Local newspapers gave Alma's place of birth as Prince Rupert, near the Alaskan frontier, but if that is correct it must have been before the first settlers established themselves there in 1906. Perhaps they meant Fort Rupert, a derelict mining town on Vancouver Island. The prospector, from one of his lone expeditions, did not return, his body was not found and nothing more was heard of him. His wife, after waiting the requisite time, married W. W. Clarke, a printer for the *Standard* newspaper in Kamloops, a pleasant town at the junction of the North and South Thomson Rivers in Cariboo – it had started as a fur-trading post, and prospered with the development of the railways : they lived in a comfortable house opposite the old post office on Victoria Street. Alma assumed the name of Clarke and went to Zetland School : there is a suggestion that she was christened Ethel, but when she showed a talent for music her mother changed it to Alma, thinking it would sound better when she was famous. Old street directories of Kamloops reveal that a music teacher, A. E. Wolf, was living in the same street : it may have been a coincidence, or he may have been Alma's grandfather, or an uncle, and in that case he was probably her teacher also.

We first become humanly aware of her when she was a very small child : her schoolmistress said of her, 'She was a brilliantly clever child, a vivid little thing full of happiness and music with such a special attraction of her own.'[1]

Her ambitious mother sent her to Havergal College in Toronto, the most exclusive girls' school in Canada : she was in the kindergarten there in 1902. There were 160 girls and two boys, one of whom was Raymond Massey, the actor, who says, 'It was named after a Victorian hymn-writer of saintly character whose principles were strenuously adhered to by Miss Knox and her chief of staff, Miss Kent. Miss Knox was a startling replica of Queen Victoria.'[2]

The next report, from family sources, states that Alma's mother beat her if she didn't practise her music for a sufficient number of hours a day, and made her perform in concerts and give recitals from the age of eight. Even this treatment could not quench her love of music; she was equally proficient on the piano and the violin, and soon became known all along the western coast of Canada as an infant prodigy. She studied under Dr Torrington, with the result that she became a professional pianist, delighting the critics with her rendering of Beethoven, Schumann, Liszt, Rachmaninoff and other composers. 'It will be difficult to find another pianist,' wrote the *Toronto Globe*, 'who can give a programme . . . with greater brilliancy and musicianly ability, and entirely from memory. Her execution is admirable, and with perfect ease, not the slightest extravagant movement being used.' The *Toronto Mail* singled out her interpretation of Chopin for special praise.[3] She is said to have appeared as a soloist with the Toronto Symphony

Orchestra at the age of seventeen, and to have played both a violin and a piano concerto in the same programme.

In 1913 she met a tall dark Irishman, several years older than herself, and fell in love: his name was Caledon Dolling and he came from an eminent Ulster Catholic family. His grandfather, Robert Holbeach Dolling, was High Sheriff of Londonderry: his mother (née Alexander) was a niece of the Earl of Caledon. His uncle Robert, Father Dolling, was a well-known social reformer. Caledon wanted to be a soldier. On leaving Tonbridge School in Kent he passed his exams for Sandhurst but failed his medical owing to defective eyesight. He therefore set out on his travels. After working on farms in Saskatchewan and Alberta, he started a real estate business in Vancouver.[4] Alma said they eloped, which seems to indicate that her strong-willed mother opposed the match, for there is no suggestion that Caledon's family raised objections although Alma was not a Catholic. Caledon's brother Harry also came to British Columbia: when he arrived in Vancouver the lovers were away on their honeymoon, but from their office window in Granville Street he saw them returning. He says:

> On the other side of the street I saw Alma first. She was dressed in a white suit and she looked absolutely radiant – a sight I have never forgotten. She looked superb. They took a small house in West Vancouver where I visited them from time to time.

All accounts agree that it was an ideally happy marriage – but it was not an easy time to be happy in. Soon the Great War came, and both the Dolling brothers immediately joined up. Caledon was given a commission and appointed second-in-command of the garrison at Prince Rupert. Alma went with him, and gave concerts for the troops.

Soon Caledon was sent to England and drafted to the 2nd Battalion Royal Welch Fusiliers, the regiment in which Siegfried Sassoon and Robert Graves served, but in a different battalion. Alma followed him to London and got a job at the War Office, so they were able to spend his leaves together. Before long, her protesting mother appeared on the scene: Alma locked her out of her lodging, but she howled under the window until she was admitted.

Leaves were all too short. Caledon was ordered to proceed to France. He was promoted Captain and given comand of 'B' Company. He duly reported to his battalion commander. There is a story that on his way back to rejoin his company, being unfamiliar with the terrain he fell into a shell-hole and swore very loudly. He had an unusual accent, basically an Irish lilt but heavily influenced by his stay in Canada: he was overheard by a lance-corporal and a private who at once sought an interview with the Commanding Officer. When it had been granted, the lance-corporal asked if it was possible that an officer of the Royal Welch Fusiliers would ever swear. The Commanding Officer agreed that it was of course impossible except under extreme provocation. The private confirmed that he too had heard the swearing, and as in civil life he was a lecturer in phonetics at Oxford University and had done research at Heidelberg University, he could state positively that there was a spy in the vicinity, an imposter in the uniform of the Royal Welch Fusiliers who had sworn and who had pronounced the ending –er in the dialect of Lower Silesia!

In March 1916 Caledon was wounded, and awarded the Military Cross 'for conspicuous gallantry in leading a night attack'. In the great Somme offensive he was wounded again. He was discharged from hospital on 2nd August and immediately rejoined his regiment: and then, on 20th August, in the morning, at Mametz Wood, he was killed instantly by a shell. His Commanding Officer wrote to Alma that she had the whole regiment's sympathy:

> They were all fond of him and relied on him and trusted his leadership. . . . He was such a man, and had no fear and loved his work. . . . I have lost a brilliant company commander and a friend.[5]

Alma was staying with Caledon's aunt, Mrs Solly, at Chislehurst. Harry Dolling, on sick leave from France, visited her there. He writes:

> I was with her when my brother's sleeping bag came from France. I helped her to unroll it, and the first item we got out were his glasses in broken pieces. That was a terrible sight for her.

There is little doubt that Caledon was the great love of Alma's life. She threw up her job at the War Office and joined the Scottish Women's Hospital based at Royaumont which operated as a unit of the French Red Cross. During the big offensives of July 1917 she worked just behind the lines as an orderly and stretcher-bearer. In a letter to her aunt, dated 24 July, from Auxiliary Hospital 301 at Asnières-sur-Oise, she wrote:

> Am working with the Croix Rouge Française. I share a barn (when here) with five other orderlies. We have 400 beds in the Seine et Oise and another 400 at Villers-Cotterêts and another at Soissons and so on up. . . . It's a pretty big business. We chop and change from post to post, but are never kept 'up' for more than three weeks at a time, the strain's too great. . . .

I do all kinds of work . . . [this included assisting at emergency operations. The first time that she had to hold a leg on her shoulder while it was being sawn off, the smell of blood and anaesthetic sickened her to the point that she thought she would faint, but she bore up because it frightened her more to think she might drop the leg and possibly kill the patient.] We never know one day from another except by Mass every Monday morning, then yesterday must have been Sunday. There is a fearful French push on at the moment and one can hardly think straight for noise. Every other night am 'Night orderly' – hours running something like this. Woke up at 4 a.m., on duty by 4.15, off duty at 4 p.m. in afternoon. Sleep till 8.45, on duty 9 p.m. till 8 a.m. next morning. Sleep??? till 12.45, duty at 1 o'clock, off at 6.30 when I have a night's rest till 4 next morning. It's a limit of a time and dreadful hours; I hardly know what I'm doing, for naturally one does not *sleep* solidly those few hours off. Am *supposed* to be asleep now . . . the noise is dreadful. . . .

On one occasion she performed a mastoid operation, complete with anaesthetic, on the camp cat; this was strictly forbidden and had to be carried out secretly after dark. The cat's miraculous recovery was noticed at once, and Alma was accused of being responsible for it: she made strenuous denials, but the cat gave the show away by following her about everywhere 'like a dog'.[6]

She described the bombarding of the Croix Rouge Auxiliary Hospital, and her work as a stretcher-bearer, bringing in the wounded at night under shellfire, and how on the previous night when they had nearly got a lad in he was hit again and killed: it made her long to be a man and fight too, she said, but then she remembered the red cross on her arm: 'Precious little protection, I'm sorry to say, but *c'est la guerre.*'[7]

Alma was twice wounded, and awarded the Croix de Guerre with star and palm.[8] She mentioned that she never saw British officers and at times was homesick for them – her husband had been dead for about a year. She corresponded with Harry Dolling, possibly saw him in France, and sent him her photograph;[9] but after she had been transferred to Salonika and he had been seriously wounded, they lost touch.[10]

It has been said that the war left Alma cynical and disillusioned, and that she took her pleasures where she could find them; of this we have found no evidence, but what has been definitely established is that during, or soon after the war, she formed an intimate and fairly stable relationship with an officer of the Coldstream Guards, Captain Compton Pakenham who, like Caledon, was a brave soldier and had also been awarded the Military Cross. He had married, in 1915, Phyllis Mona Price, daughter of Colonel Price, a prominent member of the British colony at Dieppe: she is described as exceedingly pretty with curly blue-black hair, pale blue eyes and a permanent suggestion of sunburn as she was an open-air girl, fond of golf and swimming. According to Simona Pakenham, the authoress, only child of the marriage, it was brought about by Phyllis's very assertive mother who 'had seen in this handsome Guards officer the kind of son-in-law she was looking for. As firmly, at a slightly later date, she pushed him out of the house again, threatening him with a poker, because he had taken no time at all to reveal himself as a most unsatisfactory choice.' Simona tells us he left Phyllis with a baby and no money – she was certain he was living with Alma Clarke but couldn't get the evidence for years. She obtained a divorce in 1920, naming Alma as the other woman.[11]

Pakenham was said to be a man of immense charm, and he certainly had a good knowledge and understanding of music. Everybody liked him when they met him, just as everybody liked Alma. He stood in line, albeit rather remotely, for the earldom of Longford. The family, known later as 'the literary Longfords' because of the astonishing number of books they wrote, had produced whole generations of naval and military officers, and a good crop of heroes. Ned Pakenham distinguished himself in the fighting against Napoleon and died gloriously, and uselessly, at New Orleans in 1813, unaware that peace had already been signed. Kitty Pakenham, in an era when it was difficult for a woman to win glory on the battlefield, did the next best thing and married the Duke of Wellington. Sir Thomas Pakenham was Admiral of the Red on the 'Glorious First of June' when the British under Lord Howe defeated the French in 1794: his great-great-grandson was the Compton Pakenham whom Alma married.

He was born on 11th May 1893 in Japan where his father was Naval Attaché, and he learned Japanese before he could speak English: he was at school in Kobe before the family moved to China where he attended the Mission School in Che foo.[12] On the outbreak of the Great War he made his way to England, enlisted in the Inns of Court Regiment before receiving his commission in the Coldstream Guards. He married Alma in 1921. It is curious that in spite of her obscure origin she married twice into the aristocracy and figures in Burke and Debrett, though throughout her life she was completely un-classconscious. They had a son whom they named Christopher – but the marriage wasn't much of a success. They went to the United States and settled in Long Island. Here Pakenham worked as a book reviewer for the *New York Herald Tribune*. Also, true to family tradition, he wrote a book, entitled *Rearguard*, which was largely autobiographical: it tells of the adventures of a young man who was in the Far East when the war broke out, and describes how he made his way to England to enlist. In one of his characters, 'Olga', whom the hero meets in Vladivostock, there seem to be traces both of Phyllis and of Alma.

In Long Island the Pakenhams were short of money, so Alma gave piano lessons while Compton travelled about giving lectures on economic conditions in Japan: although he had been in England for only a short time, he had acquired, and cultivated, the clipped Oxonian accent and polished manner of a British Officer and Gentleman. He frequently spoke with affection of 'his old school' Harrow although he had never attended it, and to increase his prestige as a lecturer he provided himself with an Oxford D.Phil., to which he was not entitled.

When neighbours remarked on the beautiful piano music they often heard coming from the house on Long Island, he gave them to understand that he had been playing it. Those who knew him well seemed to find his habit of petty misrepresentation engaging rather than offensive, and considered it nothing more than an endearing eccentricity, but Alma grew more and more unhappy. They were obviously unsuited to each other in many ways, and financial problems were acute. At last she swallowed her pride and wrote in desperation to her mother who came at once and took her and Christopher back to British Columbia.

CHAPTER THREE

A Jolly Good Fellow

Victoria, the capital of British Columbia, because of its architecture, its red London buses and its hanging baskets, is generally considered to be the most English of the Canadian cities, and is sometimes called 'the Bournemouth of Canada'. Its surroundings are so beautiful and its climate so mellow that hundreds of business and professional people settle there when they retire: in Alma's day they could be seen taking tea in the Empress Hotel and listening to the Palm Court orchestra. Tea at the Empress is still an institution though the orchestra has gone. This was probably the first time she had been back to her native city since she had left it to follow Dolling so eagerly to the wars. She stayed at first with her mother, then rented a small house for herself and Christopher. Here she tried to earn a living by teaching the piano and giving recitals. She was still an attractive woman and she soon began to play a lively part in the social life around her.

One evening she was sitting with a friend in the lounge of a hotel in Victoria which may have been the Empress Hotel: she was relaxing after giving a recital. They heard coming from the banqueting hall the strains of 'For he's a Jolly Good Fellow'. Alma remarked that the people were singing as if they really meant it. Soon the party broke up, and the hero of the occasion came out. Her friend knew him and presented him – he was the well-known architect Francis Mawson Rattenbury. He was nearly six feet tall, handsome, self-assured, and old enough to be Alma's father. But what appealed most to her wounded soul was that his expression was kind when he looked at her.

Perhaps this was a chance meeting, or perhaps Alma was the object of some deliberate match-making by her mother or by her aunt, Mrs Florence Criddle, who acted as housekeeper for one of Rattenbury's close friends. He was interested enough to go to one of her piano recitals, and then they met again at a dance where Alma's unfeigned admiration and magnetic personality had their effect. Rattenbury, for all

26

his popularity and worldly success, was a lonely man whose marriage had been a failure. He wrote at this time to his sister Kate:

> I don't get much pleasure out of the family and don't see much of them – but I have got used to that long ago. . . . At my age a man cannot expect to find a real life-long friend among men – and I thought it would be impossible among women. . . .

When he met Alma he very quickly changed his mind.

> Talking of women [he went on] one of them last night – at a dance in a lovely big house – a young married one about 26 – the belle of the dance and a marvellous musician – knocked me out by saying – 'Do you know that you have a lovely face?' 'Great Scott' I said – have I? I'm going right home to have a look at it – I never thought it worth looking at yet' – 'I'm not joking' she said – 'You have almost the kindest face I ever saw' – I feel that I am just beginning to be appreciated. . . .'

Francis Rattenbury, like many other leading spirits in British Columbia then, was a Yorkshireman. He was born in Leeds on 11th October 1867, and so he was probably about thirty years older than Alma. He was educated at Leeds Grammar School and Yorkshire College – he was so frugal at school that he regularly went without lunch in order to save money. It is said also that he was belligerent, continually scrapping with the other boys. His academic record, however, and his behaviour in class, seem to have been impeccable. His family, though settled in Yorkshire for two generations, came from Okehampton in Devon: they traced their descent from a Bavarian gentleman, Johannes von Rathenburg, who came to England in the year 1484. The family were described in *The Times* as a 'dynasty of Methodist ministers', but actually the dynasty included a professional smuggler who called himself 'the Rob Roy of the West', and a painter.[1]

For a long while young Rattenbury could not make up his mind what career to follow, until one day he designed a Christmas card that pleased his uncle who was an architect and a partner in the firm of Mawson and Hudson (previously Lockwood and Mawson). Consequently he became an articled clerk in his uncle's office and for four years caught the 8.32 a.m. train daily from Leeds to Bradford. The firm was doing exciting work: they had designed many of the public buildings in Bradford, including the town hall, and they were responsible for laying out and constructing the new town of Saltaire which, with its modern workers' houses and fine parks, was looked upon as a great

advance in industrial planning and social amenity. He passed his
exams with no difficulty, and had already begun to distinguish himself
as an architect when he threw up his safe job and assured career to see
the world.

In May 1892 he went to British Columbia where a project for new
Parliament Buildings in Victoria was under discussion. Architects from
all over the world had been invited to submit designs which, to avoid
any suggestion of favouritism, were to be judged anonymously by a
committee in Montreal. Rattenbury, perhaps hoping to influence the
committee in his favour, added to his design the words, 'by a local
architect'. When it was announced that he was the winner he had
been in British Columbia less than a year, and he was twenty-five
years old. It was an ambitious project that was to cost 923,000 dollars
of which his fee was to be 37,635 dollars.

It was a fortunate time for a talented young architect to settle in
Victoria which had been in existence for only about fifty years: it
was founded in 1843, as Fort Victoria, to serve as the western terminal
for the fur trade. It lies on beautiful Vancouver Island off the Pacific
Coast of Canada. The province with its flourishing towns, rich grass-
lands on the foothills and valuable mineral deposits had been shut
off from the rest of Canada by the northern ranges of the Rocky
Mountains until 1885 when the railway reached the coast, only seven
years before Rattenbury's arrival there, and it had brought about a
sudden increase of economic activity. He opened an office, used an
elevation of the projected Parliament Buildings in sepia across his
letterheads, and soon his services were in great demand: within two
years his designs had been accepted for buildings totalling 800,000
dollars – fine private houses for prosperous merchants, Court Houses
and business premises. He made all his own drawings. With restless
energy he embarked on many new enterprises, designing a new type
of portable house for which he found a market in the Canary Islands,
and devising the first practical method for shipping frozen salmon to
Europe. He also became a director of a large painting and decorating
firm.[2]

In the summer of 1896, gold was discovered in Canada's distant
north in the valley of the Klondike River. Before winter set in, the
log-cabin town of Dawson had been established where the Klondike
falls into the Yukon River near the frontier of Alaska, and by the
following year it already had 3,000–4,000 inhabitants – it was a
remarkably law-abiding place owing to the presence of a small detach-
ment of the North West Mounted Police.

Rich finds were reported in its immediate vicinity, and in the spring of 1898 the great Klondike Gold Rush began. It is estimated that 100,000 people from various parts of the world tried to reach Dawson, of whom only 30,000 or 40,000 succeeded in getting there owing to its inaccessibility and the enormous transport difficulties. Some approached it through Alaska, making their way up the Yukon River from the Bering Sea, but the most popular route was northwards through British Columbia and the Yukon Territory.

Victoria was suddenly crowded with prospectors eagerly buying supplies and equipment : for every prospector there was an average of two backers to pay for his outfit and share in his profits : prices rose, there was much bargaining and haggling, and brawling in the streets at night. The first stage of the journey was by sea to the mushroom port of Skagway on the coast of Alaska, consisting of perhaps 1,000 tents and frame buildings that were set up almost overnight at the water's edge, complete with shops, saloons and gambling dens. The North West Mounted Police established an office there, but as they were in American territory they had no jurisdiction. One of their officers wrote :

> Almost the only persons who were safe were the members of our force. . . . At night the crash of bands, shouts of 'murder' and cries for help mingled with the cracked voices of the singers in the variety halls.[3]

The place was ruled by a gangster from Colorado called Soapy Smith.

Then, when the snow had cleared sufficiently, the long trek began over the Chilkoot Pass in British Columbia, with an alternative route over the Whitehorse Pass, to Lake Bennett, from which it was possible in summer to descend by water all the way to Dawson. Police posts were set up which no one was allowed to pass unless he had brought sufficient supplies with him : the usual amount insisted upon was about a ton – it was more than a man could carry, so he had to divide his goods, pack some of them for about three miles at a time, leave them, and go back for another load. This caused great congestion on the narrow way across the mountains, and although gangs were set to work laying log paths over marshes, blasting out slippery rocks and constructing bridges, there was a long trail of dead horses and stranded men. From Lake Bennett, as soon as the ice had melted, a fleet of canoes, rafts and sailing barges carrying up to fifteen tons, started down the headwaters of the Yukon River, shooting dangerously through Miles Canyon and the Whitehorse Rapids – the men in the smaller craft had to pack laboriously round them.

Rattenbury was not content to sit back in Victoria and make a profit from the prospectors; he undertook a far more challenging enterprise – that of taking supplies up to the miners in the Klondyke, and in particular to Dawson. There was a story, apparently told by Rattenbury himself in later years, that in 1897 he was just in time to save the inhabitants from the threat of starvation by driving in sixty head of cattle after an arduous and perilous journey: we have not been able to confirm this, but in 1898 he raised £75,000 and formed the Bennett Lake and Klondike Transportation Company the purpose of which was to take passengers and freight from the foot of the Chilkoot Pass on Lake Bennett to Dawson.[4] He had three wood-burning steamers carried in sections over the pass at immense trouble and expense, assembled them on the lake and began a regular service during the summer months.[5] He had to take a larger office on the ground floor to handle the business. He also ran a steamer, the *Amur*, from Victoria to Skagway.

Because the whole area was closed all winter – anyone who stayed on in Dawson after the freeze up had to wait there until the spring thaw – he next turned his attention to the problem of winter travel. With associates in Montreal he took over the Arctic Express Company and established a series of depots all along the route thirty miles apart, each with a manager, a cook, beds and provisions. This meant that a man could leave Dawson and reach the coast in nine days without having to carry anything, at a total cost of 250 dollars. Like everything else that Rattenbury undertook, the venture was initially a great success: he wrote home:

> It only takes nine days now, Victoria to Dawson, 4 on the steamers up – one on the trail – 3 to 4 on the steamers down – So Yukon travel is revolutionized and has lost its terrors – in Summer at least – We have done good business & have taken a lot of freight in and brought out a lot of passengers – who were simply astounded at the ease and speed that they could travel with. . . . Our ships are called the Ora – Nora and Flora – & I expect your papers will now often have mentioned their names – They are household words in this part of the world – [6]

(He never bothered much with punctuation – too busy!) He went on to describe how he was opening up the winter route for mails with trading posts, and said he was working in his office usually till midnight.

In July of that year, 1898, he found time to get married. His bride was Eleanor Florence, daughter of the late Captain Elphinstone Nunn of His Majesty's 47th Regiment. She was described in the local press as 'a lady of breeding and education'. She had courage also, for she accepted Rattenbury's unconventional plan for a honeymoon: they went first to Vancouver, thence up the coast to Skagway, and rode over the Whitehorse Pass to Lake Bennett where they embarked on one of his steamers, explored the lakes and went down nearly to Dawson. We learn from his letters that Florrie stood the trip easily and that she was delighted with the scenery: she particularly liked Lake Tagish with its enormous trout and beautiful whitefish. He returned from his honeymoon with 600 ounces of gold which he deposited in his bank in Victoria. He wrote that his wife was blessed with a marvellously good temper, 'a jolly good thing for me – for as you know mine is rather short – especially when rushed with work – So we pull along well together.'

Also in this eventful year, 1898, the official opening of the Parliament Buildings was celebrated – they had already been illuminated with 3,000 electric bulbs in the previous year in honour of Queen Victoria's Diamond Jubilee. The buildings were a triumphant success and aroused enthusiastic admiration, though a few officials protested at the heavy expenditure of public money, and others thought they were too big. The Attorney-General called them a white elephant, and it is said that a distracted Commissioner of Lands and Works shouted aloud in the empty halls, 'Never in 500 years will the government have enough employees to fill this vast building!' There were criticisms too of Rattenbury's high-handed manner: he was frequently involved in quarrels and recriminations, and his work was not accomplished without serious difficulties with bureaucratic authority. This letter, from the Deputy Commissioner of Lands and Works, was addressed to him on 5th October 1897:

Dear Sir, – Dr Pope, Superintendent of Education, has called on me to protest against the removal of a partition wall in his office which he says you contemplate doing. I am somewhat surprised, as I have not heard you mention the matter and must request you to be kind enough to call at my office and show me what you propose doing before you take any steps in the matter. In the meantime I have told Mr Howell not to proceed with any alterations until I had an opportunity of conferring with you.

I beg also to remind you that as the professional deputy head of this Department I expect you to consult me on any material changes in connection with the building which you desire to advocate.

Yours truly etc. –

On the same day, back came Rattenbury's reply:

Dear Sir, – Yours of Oct 5th received re *Fittings to Education Department*. In response to your rather peremptory demand that I should call at your office and show you what I propose doing before I take any steps in the matter – I have to inform you that I have already let the contract for this work.

Should you desire any information on this matter, I shall be happy to make an appointment with you at my office as above. In the meantime, might I request that you be good enough not to issue any instructions in the Buildings, in respect to work under my control, as such instructions confuse and lead to endless trouble.

As regards your desire that I should consult you in respect to every small change rendered necessary in my opinion to ensure the due and satisfactory completion of the Parliament Buildings, I am afraid that were I to do so I should take up more of your time than you could spare. I have been accustomed, therefore, to rely on my own judgement, and I think it wiser to do so as I have found that non-professional interference in technical work produces costly and disastrous results.

I am, Sir,

Yours truly,

F. M. Rattenbury, Architect.

He probably enjoyed situations like this, but a government decision to cut down all the trees round the Parliament Buildings affected him deeply. In a letter to the Editor of the *Daily Colonist* he said :

Allow me to express to Mr Sorby my gratitude for his excellent letter last evening – appealing for the preservation of the trees round the new parliament buildings.

I entirely agree with Mr Sorby and it makes me heartsick to see each tree as it falls to the ground.

It is so rarely than an architect is fortunate enough to have the opportunity of erecting a large building amongst the delicate tracery of woodland scenery. And the peeps of high masses of masonry through the trees gives so distinctive a charm, so different to what one can usually see, that words fail me to express my grief at seeing this charm disappear.

I had no voice in the matter or I would have saved at least some of these trees; but, sir, it is not yet too late to save the magnificent poplars at the corner of James Bay Bridge, standing out in bold relief against the sky, acting as a foil to the outline of the dome and giving distance and perspective to the whole building. If they are cut down, the loss will, I feel sure, be realised too late.

The old axiom is a good one, to think twenty times before you cut down any tree.

(*Left*) Alma during her career as a pianist. A photograph taken from a concert brochure
(*Right*) Alma in her Scottish Women's Hospital uniform

Alma (*centre*) as a nurse during the First World War with two friends

(*Left*) Alma when she ma[r]
Dolling

(*Below*) Alma and Francis
Rattenbury about the tim[e]
of their marriage

Rattenbury was absent from the ceremonial opening – on a business trip to London. The Parliament Buildings continued to arouse the envy of other cities – there was even a suggestion that they were too good for Victoria and should be dismantled and re-erected on the mainland in the City of Vancouver.

It seems that Florrie, with all her marvellously good temper, was not content to have her newly-wed husband making a habit of working till midnight in his office, for we next hear of him in the following year selling all his interests in the north and taking things more easily. His letters to England, instead of being full of his projects, now describe the garden of the house he had rented, the woods, the beach, duck shooting, visits to his club. 'It's a curious feeling,' he wrote, 'to be without any little ventures – as they certainly add a zest and excitement to life.'

He invested his money in the safest securities he could find, and he built for his bride a large house at Oak Bay over-looking the sea, just outside Victoria. He furnished it with rich Turkish carpets, hanging tapestries of Arabesque design, oak tables and chairs, glass and silverware imported from England. He surrounded it with gardens in which he planted trees and thousands of bulbs, broom, honeysuckle, climbing roses and jasmine: it became part of his daily routine to walk round them and note what flowers were coming up and how much his trees had grown.

In winter there were log fires fed by an abundant supply of driftwood brought from the beach and sawn up by Foy, his Chinese gardener. He was told by an old-timer that his garden had been for centuries an Indian camping ground, beside a small spring which still sparkled among his flowers, and there was a legend that in this very spot the Good Spirit had conferred on man the gift of speech : therefore it had always been called *Iechinihl* (pronounced softly, Eye-a-chineel), meaning 'The Place where a Good Thing Happened'. Naturally he took this name for his house. In the main hall, over an ornate Tudor-style fireplace, he had these words inscribed : 'East, West, Hame's Best.' Soon a son and a daughter were born. Now he was content. He said he had a notion in his head that he had nearly finished all his work, and that he was as well off as he cared to be.

In a very short while his old restlessness returned. On a business trip to Calgary we find him writing :

The mountains always look magnificent – but I could not help contrasting the feelings with which I now gaze on them and the exciting interest that I took in them on my first trip over, when they seemed so wrapped in glamour and romance. It was almost saddening to feel that all enthusiasms had vanished and could not be reawakened.

It is not surprising to find him turning again to his architectural work and tendering successfully for a series of mountain hotels for the Canadian Pacific Railway, and then for a luxury hotel in Victoria to cost £150,000 – the Empress Hotel. These projects, together with a court house in Vancouver, a new house in Victoria for the Lieutenant-Governor, a rail terminal and numerous private residences, made him as busy as he had ever been before. He found himself 'getting awfully rich', and he frequently offered money to his mother in England.

As his children grew up he loved them and spoiled them: his letters are full of descriptions of their childish doings. Florrie is rarely mentioned, and when she is, it is usually without much enthusiasm: he apologises for her being a bad correspondent, she is making things for a bazaar, she is preparing for a garden fête, she is getting things ready for Christmas and bossing the new cook, she is talking of taking electrical treatment for *embonpoint* (this item accompanied by a sketch of her figure), or she is in difficulties with her accounts: having asked for a separate allowance, she has bought jewellery on the instalment plan without telling him. Of course he has found out, and is mischievously pretending he doesn't know why her bills are mounting up. Her interest in pots of flowers he feels to be excessive, 'the house is always smothered with them – must be 100 pots of geraniums etc., daffodils and tulips all over the place'.

Most of his letters are conventional and businesslike, but there is one that is different. He has just returned from visiting his mother in England, and he tries with some embarrassment, and with difficulty in finding the words, to tell her how much he loves and appreciates her:

Victoria B.C. 10 Sept 1905 – Dear Mother – I have been thinking a good deal of you tonight – and it was strongly impressed upon me – what a wonderful mother I have had – I suppose it will not turn your head to tell you what I thought – though as you know I am not of a demonstrative nature – & while I think a lot – I don't say much – but during my last visit to England I seemed to get to know you – better than I ever did before – perhaps having seen life – I am better able to appreciate you – I suppose that is it – It was a constant marvel to me in England to hear you expressing your opinions – & a delight to see the broad tolerant spirit with which you viewed people – apparently realising their weaknesses – their efforts – & your knowledge that the good would eventually overcome the faults – and all the time doing so in a spirit of loving kindness – Day by day I learned many lessons from you – and I hope and know that I shall be a better man from what I have learned – as I listened to you on every topic that came up – I instinctively attempted to gather from you a truer view of life . . . I only hope that my youngsters will – in some small degree – have the same feeling for me – that I have for my charming mother – I am going to finish this at once – for if I do not – my instinctive nature of self repression will make me tear it up –

Your loving son, Frank.

Then there is a long gap in the correspondence that has survived. When we pick up the threads again, he and Florrie have drifted apart. They are no longer on speaking terms although they are both living in the same house – it was large enough for each of them to occupy respectively the east and the west portions of their home without being forced into each other's company. We learn that both children sided with their mother, but the youngest, Mary, 'who seems to be all at once a woman, generally comes in after dinner for an hour or two – She still has her governess . . . She has naturally a fine character.'

Again he felt he was losing his ambition, though he was now Supervising Architect for the Western Division of the Grand Trunk Railway, and had designed terminals for them, and depots and mountain hotels. He had made additions to the Parliament Buildings which were now twice the size, and he had many other buildings to his credit including the luxurious Empress Hotel which is a landmark almost as well known as the Parliament Buildings.

By 1920, although he was only fifty-three, he seemed to have burned himself out; he lost interest in his work, became morose and lethargic, his circulation was poor, he always felt chilly, he suffered from indigestion. By 1922 he looked so old and pale that his friends thought he was dying – but then, as a result of treatment by a practitioner whom he called 'Dr Chiro', (his jocular way, no doubt, of referring to his chiropractor), he made a remarkable recovery. He describes this in a letter to his sister :

For three years I was too tired to play golf – simply could not – whilst at dances two dances were more than enough – A week or two ago I played 36 holes and not a [sign of] fatigue – Last night I was out to a dance and danced every dance till two o'clock in the morning and enjoyed every minute – the Lieutenant-Governor remarked, 'You have simply renewed your youth. . . .'

That was the night he danced with Alma for the first time. With his zest for living renewed, and with his health and youth restored, he wanted a divorce from Florrie, but it wasn't easy. At first he thought that if he could persuade her to leave their home he could charge her with desertion, but she wouldn't go. He cut off the light and the telephone, took the furniture away – still she wouldn't go. She remained there sleeping in a cot and eating off an apple box until he made her a cash settlement and gave her a house of her own, allowing her to choose the site. She had one built overlooking *Iechinihl*. In 1925 she divorced him, naming Alma. A divorce was also arranged between Alma and Compton Pakenham, so Rattenbury was able at last to marry her and install her and Christopher in the home at Oak Bay.

In spite of the friendliness of the Chinese cook and the Chinese gardener, who is described as 'a fine old man, a master gardener and a family friend,' Christopher, aged three, felt ill at ease at first in this palatial building after their tiny house in Victoria : to prevent him getting into places where he was not allowed, Rattenbury had all the door handles raised. For some time Alma had been suffering from severe headaches : she had always kept going in spite of them, but now she became rather seriously ill. Rattenbury called in several doctors, but none of them could diagnose her condition. One of them put it down to drink, which made him very angry : 'She never takes any !' he protested. He sent the doctors away and called in his chiro-practor who not only diagnosed an abscess on the brain behind one eye, but succeeded in dispersing it. The treatment took several weeks and then she was completely cured.

On 2nd June 1925, two months after they had married, Rattenbury wrote to his sister, '. . . I have a wonderfully happy home – bright and joyous and full of fun all the time – and apparently Alma likes it as much as I do.' He describes her as intensely in earnest over whatever she is about, full of sympathy, keen to see the nice side of everyone, and she flares up with rage over any meanness; she is talented in literature and poetry and 'gets a world of amusement out of every living thing'. She looks 'like a fragile Madonna – rather sad, but is really full of fun'.

The next part of the letter, almost indecipherable now, tells of her education, a musical prodigy at five :

Musicians say that she is a divine player – that there is none who can surpass her – quit her music at twenty – & volunteered to go to France as a VAD – was stretcher-bearer in the trenches – wounded several times – married a Captain Pakenham – son of Admiral Pakenham – has one son – who will be Lord Longford – [This was highly improbable, but at least he was in the line of succession.] – I'm becoming quite appreciative of music – and beginning to understand – In short a very interesting – most lovable – human soul – and best of all – simply adored by all her girl friends – including those who lived with her in France – and by all the elderly people as well – I can't tell why she linked up with me – at her age it seems unreasonable – for she had the world at her feet – Perhaps the restful life appealed – and she seems to find all kinds of qualities in me – that she likes – that I never knew of. *However* – It looks like some years of happiness and interest instead of the loneliness I see so much around – I look years younger than when I came to England. . . .

In September of the following year he is still writing in the same tone (and with the same system of punctuation) :

We are very happy – Alma is a brick – and a wonderfully bright and lovable companion – I can't imagine life without her now – and fortunately she seems as contented with me – with the disparity in years – it seems astonishing to me – but we seem to enter into everything together – as if we were the same age –

I don't know when we will come to England – it is an [expensive?] trip and I think it will have to wait – until I get some compensation from the Govt. – which I hope to do before long – They certainly robbed me in good style –

In the meantime we have already renovated the house – and added on a music room – which acoustically is marvellous – I built the walls and ceiling on the principle of a drum – and the huge concert grand piano – sounds almost like a glorious organ – This really is a wonderfully happy home – Alma has the knack of eliciting love – and the servants are devoted to her – and the place is full of animals and birds – all of them – next door to human. . . . I hate to think what my life would have been like – had she not come along – it was pretty hateful – & of course – would have got much worse. . . .

Another year passes, and then :

I'm sitting in the garden on a beautiful day – by the side of the sea – whilst Alma is busy with her flowers and dogs & cats . . . she slipped and had a badly sprained ankle – kept her a month in bed & it will trouble her for months – but she doesn't seem to mind it a bit. . . . Lo and behold – her great wish of years is coming true – & she is going to be a mother – she is delighted beyond measure – and that child will certainly get lots of love *showering* – he ought to be some child. . . . I've had a wonderful five years. . . .

To judge from these letters, neither of them seem to have been unduly worried by an insidious smear campaign that was being waged by Rattenbury's discarded family. Alma was always spontaneously generous.

and when she helped people this was called 'filching money from her husband by pretending she knew people who were in need'. When Alma drove her car into a basement shop window (Christopher who was in the back seat still bears the scars on his face caused by the flying glass from the shattered windshield) they spread the story that she was drunk. They scored a signal triumph when she was refused membership in the Victoria Musical Society – which demonstrates how little the qualifications for membership had to do with music. It seems that quite apart from family resentments, the society in which Rattenbury had been a leading light did not at all approve of his liaison with Alma and their subsequent marriage. His son Frank, who had tried to dissuade him from it, was particularly bitter, prophesying disaster.⁷

The compensation expected from the Government, mentioned in one of his letters, refers to a long and troublesome dispute about 40,000 acres of land that he had bought in 1907 along the line of the Grand Trunk Railway survey: he planned to develop the area and attract settlers to it after the railway had been completed. In 1917, under new legislation designed to keep land settlement in control of the Government, very heavy taxes were imposed on private speculators. Rattenbury sued the Land Settlement Board, but lost the case and with it the bulk of his fortune. At about the same time he was involved in a dispute with the Canadian Pacific Railway. He had always intended to go back to England eventually, and this seemed a good time to do so. Alma encouraged him to make the move, observing perhaps that his splendid career had degenerated into a series of disputes and recriminations: or perhaps she too had a longing for England. She told him she wanted their son John to be christened in the ancestral church at Okehampton in Devon.

Before leaving British Columbia, Rattenbury donated some land in Oak Bay to the municipality, giving the public the use of 1,500 feet sea frontage with access to the beach, and also a five acre island off *Iechinihl* called Mary Tod Island to be preserved as a public park.

His eldest son, Frank, Alma's bitter opponent, says that the second marriage made his father so unpopular that no one but himself saw him off at the docks – a sad leavetaking for British Columbia's most eminent architect whose work and ideas had done a great deal to transform the capital from a shabby little town into a city of monumental beauty. He kept the Chinese gardener, Foy, on the payroll after they had left. Christopher writes: 'I still remember his crying when we departed . . .'

CHAPTER FOUR

The Bournemouth Triangle

The Rattenburys were in no hurry to reach England and begin the final chapter of their lives: they decided to see a bit more of the world first. Instead of taking the direct route across Canada, they went round via the Panama Canal to Cuba where they stayed for a while. Then, on the passage from Havana to New York Rattenbury was taken in by some professional black jack artists and ended up heavily in debt – it seems quite out of character for him. His situation, as they waited in their hotel for a passage to England, was extremely embarrassing, for his late gambling companions were awkward customers and made no secret of what they would do to him if they didn't get their money. In this emergency his old determination did not desert him: he awakened his family at dead of night and they left New York by train for Montreal where they boarded a ship and escaped, gambling debts unpaid.

The ship was bound for the Mediterranean. For years Rattenbury had been promising himself a holiday, not in the scenic beauty spots of Europe – for he thought no country in the world could be as beautiful as British Columbia – but amid the architectural splendours of Northern Italy. After lingering in Monte Carlo they went to Venice where Alma wanted to visit the palazzo where Gigli lived, the famous operatic tenor. She quickly attracted an escort of admiring gentlemen who trailed after her wherever she went.

Many weeks had passed since they started on their travels, but still they hesitated to make for England. For several months they stayed in Northern France where Christopher attended school. At last, after they had wandered for nearly a year, we find them at Okehampton where John was duly baptised in the parish church.

For their permanent residence, instead of settling in Yorkshire where Rattenbury was born, they chose Bournemouth which Thomas Hardy once described as a 'Mediterranean lounging place on the English Channel'. It was the place in England that most resembled Victoria

BC. In a beautiful setting on the Hampshire-Dorset border, its long beaches, gentle climate and acres of pine woods gave it an attractive continental look, yet its tone and character were essentially and unmistakably English middle-class. It reached its heyday between the world wars when it became a fashionable place of retirement much favoured by military men, and ladies in reduced circumstances, who wished to live out the remaining years of their lives in an atmosphere of untroubled gentility. It suited Alma particularly well because it was the home of a world-famous symphony orchestra, and it was only a couple of hours by train from London. The Villa Madeira, which they rented from a Mrs Price, was at 5 Manor Road, a few minutes' walk from the cliffs and beach. Her concert grand piano was brought from *Iechinihl* and installed in the drawing-room. They engaged a small domestic staff to help with the running of the house.

Although the war had ended Alma's career as a concert pianist, music was still her grand passion. From an early age she had been in the habit of jotting down on menu cards or the backs of old envelopes scraps of melodies that occurred to her: now she began adding sentimental words to them, mourning for lost love, dreaming of the future:

> Day with her hopes and fears
> Fades when the light is done,
> Breezes that sang in trees
> Sleep at the set of sun.
> Love close thy weary eyes
> Kissed by the falling dew,
> While in the dark, hungry I dream,
> Love of my heart adieu![1]

These were not the emotions of a woman who was entirely satisfied. Rattenbury took a great interest in her music and did everything in his power to interest a publisher. In a letter to his sister, dated 12th December 1931, he described how they finally succeeded:

Dearest Kate, – This has been a most astonishing week. For a long time we have been trying to get in touch with a publisher – I even went up to London and had a talk with Boosey – who was very nice, but frankly said – It was no use trying at present, they were selling nothing and publishing nothing, did not even want to look at the composition.

Poor Alma was in despair. It seemed like hitting a stone wall. Then I got an inspiration – with an intro: we went to see Sir Dan Godfrey (Conductor of the Bournemouth Symphony Orchestra) – he advised getting other introductions & then go to London to the Keith Prowse Co. who he said were *the* people for this style of music. So I got introductions from the 'Agent General' & others – & last Tuesday we called on Mr Van Lier, the head of the huge K.P.Co. We waited in an outer office – full of busy clerks – then were ushered into the private office.

Van Lier was a nice fellow (he is a great musician himself). We talked for a time – he then said – indifferently – Well play over one of the numbers – the one you think best.

Alma in 2 minutes had him enthralled – at the end of 10 minutes I said to him – well what do you think? He said, 'I am greatly impressed' – and said he would publish 1 number, have it orchestrated – & broadcast all over, and 2 other numbers for the piano only at present.

He then asked us to dinner – And last night we had dinner with him & his fiancée (a singer at the BBC) & who was as keenly interested as Van Lier.

We had an interesting time – he opened right out – told us all about the difficulties of a Publishing Concern – and when successful the huge results. He discovered – and put out 'The Druid's Prayer', the 'Stein Song' (500,000 copies sold) & is supposed to be the best judge of this style of music in the world.

At present he is at Alma's feet. He told me, 'She is marvellous! I have travelled all over the world – & into all kinds of places – for tunes – there are few of them – it is one of the scarcest gifts of humanity – & here is your wife – her mind teeming with exquisite tunes.'

We were dining at the Mayfair – the latest and most beautiful & fashionable of London Hotels – with a splendid orchestra, 'Ambrose & his Band' who are the most highly paid musicians in London – & the floor was brilliant with the gorgeous costumes of the dancers. Van Lier had evidently sent out word – that a great new composer was present.

It was most amazing – Ambrose himself – came forward to apologise for his music – it being an off night (Saturday) – fancy Ambrose apologising – he is going to broadcast Alma's music.

Van Lier has given us the entrie [sic] to BBC House – and an entrie elsewhere music is performed – & to the great singers etc.

Miss Yvette Darnac (his fiancée) said, 'Do you realise in future – that when you enter this room – the Band will break off and play your music to you?'

Van Lier gets 200 compositions submitted to him each week – & his outer office is thronged with poor devils all anxious – And here we walk in and in 2 or 3 days – the Greatest Publisher in London is absolutely at Alma's feet – acclaiming her as a genius – in the centre of London life – said they would spend thousands of pounds putting out her work – and anxious beyond words that we won't trot away.

He asked me – 'which is it that you want – is it money? or what is it? You must stay here – don't go.'

We go this afternoon at 4 p.m. to meet his 'Arranger' – He said, 'We have dozens of Arrangers – but not one can write a tune.' He also told Alma – he would give her an hour a day of his time – putting her wise – to all the tricks of the trade.

Alma has arrived & in a moment – she is almost dizzy with it all – but still as simple as ever – of course it means coming to London to live – it is inevitable. She will be called upon to write music for the Theatres and for Elstree (film studios). And a week ago we were wondering how on earth we could get a publisher to even listen to them.

Now we have a Publisher.
Then a friendly   „
Now an enthusiastic „   2

The song Van Lier particularly like was 'Avelette'. The 'enthusiastic publisher' said in an interview that when he accepted it, Rattenbury almost danced for joy and clasped his young wife affectionately.

Alma's success spurred her to further efforts: she was ambitious more because of her children than herself. Under the name Lozanne she wrote and published a whole series of songs, 'Zanita', 'You brought my Heart the Sunshine', 'Dark-Haired Marie' . . . She bought a selection of gramophone records of tenor voices, and when she heard one sung by Frank Titterton, a popular singer with a sensitive ear, she exclaimed, 'That is the Voice for my songs!' Whereupon Rattenbury wrote to Frank Titterton and invited him to meet them for lunch at a London hotel. He arrived with his secretary and accompanist, Miss Esmond, and this is how he described their first meeting:

> We found Mr and Mrs Rattenbury to be a striking looking couple. Mrs Rattenbury was very smartly dressed, and her conservation was that of a well-travelled cultured woman with keen powers of observation. Her intense emotionalism, which since has impressed itself on me over and over again, was apparent at that first meeting. At one moment she would be wildly gay, and would fling her arms in the air to emphasize her voluble flow of words. The next moment she would be silent and subdued. Her eyes, so grey and magnetic, compelled attention to everything she said. I noticed particularly – as I have since noticed often – the very intense way in which she looks into one's face and her eyes become large with emotion or excitement. . . .'3

He said they met frequently from them on, for lunch or dinner and little gala evenings for dancing and the theatre. Alma was fond of festivity, but she did not drink; she never took anything stronger than orange juice, except on one occasion when she had a little champagne to celebrate the broadcasting of some of her music. At one of these parties, Rattenbury announced that he thought it would be a good idea if he could write the words to his wife's songs. He said he had written a lyric, but that Lozanne had not seemed very keen about it. He then proceeded to recite the lyric with great feeling: there was a moment's awkward silence, and then everyone burst into laughter. They could not control themselves, it was such sheer doggerel. He took it very well. He laughed, and said, 'Well, perhaps I had better stick to architecture and not become a poet.'

In connection with some publicity he was trying to get for her, Titterton asked her about her life in British Columbia. She told him of her youthful romance, of the death of her first husband in the war, and she scribbled some autobiographical notes for him on the back of a menu card – that she had a natural bent for music and started composing at an early age; that when she was only seventeen she played a violin concerto and a piano concerto on the same evening at a concert in Toronto. Frank Titterton liked her songs, broadcast them, and recorded them. For his record of 'You Brought my Heart the Sunshine', she played the accompaniment herself. It was probably through him or Van Lier that she met and became friends with Richard Tauber who visited her at the Villa Madeira.

A cellist from the Bournemouth Symphony Orchestra, who had heard she was a brilliant pianist, also visited her and asked her to play a Liszt Rhapsody; she surprised him by asking which key he would like to hear it in and then by playing it with complete assurance in the one he chose. She had the unusual gift of being able to get inside the music and transpose it at will into any one of the eighteen different keys.

This period of Alma's life was a happy one. Besides enjoying this success with her music, she derived immense pleasure from her children, both Christopher, her son by Compton Pakenham, and John, Rattenbury's son. They have vivid recollections of the affection she lavished upon them: there were trips to the New Forest where they sat in the clearings while she played the violin for them; in summer she would awaken them before dawn and the three of them would be swimming in the sea as the sun rose, little John riding on his mother's back. John still recalls how his mother taught him to read, and taught him to help in the garden, and to dance for his father. When he was old enough he went to a day-school and then to a prep school as a weekly boarder, returning for weekends to the Villa Madeira. His father always drove him back to school and collected him at the end of the week.

The Rattenburys did not associate very much with their neighbours who were perhaps inclined to resent Alma's fine clothes, her Daimler, her frequent visits to London, her free and easy ways and her style of living that was rather Bohemian by local standards – she never thought of keeping regular hours, and sometimes her lights were on all night while she played her piano or listened to records. One day she telephoned Miss Esmond and told her she had written two more songs she wanted Frank Titterton to hear : she had started afresh, she said, as her husband had lately taken up some new scheme and had lost interest in her music.

He seems at this time to have lost interest in Alma as well. She had hoped that these songs would arouse his old enthusiasm, but she was disappointed; he remained uninterested and apathetic. His new scheme, for the construction of a block of flats, was not pursued with anything like his old flair and determination : it became merely an additional source of worry. He was evidently suffering from the same ailment that had afflicted him in British Columbia during the three years before he met Alma, but this time there was no 'Dr Chiro' to set him on his feet again. Alma was left to her own devices. He seems to have made only two friends, the local practitioner, Dr William O'Donnell, who was the old-fashioned type of family doctor with a genuine and personal interest in his patients; and there was a Mr Jenks, a retired barrister who had a house at Bridport and was in some way connected with the building project.

Alma had made a close friend of Irene Riggs who entered her service in 1931 : although she was about her own age, the resemblance ended there, for Irene was shy and rather plain : it was typical of Alma to treat her as an equal, not because she thought it was her social duty, but because it would have seemed unnatural for her to have behaved otherwise. There was a genuine affection between them. They went to London on shopping expeditions together, and once to Oxford, staying away for two or three days at a time.

In August 1932 Alma fell ill. Dr O'Donnell sent her to a nursing home for two weeks observation. She was X-rayed and found to be suffering from pulmonary tuberculosis. This didn't affect her life style in any way, except that she began to drink cocktails, sometimes to excess, but then she wouldn't drink again for a month or so. She had always been attracted to men of talent and initiative, and it may be that when these qualities manifested themselves less and less in her husband the strength of her feeling for him began to wane also. The difference in their attitude to money became a constant source of irritation. Rattenbury was increasingly worried about his financial situation : he had never been poor, whereas she had been, frequently, and was not alarmed by the possibility of being so again. Her generosity, her concern for everybody's welfare and for all living things, which once had endeared her to him, began to cause him anxiety now that he was no longer wealthy. As a practical businessman he took exception to her carelessness in financial affairs: anyone in need, friend or complete stranger, could get money from her merely for the asking, and she had a habit of giving away her things to anyone who admired them. He allowed her about £1,000 a year, but out of this she had to meet the household expenses, clothe herself and her family, pay the staff and the school fees and the wine merchant and the doctor's bills: he seems to have given up in despair any attempt to teach her to keep her accounts in order: she had a totally unmathematical mind. She was always overdrawn, and always trying to coax more money from him, inventing some likely story to suit every occasion.

Her son Christopher once said, with laughing affection, 'She was half genius, half moron. Strike a chord on the piano, and she could identify every note in it, but she had difficulty in counting above ten because she would run out of fingers!'

She received small sums occasionally from her mother, and when cheques arrived from the music publishers and record companies, she cashed them at once and spent the money: these cheques became larger and more frequent – she seemed to be on the high road to success. On Saturday, 29th April 1935 there was a special performance of music by Lozanne on BBC Radio; Sidney Baynes and his orchestra played their arrangements of 'Night Brings me You', 'Avelette', and 'Zanita'. The most popular of her records was 'Dark-Haired Marie', sung by Peter Dawson:

> Are you waiting in your garden
> By the deep wide azure sea?
> Are you waiting for your loveship,
> Dark-Haired Marie?
>
> I shall come to claim you someday,
> In my arms at last you'll be,
> I shall kiss your lips and love you,
> Dark-Haired Marie.[4]

Although she chose the times for making her requests for money when Rattenbury had had several whiskies and was feeling mellow, occasional rows about her extravagance were unavoidable. Their only serious quarrel, however, was the direct result of his morbid depression. It happened on 9th July 1934, when he was even gloomier than usual. In his worst moods he would talk of suicide and threaten to put his head in the gas oven : on this particular evening he went on about it at greater length than usual until Alma, exasperated, told him it was a pity he didn't do it instead of merely harping on about it. This roused him from his apathy. He struck her in the face, she bit his arm, and he stormed out of the house.

In great alarm she called Dr O'Donnell : he treated her for a black eye and put her to bed with an injection of a quarter of a grain of morphia, then notified the police that Rattenbury was missing and went out with Irene to search for him along the cliffs. They didn't find him but, as it happened, Rattenbury decided against suicide that night, and returned home at about two o'clock in the morning. It would be unfair to judge a marriage by an occasional crisis, and this was the only time they came to blows. They bore one another no grudge as a result of that evening, and continued to live as they had before, on cordial, even affectionate terms. Alma's health was still poor. The doctor called frequently, and on four separate occasions she was operated on for tubercular glands.

In September of that year, 1934, because Rattenbury no longer wished to drive the car, they advertised for a willing lad, preferably scout-trained, age 14 to 18. As a result they engaged George Percy Stoner, who gave his age as twenty-two. He was a likeable sort of chap, pleasant and friendly; quite good-looking too, the son of a bricklayer. Alma, devoid as usual of any class-consciousness, accepted him as an equal, and soon he was behaving like one of the family, smoking Rattenbury's cigars, playing cards with him and discussing his business problems with him. His duties were to drive the car, take the little boy to school and call for him, attend to the garden and do a few small jobs about the house. His wages were £1 a week, but instead of paying him regularly, Alma would send him to buy things in the shops and give him a cheque for £5 or £10 telling him to deduct his wages and bring her the change.

As Rattenbury would seldom go out, it was Stoner now who drove Alma and Irene to the country, or to London on their shopping and theatre expeditions. Alma had liked him from the first. Something about him touched a sympathetic chord in her nature. She had never forgotten her early love and her brief happiness so abruptly terminated by the war, and her youth squandered in the pain and squalor of Auxiliary Hospital No 301 behind the front line – but perhaps not yet quite gone beyond recall? Irene observed with dismay and some personal distress that her mistress was beginning to prefer Stoner's company to hers. In November 1934 they again spent three days in Oxford, and it was still Irene who occupied the room at the Randolph Hotel communicating with Alma's, but before the end of that month everything had changed : Alma and Stoner had become lovers, and he had moved into the Villa Madeira.

She was not worried about what Rattenbury would say. In this matter at least he was understanding and considerate. He had told her long ago to make her own arrangements about her physical life, and now she told him she had done so, without specifically naming Stoner. The house was small. There were three bedrooms on the first floor : Alma's was at the back with french windows opening onto a balcony that overlooked the garden; Stoner's was just across the landing from it, and Irene occupied the smaller room above the kitchen : it would have been difficult for Rattenbury not to know what was going on, but he does not appear to have been interested. He spent most of his time in the drawing-room, which was next to his bedroom on the ground floor.

Soon Alma was deeply in love with Stoner; she was experiencing a renewal of her youth and a new awakening – 'My Heart comes to Your Heart in the Darkness' she sang, and lovers all over the country responded to the recorded words and the melody.

It is not likely that Stoner would have dared to make love to her unless she had taken the initiative and deliberately encouraged him, but after she had become his mistress, a remarkable change took place : the unassuming youth, having by chance gained possession of a cultured and still beautiful woman – a conquest which he had done nothing to deserve – found himself in a situation for which his understanding and his experience of life were insufficient. He became self-assertive, inconsiderate, domineering. She seemed to like this. He told her to give up drinking cocktails as they were bad for her, and she obediently did so. Almost at the same time as the affair was consummated, she had discovered that, although he had given his age as twenty-two, he was in fact barely eighteen. She tried to break off their intimate relationship, but Stoner would not hear of it. They frequently quarrelled about this, but Stoner always had his way. Once he lost his temper and caught hold of her so violently that Irene intervened and separated them. She confided to Irene that he carried a dagger with a four-inch blade, and that he had threatened to kill her – it was exciting, as well as frightening, to be the object of a man's jealousy after years of neglect.

In February 1935, evidently to alarm her, he hinted that he took drugs : she at once sent for the invaluable Dr O'Donnell, confessed that she and Stoner were living together, that he was sometimes violent, had threatened to strangle her, and that she had reason to believe he was taking drugs. She asked the doctor to have a talk with him and warn him of the effects. The doctor did so. Stoner admitted to him that he was taking cocaine. O'Donnell offered to help him if he wished to give it up, but this was not well received. Shortly after this, Stoner told her he had had an impulse to throw himself from the train as it was crossing the River Avon near Christchurch – it was a spot she afterwards remembered.

It is difficult to determine to what extent Stoner put on these apparently neurotic symptoms deliberately, but it is obvious that consciously or unconsciously they were all directed towards playing on Alma's emotions and increasing his domination over her.

About twice a year Alma's account was so overdrawn that she had, on one pretext or another, to wheedle quite a large sum out of Rattenbury to pay the tradesmen, perhaps £100 or £150. In March of that year, 1935, she asked him for £250 'because she had to go to London for an operation'. She thought it sounded fairly plausible because her last operation for tuberculous glands had been about two months ago. No doubt he understood that this was a fiction for he showed no solicitude, or interest in the proposed operation; he merely grumbled that it would entail sacrifices for him, and gave her the money.

She used some of it to pay off the outstanding bills and then set out for London with Stoner, this time without Irene. The car broke down at Southampton so they left it there and went on by train. They took separate rooms at the Royal Palace Hotel, Kensington, calling themselves brother and sister, then they went to Harrod's and hurried from one department to another, buying Stoner silk pyjamas, shoes, shirts and a grey suit; then he chose a ring for her, which she wore. They spent the next three days going to theatres and cinemas, and returned to the Villa Madeira on the evening of 22nd March, at about 10.30. Rattenbury was already in bed, so she went in and kissed him goodnight. He asked nothing at all about the operation or what had happened in London : he had had a good deal of whisky and was feeling jolly.

Sunday morning, 24th March, found Rattenbury in one of his frequent bounts of depression. To cheer him up Alma persuaded him to have Stoner drive them to the Tree Top Kennels to see a litter of puppies that her dog, Dinah, had recently produced. They spent a reasonably happy morning at the kennels and returned to the Villa Madeira for

Rattenbury's design for the Parliament Buildings in Victoria B.C.

The Parliament Buildings today

John's christening

Alma and Francis Rattenbury with their son John

lunch; then Rattenbury took a nap while Alma amused herself with her favourite pastime, playing with her youngest son, and reading to him. As Irene was out, it fell to Stoner to serve tea, which he did at 4.30 p.m., with cake and sandwiches, upstairs in Alma's bedroom. It must have been a depressing meal, for Rattenbury insisted on reading aloud passages from a library book entitled *Stay of Execution* by Eliot Crawshay-Williams. In this novel the main character, Stephen Clarke, seems also to have needed the services of a chiropractor. At the beginning of the book he feels old and depressed, and his thoughts turn to suicide. The following extract could have been a description of Rattenbury as he was then:

> Bitterness crept into Stephen's soul. He hoped less and trusted less, and desired less, and descended gradually, as most men do under the influence of age and experience, from the lofty levels where his young spirit used to dwell. Where once had been the joyous desire for adventure, came a restless seeking for sensation. His old energy began to weaken; his capacity for steady and good work diminished with his belief in its being worth doing. He failed himself, and others failed him. There had been an attempt at marriage, but it had ended in disaster.[5]

Rattenbury concluded his lugubrious narrative by observing that he admired a person who had the courage to do himself in before he became old and doddering.

It was clear that he was in one of his worst moods and it would take more than an hour at the dog kennels to get him out of it. Alma suggested a trip to London, but he didn't like the idea. She then suggested they should visit Mr Jenks, his friend and business associate at Bridport. He liked this better, because he wanted to discuss with his friend the financing of the block of flats that was causing him such concern.

After tea, according to her evidence at the trial, Alma went down to her husband's bedroom, in which the telephone was, to make arrangements for the visit. Mr Jenks said he would be delighted to see them, and suggested they should stay at his house, Plasdene Manor, for the night. She accepted this offer and put down the receiver. At this point she seems to have been rather pleased with herself – looking forward to the change in their usual routine that the visit would bring, and to the possibility that Ratz would start work again. He was always better when he was working on a project. His depressions and continual talk of suicide must have been very hard to live with, and perhaps increased her dependence on Stoner.

Meanwhile Rattenbury had taken *Stay of Execution* downstairs with him, and remained absorbed in it, seated in his overstuffed armchair. The book went on to describe how a friend, to raise Stephen Clarke's spirits, invited him to visit his country house. The plot then became rather involved: at one stage Stephen was attacked by an intruder who entered through the french windows; and then a girl, Cecily, who had fallen in love with him, committed suicide in a rather dramatic and ostentatious fashion. Towards the end of the book there was a passage in which the author, in the form of a dialogue between Stephen Clarke and a girl he is trying to dissuade from marrying him, gave his views on elderly men with young wives:

> . . . elderly men like to marry young girls, and after a bit it's hell for both.
> 'Why?'
> 'Because it's naturally annoying to a young girl to see her husband mouldering while she still feels frisky. To see the bare patch on the back of his head growing bigger and shinier. To have the shock, one day, of coming across most of his teeth grinning at her out of a glass of water. And there are other things, besides.'
> 'What things?'
> 'Well – if you will have me enter into physiological details – a woman, let's put it, always wants more than a man. And when a man's a good deal older, she wants a good deal more than him. A good deal more than he can give her. It takes all his time for a young man to keep pace with a young girl. And an old man hasn't a chance of doing it. And then – she usually goes somewhere else to make up the deficiency.

At this point, at page 291, Rattenbury laid the book face downwards on the piano, perhaps to pour himself a drink – or perhaps Alma joined him just then for their evening game of cards.

CHAPTER FIVE

The Investigation

It was not until 28th March that Alma really understood what was
happening to her, or became aware of her surroundings. At some time in
the course of the morning she awoke, her mind struggling back to
normal, and she found herself lying fully dressed on a hard bed in a
narrow whitewashed room : at one end of it there was an arched
window with bars, high up in the wall; at the other a heavy door in
which there was a sliding panel with a round observation hole above it.
The room contained only a wooden chair, a folding table, a wash-basin
and a water-closet.

It was all part of the nightmare that had beset her when she rushed
downstairs and found Rattenbury leaning back in his armchair terribly
injured, but now she knew it was real. She remembered chafing his
hands and trying to get him to speak to her, and then the horror of
treading on his false teeth on the bloodstained carpet. She remembered
also taking a drink to stave off the nausea that assailed her, being sick
and pouring herself another one, but whether she had drunk the second
one or not, she wasn't sure. Evidently she must have. Everything about
that night was swimming in her mind like a dream one knows one has
dreamt and still has the shadowy outlines of, but can't recall. She
recaptured one or two detached fragments : she saw herself winding a
wet towel round Rattenbury's head, she saw herself driving away from
the villa, looking back and seeing little John standing in the doorway;
she didn't know in whose car, or where to. She remembered also making
out two cheques, each for five pounds, one for Irene and one for
Stoner. What she did with them, or how she got her cheque book, she
didn't know.

Keys jangled outside, the door swung open and a woman in uniform
entered. 'Better get up,' she said. 'You've to see the Governor.'

She was conducted along an immense echoing corridor. There were
high walls on either side with galleries connected by spiral staircases.

They passed a centre point from which three more identical corridors radiated; and eventually they came to a room in the hospital block in which the Governor, Dr Morton, was seated at a desk.

Alma was fortunate to be in the custody of this wise and understanding public servant who worked unceasingly to help the prisoners entrusted to his care, and to improve their conditions. He had seen her first two days ago, on the morning of the 26th, when she was still under the influence of morphia and couldn't understand what was said to her but kept repeating the same sentences again and again. Now that she was better he found, as he had expected, that she had no recollection of what she had said then, or of how she had behaved since her arrival. He had to inform her that she was in Holloway Prison, charged with the attempted murder of her husband, and that she had made statements to the police incriminating herself. Rattenbury had died that morning. The news did not come as a shock – as a Red Cross Nurse in Auxiliary Hospital 301 behind the lines, she had seen many men die, and she had known from the first, instinctively, that there was no hope for him. It meant now, Dr Morton explained, that she would be charged with murder.

He was entirely convinced that she was innocent, and he knew from the tests he had applied to her that until that morning she had been unaware of what she was saying. She would have to stand her trial, but he was confident she would be acquitted if she would now tell the truth about what had happened: it was the only way to clear herself, and he trusted she would do so. Alma thought for a long while, and then answered: 'The truth is, it was my fault – absolutely.'

On the following day, at 5.40 p.m., Detective-Inspector Carter came to Holloway Prison and in the presence of Alma's solicitor, Lewis Manning, charged her with the murder of Rattenbury. She made no reply.

Meanwhile Irene had taken the little boy back to the school where he was a weekly boarder, and now she was alone in the Villa Madeira with Stoner. In order to escape for a short time from their gloom and depression they decided, on Tuesday, 26th March, to drive to the nearby town of Wimborne Minster. She had given him Alma's message about the mallet, but even as she was doing so she remembered the police already had it, so there was no point. She had informed Stoner of this also and he made no comment: but the outing had put him in a more expansive mood. On the way back, passing through Ensbury, he pointed out the places where he had lived and the houses of people he knew. When they passed his grandparents' house he mentioned that he had collected the mallet there at about 8 o'clock on the Sunday evening, but that it would not carry any fingerprints because he had worn gloves. Irene, plucking up courage, asked him why he had done it. He replied that he had seen Rattenbury making love with Alma that afternoon and had determined that he must be put out of the way.

Now Irene knew the truth and might be able to save her mistress, but she had no evidence yet and could not be sure whether Stoner, if confronted by the police, would repeat his confession or simply deny that he had told her anything. Next day her mother and brother moved into the villa to keep her company. Although Irene was not a Catholic, she went that evening to see a priest. When she returned at about 10.30 p.m. she learned that Stoner had got drunk and rushed out of the house shouting, 'Mrs Rattenbury is in jail, and I put her there!' Stoner was not habitually drunk, he didn't drink at all, but apparently he had received a letter from Alma that upset him. Later, he was brought back by two taxi drivers and he behaved so wildly that Irene was frightened and phoned the police. By the time a constable arrived he had calmed down, and they had put him to bed. He told Irene he was going to London in the morning to see Alma, and that he would give himself up. He asked her not to let him oversleep.

In spite of his self-indulgence on the previous evening, Stoner got up at 6.30 and caught the London train – it was Thursday, 28th March, the day Rattenbury died. Early in the afternoon Dr O'Donnell called at the villa and, finding Irene alone, was able to talk freely to her. He could sense that she was hiding something. When he asked her if she thought Alma had killed her husband, she replied firmly: 'I know she did not!'

He then impressed upon her that if she had any information about the case it was her duty to give it to the police, and that if she did not she might find herself implicated. Poor Irene, who did not know that the doctor was already aware of Alma's liaison, still hesitated. At last he persuaded her that discretion was of little importance in comparison to Alma's life which was at stake; and so she confided to him that Stoner had confessed and even told her where he got the mallet. The doctor immediately rang the police who came at once and took down Irene's statement.

Detective-Inspector Carter arrested Stoner that evening at Bournemouth Station as he stepped off the London train. His journey had been in vain as he had not managed to see Alma. He was taken to the police station and formally charged with Rattenbury's murder. He had in his pockets a letter from Alma asking him to come to her, two photographs of her and a heavy gold watch.

'Be careful of that watch,' he said 'It was given to me by Mrs Rattenbury and it is worth twenty pounds.'

Next day, at about 11.30 a.m., he said to Constable Gates who was in charge of him, 'You know Mrs Rattenbury, don't you?'

'Yes, I do,' came the reply.

'Do you know Mrs Rattenbury had nothing to do with the affair?'

He was cautioned, but still he went on: 'When I did the job I believed he was asleep. I hit him, and then came upstairs and told Mrs Rattenbury. She rushed down then. You see, I watched through the french windows and saw her kiss him goodnight, then leave the room. I waited, and crept in through the french window which was unlocked. I think he must have been asleep when I hit him, still, it ain't much use saying anything. I don't suppose they will let her out yet. You know there should be a doctor with her when they tell her I am arrested, because she will go out of her mind . . .'

On the following day the *Bournemouth Daily Echo* reported: SENSATIONAL EAST CLIFF TRAGEDY DEVELOPMENT. RATTENBURY'S DEATH. HIT ON HEAD WITH MALLET. MAN REMANDED AT BOURNEMOUTH.

There have been swift and sensational developments in the case of alleged attempted murder which came up at the Bournemouth Police Court on Monday. Yesterday the man died, and today a man was brought before the magistrates on a murder charge. . . . He stepped lightly into the witness-box and smiled recognition to one or two people in the public seats. He was smartly dressed in a broad grey striped suit with blue tie and blue striped soft collar. His hair was brushed back smoothly, and his face was pale.

The charge was read by the Clerk – 'that you did by wounding murder one Francis Mawson Rattenbury on 24th March 1935.' Someone at the back of the court murmured, 'It's a lie!' During the proceedings which lasted only a few minutes, Stoner stood with his arms resting on the side of the dock. . . . (*Bournemouth Daily Echo, 29th March 1935*)

Inspector Carter asked for a remand until the following Tuesday, 2nd April, which meant that he and Alma would appear together before the magistrates on that date: consequently the public interest was very great. The remand was granted, and Stoner was taken to Dorchester Jail. On 1st April an inquest on Rattenbury was opened:

The Coroner (Mr Lefroy), addressing the jury, said that the circum-stances relating to his death were now a matter of criminal proceedings, and therefore the enquiry would be confined to one of identity, to evidence of death and medical evidence of the cause of death.

(Bournemouth Daily Echo, 29th March 1935)

The curiosity aroused by these reports caused members of the public to gather outside the law courts when Alma and Stoner were due to appear. The reports continued :

TWO CHARGED WITH MURDER. As early as 9.30 in the morning – an hour and a half before the court was due to open – a little group of women had gathered outside the law courts in Stafford Road in their eagerness to secure seats, and an hour later the queue had grown to about 150. . . . Only a small section of the crowd was admitted.

Mrs Rattenbury appeared in the dock accompanied by a wardress. A plain clothes officer appeared beside Stoner. The man appeared com-posed, but the woman showed signs of languor and leant her head on an upraised hand. . . . *(Bournemouth Daily Echo, 2nd April 1935)*

The proceedings lasted only a few minutes – the couple being remanded until 11th April.

By the following week the case had attracted the national newspapers and on 11th April there were twenty-five journalists in court. The spectators had began to line up several hours before the doors were due to open; the queue was controlled by four police officers and a sergeant. Stoner was the first to arrive, at the rear entrance of the law courts; then Alma came, at about 11 o'clock, in a large saloon car that had brought her from Holloway : seeing the crowd awaiting her, she leant back as far as she could, and a wardress who was with her hurriedly drew the blinds, screening her from view until the car drew up and she was led into the building.

The Chief Constable of Hampshire had a seat on the bench with the magistrates : in front of them was a table on which were laid out various exhibits – a pair of folded brown trousers, two suitcases, green and brown *crêpe de chine* pyjamas, blue-striped and other shirts, red and blue ties and other garments of men's wear, a stained pack of playing cards, and a large wooden mallet. Beside the table stood an armchair with faded cushions.

The Director of Public Prosecutions had decided to go on with the case against both the accused, each of them being a self-confessed murderer : he did not charge them also with conspiracy to murder, which would have entailed proving some sort of agreement between them for which no evidence had come to light. Each was to be charged individually with murder but in the same indictment so that they would be tried together, unless the judge ordered otherwise.

Mr E. Marshall Harvey appeared for Stoner; Mr Lewis Manning for Alma: both were highly respected local lawyers. Alma wore a large pink carnation in the corsage of her beige dress as she preceded Stoner into the dock: for a fleeting second their eyes met, but there was no sign of recognition.

Before they were charged, Mr Manning asked that the name of Stoner should be read first as he had been the first to be charged with murder. Mr Marshall Harvey opposed this; he said that Mrs Rattenbury had been charged earlier with attempted murder, and it automatically followed that she would be charged with murder on her husband's death.

There was perhaps some small psychological advantage in not being named first in the charge, in not appearing to be the principal suspect, but when it came to the real trial at the assizes the advantage would be the other way round because the counsel defending the accused named first would have the right to address the jury last, and therefore his words would be more freshly in their minds while they were considering their verdict. The main significance, however, of this incident for an observer was as an indication that the lawyers were seeking advantages over each other and were not attempting a joint defence of their clients though they were being tried together.

The Chairman said he saw no reason to make any alteration. The Clerk thereupon read the charge, naming Alma first. Acting on the advice of their lawyers, they both pleaded not guilty. Stoner stood relaxed and apparently unconcerned: Alma fidgeted nervously with the collar of her fur coat.

Opening the case for the prosecution, Mr Paling explained that the deceased man was aged about sixty-seven years, he was a retired architect and lived at 5 Manor Road, Bournemouth. The female accused was his wife. They were married some seven or eight years ago – and he gave a brief résumé of their previous marriages, their children, and who lived in the Villa Madeira at the time of the assault.

Alma looked as if she ought to be in hospital undergoing treatment instead of facing the ordeal this public enquiry which was being held so that the magistrates could decide whether she and Stoner should be committed for trial at the assizes. She listened calmly while the prosecutor dealt with the most intimate details of her private life and reconstructed from the police reports what had happened on the night of 24th/25th March. Although she didn't remember signing a confession, or re-affirming it at the police station, she had refused to go back on it. She was in love with Stoner, she had involved him in her emotional life, she was twice his age: she wanted to assume all the responsibility for what had happened. Mr Paling read out all her statements and confessions, then held up the mallet and commented, 'To say the least of it, this seems to be a formidable weapon.'

He then read Stoner's statements and remarked that the first one, to the effect that he had gone to bed at 8.05 p.m. could not have been true because it had been shown that at 8.30 p.m. he collected the mallet at his grandparents' house. He pointed out that the relationship between the accused was not confined to that adopted or expected between a servant and the wife of his master. He suggested that Alma's statements as to who had struck the blows were not strictly accurate. He concluded:

When you come to view the evidence as a whole I shall ask you to bear in mind the motives that ordinarily actuate human beings in the conduct of their affairs, and to come to the conclusion that there is evidence which ought to go before a jury to show that Mrs Rattenbury as well as Stoner is a principal in the commission of the offence with which they are both charged.

His speech lasted nearly a whole day. Another two days were taken up in hearing the witnesses called by the prosecution. A great thing was made of Alma and Stoner's visit to London just before Rattenbury's death: the salesmen from the various departments of Harrod's where they had bought Stoner's cap, shoes, silk pyjamas, shirts, etc., each in turn gave evidence in the minutest detail – one of them identified the suit Stoner was wearing as the one Alma had bought for him. The receptionist at the Royal Palace Hotel described how they had come up to the desk together, how Alma had signed for 'Mrs Rattenbury and brother', but he had requested Stoner to sign also. With the aid of the chief cashiers of the banks concerned, they even traced a five pound note to Messrs Kirkby & Bunn, Old Bond Street jewellers, that had been issued to Alma in Bournemouth. After the police had told their story of what they found at the Villa Madeira, the medical evidence went on and on, and 'with telling gestures, the doctor (Rooke) indicated on his own head where Mr Rattenbury was wounded.' (*Bournemouth Daily Echo*)

At the end of the third day, the magistrates committed both Alma and Stoner for trial at the Hampshire Assizes. Mr Manning applied for the trial to take place at the Central Criminal Court because the Hampshire Assizes would not be held until July, and it would be, he submitted, a very great hardship for Mrs Rattenbury to wait that length of time before taking her trial. Mr Marshall Harvey supported his application. Mr Paling offered no objection, except to point out that the defence would probably not be ready in time for the next sitting there, which would commence on the following Tuesday. Proceedings were therefore adjourned until the following Wednesday, upon which date the prisoners were again brought before the magistrates' court at Bournemouth; and this time they were committed for trial at the Central Criminal Court in London, better known as the Old Bailey.

After every session of the magistrates' court there had been headlines: SENSATIONAL ALLEGATIONS BY PROSECUTOR. MR RATTENBURY'S HEAD WOUNDS. MRS RATTENBURY'S PINK CARNATION. ALLEGED PURCHASES BY ACCUSED COUPLE AT LONDON STORE, followed by pages of verbatim reports punctuated by sub-titles such as BANK TRANSACTION. A GOODNIGHT KISS. THREE SEPARATE BLOWS. PYJAMAS AT 60/- A PAIR etc. It took three long columns of newsprint to describe the gruesome details of Rattenbury's injuries and the post mortem. A local newspaper in Alma's home town, Victoria BC, called her a twentieth-century Circe who lured men to their destruction to further her own ambitions.

As has so often happened, details of the preliminary hearing, during which no word was said for the defence, were widely reported. They had the effect of creating violent prejudice, particularly against Alma. A very enlightened observer, Miss Tennyson Jesse, well-known author and criminologist, formed the opinion that she was 'a coarse, brawling, drunken and callous woman'.[1]

When the school holidays were about to begin, the question arose, what was to be done with the children? It was arranged that John would be looked after by Keith Miller Jones, Rattenbury's nephew, at the London flat he shared with his sister. Mrs Daphne Kingham, who was Compton Pakenham's sister and therefore Christopher's aunt, received a letter from the family solicitor, asking her if she would look after the lad, and asking her also if she could do anything to help Alma. She therefore collected Christopher from his school and took him to her home in Berkshire. Then she went to see Alma whom she had never met.

In the bare interviewing room they had to sit one each side of a large wooden counter which stretched from wall to wall. They took to each other immediately. The visitor put her handbag down on the counter and invited Alma to use her make-up: the wardress in attendance said nothing. Alma seemed to be popular with the staff, perhaps because she was so docile.

When Mrs Kingham had told her all about Christopher, she asked her what she did all day, and 'How have they been treating you?'

'I've been scrubbing floors,' Alma said. 'I don't know whether I should have been made to do this as I am officially innocent unless and until found guilty, but it was easier to acquiesce than to have a row about it.'

Mrs Kingham was impressed by Alma's personality and good nature but she didn't find her brother's ex-wife particularly beautiful – which is perhaps not surprising considering what she had been through – neither were her songs much to her liking.

The next visitor was the enthusiastic admirer of her music, Frank Titterton, who had done so much through his records and broadcasts to make her name known to the public. He subsequently wrote an article for the *Daily Express* in which he said,

> . . . the charges of murder against Lozanne and Stoner staggered me. I had never even heard of Stoner. Lozanne had spoken to Miss Esmond about him only once. She thought she was joking and laughed at her.
>
> Miss Esmond and I went to see Lozanne in Holloway Prison. She was brought from the hospital by a nurse into the bare waiting-room where we were. 'How dreadful it is to meet like this!' were her first words.
>
> She looked wan, and was worried about her children. She spoke little about the charge against her, but from her conversation it was plain she had not the slightest doubt what the outcome would be.
>
> She discussed plans for the publishing of her songs, and again and again she spoke of what she would do 'when it is all over and I am free again'.
>
> Towards the end of the brief interview she said to me wistfully, 'Oh! I am so hungry for some music.' I bent towards her and softly sang in her ear a verse from one of her songs. Lozanne went into ecstasies. It was pathetic to see her.
>
> She told me she was sleeping badly, and that it would help her if she was allowed to compose songs while in prison. I sent her a bundle of lyrics, but the Governor returned them to me. The Prison Commissioners had decided that she could not have them.[2]

Alma did, however, compose a song in her prison: it was to her own lyric – a love song to Stoner, which she kept on repeating again and again. It was 'to help me to keep my mind sane', she said:

> By some mistake my spirit held you dear,
> But now I wake in agony and fear

To fading hope, and thought distressed and grey,
With outstretched hand I put your face away.

By some mistake you filled my empty days,
But now I wake to face the parting ways,
I see your smile, I hear the words you say,
With no reply I hush your voice away.

By some mistake, by some divine mistake,
I dreamed awhile, but now I wake, I wake.
Yet, dying, dream you kept my vision true,
I seem to climb to heaven in loving you.[3]

The next time Mrs Kingham arrived at the battlemented walls and
crenelated towers of the fairy-tale castle that was Holloway Prison, she
was told the Governor wished to see her. She had an interview with him
in his Tudor-style lodge at the main gates. He told her he was very
sorry for Alma, and that he felt very strongly she should not have been
pressed by the police to make statements while she was under the
influence of alcohol and morphia. The trouble was now, he said, she
was sticking to her story – that she had murdered Rattenbury – and
there was nothing that he or her legal advisers could do about it,
although they felt certain she was innocent and believed they could
establish it if only she would tell the whole truth about what had
happened. They had been to see her again and again, and had assured
her that by shielding Stoner she would only get herself hanged without
being able to save him, and that there was nothing she could do to
help him. It had all been useless. She continued to insist that responsibility for the crime was hers alone, and nothing would persuade her to
say a word against Stoner. Would Mrs Kingham please help? Morton
added he was allowing Alma no visitors beside herself because members
of the press and of the theatrical profession had obtained access to her
and were selling their stories to the newspapers.

Mrs Kingham continued to visit Alma regularly. She was a forcible
character. She talked to her about the interviews with the press, and
got her to admit that she had been offered £500 for her story by a
leading newspaper. 'If you accept it,' she told her, 'I'll have nothing
more to do with you.' And that was the end of it.

She adopted the same tactics about Stoner – 'It's not fair to the
children!' she said. 'They have all their lives before them – are they
to be known as the sons of a woman who was hanged for murder?
You have no right to blast their lives to shield Stoner. You owe it to

them to tell the whole truth, hiding nothing – and if you won't do anything for your own children, why should anybody else? You needn't expect me to go on looking after Christopher for you!' (I had to speak to her like that,' she said afterwards. 'It was the only weapon I had.') She went on questioning her about the crime which seemed to her to have been totally unnecessary: Stoner had had no reason to be jealous of Rattenbury who had made no physical demands on her for several years.[4]

During all this time, Alma wrote to both her children very touching and affectionate letters with little tunes in musical notation at the end.

A few days before the trial, Mrs Kingham brought Christopher to Holloway to see his mother, and this broke down her resistance. Christopher recalled only that she had one eye bandaged because of an infection, and that she appeared quite cheerful, but the effect of the visit on her was devastating. She knew now that she could not go through with her plan to sacrifice her life for the man she loved: the children must come first, and she must fight for their future by clearing herself of the murder charge – but the thought of failing Stoner and leaving him to take all the blame – for that was the only way to save herself – was bitter and hard to accept. And how disillusioning it was to find that in the eyes of this woman of the world her intention of sacrificing herself was not a splendid gesture but a selfish indulgence to which she, as a mother, had no right!

'I wish I had brought Christopher to her sooner,' Mrs Kingham told us. 'Alma adored her children, and they in return were always asking about her and champing to be with her.'

The first indication of Alma's change of heart was in a letter written to Irene immediately after her elder son's visit. Her solicitor had advised her to write about nothing except clothes, and in the first part of the letter she dutifully did so, but then her emotions gradually took charge:

> . . . Oh Lord, and to-morrow Good Friday and I dare not think of the children. I even pretend I haven't any here. If one thought for five minutes they'd go mad. I saw nothing in the papers yesterday except what was cut out; I seem to see nothing but the missing parts. Darling, will one ever be happy again? Friday will be like Sunday here. Of all days in the week, Sunday is the worst. I have to control my mind like the devil not to think of little John. Yes, take him out on Sundays, darling. C was awfully pleased to hear from you. . . . If I feel awfully sad, being separated in such a ghastly way from everything one loves, S's feelings must take some weighing up, but he'll be the same and not allow himself to think. Should think his remorse at what he's brought

down on my head, the children's, etc., – smashed lives – would drive him a raving lunatic – a frightful responsibility to hold in one person's hands. God deliver me from such a hellish responsibility. I couldn't have courage to bear *that pain;* my own is more than enough in a hundred lifetimes as it is. Two times have found my feelings very hard and bitter – Oh, my God, appallingly so – but have managed to drown these feelings and get one's heart soft again. Darling, God bless you, bless us all and get us out of this nightmare. My love to your M. and F.

My love be with you always.

Lozanne.

When she saw her solicitor again she told him that for the sake of the children she would tell the whole truth. She no longer denied that Stoner had committed the murder.

To present her case in court, Lewis Manning briefed a well-known KC, Terence O'Connor. Stoner, under the Poor Prisoners Defence Regulations, was given the services of a very experienced barrister-at-law to defend him – J. D. Casswell. He had lately been in the news for his very determined defence of a Dorset farm labourer, Reginald Woolmington, accused of the murder of his wife and sentenced to death: Casswell had taken the appeal against the sentence right up to the House of Lords, at which stage Terence O'Connor was briefed to lead the defence. Together they had presented and argued the case for two days before the Law Lords and won the appeal. This decision made legal history and established that the prosecution, to secure a verdict of murder, must prove malice.

Now these two able barristers were again working on the same case, but representing opposing interests, for it was Alma's guilt or Stoner's that had to be decided: no one thought both of them had committed the crime. Casswell explained the problem of Stoner's defence thus:

I knew from my written instructions that Stoner was going to insist on a defence which in no way threw the responsibility upon his co-accused; he was not really interested in establishing his innocence, but in ensuring that Mrs Rattenbury was not convicted. The only defence which we were instructed to put before the jury was that he had committed the murder when under the influence of cocaine, but no one, I think, really believed this. On one occasion when asked by Dr O'Donnell what the drug looked like he had replied that it was brown with black flecks*, which showed that he had not even seen the drug, let alone regularly taken it, as he wanted us to believe.[5]

* It was actually to Dr Grierson that he made this remark.

On the Saturday morning before the trial was to open, Casswell and his solicitor's managing clerk went to see Stoner in Brixton Gaol:

> He sat in the barred conference room in the gaol silent and almost completely unco-operative. For my part I did not press him to speak or encourage him to give his personal account of what had happened; I knew he might so easily insist on telling me that he had committed the murder and that he alone was the culprit. If he had done this, my hands would have been tied; by the rules of my profession I should not have been allowed to call any evidence to prove that he was innocent and should have been restricted merely to trying to show that the evidence against him was insufficient. In my own mind I was not sure whether he was guilty or not and I did not want to say anything which might precipitate him into a rash statement – even to me.
>
> I had decided before I went to Brixton that I would not call Stoner as a witness, and his demeanour when I saw him confirmed me in my decision.

He went into Stoner's past, but there was not much to be learned about it. As a child he had been backward and did not learn to walk till he was three years old. His performance at school was very poor, mainly because of his academic deficiencies but also because his parents went to various parts of the country to find work. He spent much of his early life with his grandparents until his own parents finally settled down at 104 Redhill Drive Bournemouth. To his parents he seemed a model son; as a teenager he never behaved badly and was never in trouble. Certainly he was in no way prepared for the dramatic change that came into his life when he took the job at the Villa Madeira.

In Casswell's opinion it was a mistake to order Alma and Stoner to be tried together: only prejudice and bias, he thought, could result from this middle-aged woman and her teenage lover being tried together. He determined to persuade the judge, if he could, to order separate trials. His resolve was strengthened, and his perplexities increased, when he received from Alma's solicitors a copy of her most recent letter to Irene Riggs. Until that moment he had thought she would continue resolutely to accuse herself, but in that letter she had implied in such moving terms that it was Stoner who had killed Rattenbury that it could scarcely be disbelieved.

CHAPTER SIX

Alma Faces Her Judge

On 28th May 1935 it was announced in *The Times* that Mr Justice Humphreys at the Central Criminal Court had fixed next Monday 'for the opening of the trial of Alma Victoria Rattenbury, 31, and George Percy Stoner, 18 . . .' The application was made by Mr Anthony Hawke who was appearing for the prosecution with Mr R. F. Croom-Johnson, KC.

Justice has been administered for more than a thousand years on the site of the Old Bailey, but the present building dates only from the year 1907: its copper dome surmounted by a gilded symbolic figure of justice is a familiar landmark for the citizens of London, who are keenly aware of what passes there. The case of Alma Rattenbury and Stoner had captured their imagination. On the night before the trial some men who were unemployed lined up before the entrance to the public galleries in order to sell their places next morning to later arrivals: they tried to sleep in the doorway but were constantly awakened by the policemen's flashlamps. One enterprising individual set up a stall and supplied hot coffee and rolls.

By 8 a.m. on Monday, 27th May, there were a hundred people in the queue. Among those who were determined to get in was Mrs Daphne Kingham – she had asked for a place in the courtroom to be allocated to her, but this had not yet been done. Two women beside her in the queue were discussing Alma's remarkably fascinating personality, particularly for men, and one of them told the following story: a friend of hers was on his way to Canada with his father's ashes. On the train he happened to get into conversation with Alma. At Liverpool, still chatting, they boarded the liner: only when it had sailed he remembered he had left his father's ashes on the rack of their compartment in the train.

The *Daily Mirror* announced:

No 1 Court at the Old Bailey, the scene of many famous trials, was crowded yesterday for the opening, before Mr Justice Humphreys, of the trial of Mrs Alma Rattenbury, aged thirty-eight (Lozanne, the song writer), and George Percy Stoner, nineteen, her chauffeur, who were accused of murdering the woman's husband, Mr Francis Mawson Rattenbury.

Accommodation was limited. The courtroom had been designed for the administration of justice, not for the interest and entertainment of the public: they would have their entertainment when they read the newspapers. On one side, under three large windows was the jury-box where the 'twelve good men and true' sat solemnly in two rows, very conscious of their importance; opposite them, the benches for the lawyers; at one end, at a higher level than the jury-box, the dock for the prisoners; at the other, on the highest level of all, the presiding judge with the witness-box at his right hand between him and the jury. A large section of the remaining space was allocated to the press.

An Usher of the Court opened the proceedings by announcing:

If any one can inform my Lords, the King's Justices, or the King's Attorney-General, ere this inquest be taken between our Sovereign Lord, the King, and prisoners at the bar, of any treasons, murders, felonies, or misdemeanours, done, or committed by the prisoners at the bar, let them come forth and they shall be heard; for the prisoners now stand at the bar on their deliverance. And all persons who are bound by recognizance to prosecute or give evidence against the prisoners at the bar, let them come forth, prosecute, and give evidence, or they shall forfeit their recognizances. God save the King.

The Court then rose as Mr Justice Humphreys entered, a small alert figure wearing the customary full wig, red robes and white gloves. He carried with him the triangular piece of black material known as the Black Cap and donned by judges whenever they passed sentence of death. He also carried a small nosegay; this tradition goes back to the time when cases were heard in the adjoining Newgate Prison, originally a fortified gate in the walled medieval city, where conditions were so foul that judges carried a small posy of sweet herbs to sniff at to counteract the stench and also as a protection against the ever-present danger of gaol fever.

Before he became a judge, Mr Travers Humphreys had been well known as a prosecutor – he was said to have a mind that was 'the hardest, brightest and most exact of those engaged in criminal work for the Treasury'.[1] Thirteen years ago he had appeared for the prosecution, with the Attorney General, in a famous trial that had certain points of similarity with Alma's – that of Edith Thompson and her younger lover, Frederick Bywaters. In that case too the lover was accused of murdering the woman's husband; and the wife, a highly imaginative woman, who had often indulged in the fantasy of wishing her husband dead, and had written in her letters that she had tried to poison him – though the autopsy did not bear this out – was accused with him. The actual killing seems to have been a spontaneous act of jealousy on the part of her lover. Both were hanged. Grave doubts were expressed at the time as to whether Edith Thompson was in fact guilty, and graver doubts have been expressed since. Humphreys had read out her love letters in court with deadly effect, convincing the jury that she had dominated Bywaters and was therefore equally guilty with him. According to Miss Tennyson Jesse, 'The memory of the earlier trial haunted the Court-room like a ghost.'

The prisoners were brought up from the cells below, into the dock. The spectators craned their necks to get a better view. One young reporter, Barbara Back, who had never before covered a murder trial, gave her impressions as follows :

I was surprised when I got into my seat at the smallness of the court. I don't know why, but I had always imagined the Old Bailey to be enormous.

The kindness of the officials and of everybody present, and the dispassionate look on the faces of the jury, seemed as it should be. The human element was missing. But the moment the prisoners were brought into the dock, everything changed. I began to think I would not be able to bear it. . . . After the first glance she gave round the court, Mrs Rattenbury remained half-hidden by her fur, and apparently quite unmoved. She is more than a pretty woman : her face is attractive with its large perfect eyes, short nose and thick-lipped mouth. She was said to be thirty-eight. She looked much younger. She wears her dark-blue coat and hat with gloves to match with a certain chic.

Stoner looks even less than his eighteen years. . . . He has a pale gentle face. (*Daily Mirror, 28th May 1935*)

The Clerk of the Court said :

Alma Victoria Rattenbury and George Percy Stoner, you are charged with the murder of Francis Mawson Rattenbury on the 28th March last. Alma Victoria Rattenbury, are you guilty or not guilty?

ALMA : I plead not guilty.

CLERK OF THE COURT : George Percy Stoner, are you guilty or not guilty?

STONER : I plead not guilty.

Stoner's counsel, Casswell, was sitting absorbed in the difficult task that lay ahead. Alma's counsel, O'Connor, leaned along the counsels' bench and said to him, 'Mrs Rattenbury is going to give evidence against your boy.'

'This was the first I knew,' Casswell wrote, 'that Alma Rattenbury was going so far in her efforts to save her own neck as actually to give sworn testimony against her ex-lover. . . .'[2]

He was so taken aback that for a moment he forgot he had an application to make to the judge. When he remembered, one of the jurymen had already been sworn. He hurriedly rose to his feet and said :

CASSWELL : My Lord, there is one application which I think I should make to the Court before the jury is sworn, which is that these two persons be tried separately.

THE JUDGE : It would have been better if you had made it before any of the jury were sworn. I will hear your application now. Which accused do you appear for?

CASSWELL : I appear for the accused Stoner. It is an application which perhaps had better be made in the absence of the jury.

THE JUDGE : Very well, if you think so.

The jury retired, and Casswell made his application for separate trials on the grounds that Alma's letter of 18th April, if read out, might have a very bad influence upon the minds of the jury as regards Stoner. It would be difficult, he submitted, for them to disabuse their minds of it. Whereas if Stoner were tried alone, the letter could not be used as evidence, and the jury would not hear it.

The judge asked O'Connor if he supported the application : the reply was that he did not oppose it. He then asked the prosecutor, Mr Croom-Johnson, if he intended to use this piece of additional evidence. The prosecutor submitted that the letter was no different from the other evidence in the case; he had intended saying something himself about it to the jury, but that was entirely in his lordship's discretion.

THE JUDGE : No, Mr Croom-Johnson, it is for you to decide whether any particular matter brought to my attention is admissible in evidence or not. It is not for a judge to advise either side how they should conduct their case . . . I much rather prefer to leave them to conduct the case themselves and I am in a position, so to speak, of an umpire . . . Very well, I am much obliged . . . When that letter is tendered in evidence, I will rule whether it is evidence or not . . .

and with regard to the application he ruled, 'rather tersely', Casswell wrote, 'I see no ground for directing that there should be separate trials in this case.'

For the judge there was no problem at all. The jurors had taken an oath to give a verdict 'in accordance with the evidence'. The letter was not evidence as regards Stoner, and therefore could not influence their decision. It is basic in English law that it is not the business of the jury to decide whether the accused are guilty, but whether they have been proved to be guilty.

The jury now returned, and the rest of them were duly sworn. There were ten men and two women. Casswell was so concerned at the way things were developing that it was only when he recognised a friend sitting in the front row of the jury-box that he remembered he had omitted to consider whether he should have challenged any of the jurors: his friend was Miss Webb-Johnson, sister of the late Lord Webb-Johnson, eminent surgeon. He says that had he realised her name had been called he would certainly have challenged her – not in their decision. It is basic in English law that it is not the business of busy social worker and he would gladly have saved her from spending a week on this unpleasant trial.' In fact, counsel usually object to a juror who is known to them, for various reasons.

THE CLERK OF THE COURT : Members of the jury, the prisoners at the bar, Alma Victoria Rattenbury and George Percy Stoner, are charged with the murder of Francis Mawson Rattenbury on 28th March last. To this indictment they have separately pleaded not guilty, and it is in your charge to say, having heard the evidence, whether they, or either of them, be guilty or not.

Prosecuting counsel, Mr R. C. Croom-Johnson, KC, now rose to present the case for the Crown. He began by explaining to the jury the circumstances out of which the charge of murder arose against Alma and Stoner. He described Alma's and Rattenbury's careers and previous marriages, and that they had settled in Bournemouth in 1928. Then:

In September 1934, Stoner was taken into Mr Rattenbury's employ. At first he appears to have lived outside, but shortly afterwards he took up residence in the house. On 24th March, therefore, the people living at the Villa Madeira were Mr and Mrs Rattenbury, Miss Irene Riggs, who was employed as a companion help to Mrs Rattenbury, Stoner, and the boy John.

Apparently Mrs Rattenbury had a banking acount of her own. It was fed from time to time by payments into it, usually of round sums like £40 or £50, from Mr Rattenbury's account. On 18th March her account was substantially overdrawn. For some reason, on 18th March, a sum of £250, much in excess of anything paid in for some time, was paid into Mrs Rattenbury's account from Mr Rattenbury's account, and on the same day Mrs Rattenbury drew a cheque for £50 which Stoner took to the bank and cashed. The next day Mrs Rattenbury and Stoner came to London, and stayed in adjoining bedrooms in the Royal Palace Hotel, Kensington, passing as brother and sister. They went shopping, and Mrs Rattenbury purchased a large number of articles, apparently for Stoner, including pyjamas, underclothing, suits of clothes, and boots, and Stoner also purchased for himself a diamond ring for £15 10s., while at the same time Mrs Rattenbury appears to have given him a gold watch.

It is the submission of the prosecution in this case that the relationship between Mrs Rattenbury and Stoner had ceased to be that of the wife of the employer and the man employed but had become an adulterous intercourse.

On their going back to the Villa Madeira, where Mr Rattenbury, the somewhat elderly husband, was residing, the situation was likely to be one of some difficulty, and the prosecution submits that Mr Rattenbury stood in the way of their indulgence in this guilty passion.

Coming to the night of the murder, he described how Irene Riggs, returning to the Villa at 10.15 p.m. heard the sound of heavy breathing: he suggested it was the heavy breathing of a man who had suffered the injuries they would hear about. And he described how she had seen Stoner leaning over the bannisters:

After Irene Riggs had gone to bed, Mrs Rattenbury came into her room and talked to her for about ten minutes or so, saying that she had arranged to go, apparently with Mr Rattenbury, on the following day to visit a Mr Jenks, who was a business friend of Mr Rattenbury, living at Bridport. I suggest that Mrs Rattenbury made these statements to Irene Riggs to prepare the notion, which was to be developed later, that some unknown person had come into the house and committed an assault upon Mr Rattenbury, and that she knew nothing about it.

Then he described Alma running downstairs, shouting 'Irene!' and telling her to telephone the doctor. A little while afterwards, after Irene had found Mr Rattenbury in his chair injured and Mrs Rattenbury in her pyjamas, they had called Stoner down. He went off in the car with a view to fetching the doctor more quickly.

Stoner therefore, on this night – and I want you to appreciate the full force of this – from the moment he is seen leaning over the bannisters is only on the scene for a few minutes comparatively late in the story, Mrs Rattenbury apparently not having called Stoner, the man who in the circumstances you might have supposed she would have called if it were nothing more than a case of illness . . .

There were three wounds on Mr Rattenbury's head, and these three wounds were caused by a heavy instrument. I suggest that the instrument which caused these wounds that Dr O'Donnell found on Mr Rattenbury's head was a mallet which Stoner had borrowed from the house of his grandparents by saying that he wanted it to drive some pegs in the garden. The mallet had been borrowed that evening, and it was found in the garden next morning by a police officer. There were human hairs adhering to it and also a piece of skin. It is my duty to submit that there can be no doubt that the hairs found adhering to the mallet were hairs from the head of Mr Rattenbury. [Here the mallet was handed to counsel, who held it up for the jury to see.]

Next, Counsel drew attention to a series of statements Alma had made, the first being to Dr O'Donnell: 'Look at him. Look at the blood. Someone has finished him.'

Now, at 2 a.m., after Mr Rattenbury had been removed to a nursing home, Police-constable Bagwell arrived at the house and saw Mrs Rattenbury. There is no doubt that she was under the influence of drink. She certainly was very excited, but not incoherent, and she said to Police-constable Bagwell, 'I was playing cards with my husband until 9 o'clock. I then went to my bedroom. At about 10.30 I heard a yell, and came downstairs into the drawing-room. I saw my husband sitting in the armchair, and sent for Dr O'Donnell.'

After this Mrs Rattenbury told Inspector Mills that she had heard someone groaning and found her husband unconscious with blood flowing from his head. Inspector Mills then noticed that the french windows were open, and he asked if they were open when she came down for the first time. Her answer was, 'No, they were shut and locked.' If that is right it would preclude the possibility of a person with murderous intention having come in through the window to administer the blows and afterwards to escape through the window into the garden.

A search of the garden was then made, but Police-constable Bagwell remained in the house. While he was there, Mrs Rattenbury made another statement. She said, 'I know who did it.' The officer cautioned her, and Mrs Rattenbury went on, 'I did it with a mallet. It is hidden. Ratz (referring to her husband) has lived too long.' She then corrected herself and said, 'No, my lover did it. I will give you £10. No, I won't bribe you.'

Up to this, no weapon had been found; so far as we know, Stoner had not been seen, except to go to the doctor, and if the blows were delivered when Mrs Rattenbury was upstairs in her own room, how would she know that the mallet was hidden?

It may be suggested that Mrs Rattenbury was distraught and hysterical, that she had been drinking and did not know what she was saying. At 3.30 Inspector Mills told her that her husband's condition was critical, and she asked, 'Will this be against me?'

Having been cautioned by Inspector Mills, she said, 'I did it. He gave me the book. He has lived too long. He said "Dear, dear." I will tell you in the morning where the mallet is.' She then added, 'I shall make a better job of it next time. I made a proper muddle of it. I thought I was strong enough. Irene does not know.'

In the submission of the prosecution, if those words are right, blows were struck, according to this statement, by Mrs Rattenbury, and the reason why they had not killed Mr Rattenbury outright was that her physical strength was not sufficient. She was, when she made these statements, in a state of hysteria and semi-collapse, and the doctor thought it right to give her an injection of morphia. She was put to bed, but apparently came round later, and said, 'I know who did it – his son.' The inspector asked how old his son was, and she replied, 'Thirty-two, but he is not here.'

Counsel then summarised a statement alleged to have been made by Stoner next day, saying that he went to his bedroom at 8.05 p.m. on the Sunday, and that he was aroused at 10.30 p.m. by Mrs Rattenbury shouting to him to come down; but in fact at 8.30 he was at the house of his grandparents borrowing the mallet. He went on :

Then there followed an interview between Inspector Carter and Mrs Rattenbury, and in the course of this interview she made a written statement :

> About 9 p.m. on Sunday, 24th March 1935, I was playing cards with my husband when he dared me to kill him, as he wanted to die. I picked up a mallet. He then said : 'You have not guts enough to do it.' I then hit him with the mallet. I hid the mallet outside the house. I would have shot him if I'd had a gun.

When Mrs Rattenbury was leaving with Inspector Carter, she was met by Irene Riggs and Stoner, to whom she said, 'Don't make fools of yourselves.' Stoner replied, 'You have got yourself into this mess by talking too much.' Later, when charged at the police station, Mrs Rattenbury said, 'That is right. I did it deliberately, and would do it again.'

Croom-Johnson then read out the completely different statement that Stoner made after arrest on 28th March :

> 'You know Mrs Rattenbury had nothing to do with this affair? When I did the job I believe he was asleep. I hit him and then went upstairs and told Mrs Rattenbury. She rushed down then etc . . .'

He concluded his speech, which had lasted an hour and twenty minutes, as follows :

> Ladies and gentlemen, it looks as though Stoner, having borrowed the mallet, which undoubtedly was the instrument used to inflict the head injuries, brought it back, naming some purpose or other, to the house, and it is the contention of the prosecution that one or other of the accused delivered the blow or blows at the head of Mr

Rattenbury; and, if that is right, the prosecution suggests for your consideration that these two people, Mrs Rattenbury and Stoner, with one common design set out to get rid of Mr Rattenbury who, as I suggested earlier, stood in their way. That, members of the jury, is the contention of the prosecution in this case.

The young *Daily Mirror* reporter, Barbara Back, was fascinated she says, by this opening speech for the Crown :

> . . . telling the story of the lives of those people so simply and clearly, lives not unlike our own. . . . After sitting in the court for several hours you become unconsciously part of the machine. Your heart stops aching for the prisoners. You can look at them without feeling cruel or inquisitive.

At first she had watched the judge, wondering if he would show, by the flicker of an eyelid, what he was feeling. Now she doesn't bother. She has been lulled into a sort of coma by Croom-Johnson's droning voice. He was a very dull speaker, but he was seeking to establish a theory, not to make an effect. His most important witness, except the police, was Irene Riggs. She entered the witness-box, looking very smart in a bright green dress and a white hat.

When she had answered the routine questions regarding her address and the circumstances of her employment, Croom-Johnson asked her to describe the villa, the situation of the bedrooms, the daily routine of the family, the duties of the staff; and he took her methodically through the events leading up to the crime. She answered all his questions without hesitation, and gave him no support at all for the theories he was trying to establish – that Alma had come into her bedroom and chatted to her that night, simply as a blind to pretend everything was all right when in fact she knew that Rattenbury had already been attacked; that she had struck the blows with the mallet that Stoner had fetched at her request; and that both of them had wanted Rattenbury out of the way in order to indulge in their 'guilty passion'. As a result of Irene's evidence, Alma appeared as an altogether more sympathetic person than before; but her account of how Stoner had confessed to her weighed heavily against him. Miss Back continued her story :

> Mr Croom-Johnson appeared to be rather at sea with Miss Riggs' description of a jumper, and nothing could make any of the learned counsel understand what a three-piece suit was until it was produced as an exhibit and held up piece by piece in front of the witness-box.

The pathetic little crumpled thing – that probably gave Mrs Rattenbury great pleasure. How she must have hated seeing it! She listened attentively to Miss Riggs's evidence and watched her all the time she gave it. But not once during the day did I see the boy or she glance at each other (*Daily Mirror, 28th May 1935*)

At last they came to the crucial question. Croom-Johnson asked her if she had received a letter from Mrs Rattenbury after she was arrested. At once Casswell intervened :

CASSWELL : My lord, if it is proposed to put his letter in, in my submision, it is not evidence. We have now come to that piece of additional evidence which I have already drawn your lordship's attention to before. In my submission that is not evidence; it cannot be evidence either against Mrs Rattenbury or against my client Stoner.

THE JUDGE : It quite clearly cannot be evidence against your client, and nobody suggests it will, I gather. Why do you say, if it is necessary for you to argue it, it is not evidence against the person who wrote it?

CASSWELL : Because in my submission there is nothing in that that can be evidence against her in any sense of the word, and therefore in my submission that letter ought not to go in.

THE JUDGE : Surely it is not a reason for excluding evidence because there is nothing whatever in it. That is for the jury, if it is about this case at all.

CASSWELL : My lord, if the reading of that letter is in any way going to prejudice my client then it ought not to be read.

THE JUDGE : Of course it will not prejudice your client. It is not evidence against him. The letter is *prima facie* admissible in evidence against Mrs Rattenbury if it is a letter in her handwriting. It may help her or be against her – one does not know anything about it at present.

He brushed the whole thing aside with the words, 'No objection is taken.' Then he instructed the jury as follows :

THE JUDGE : Members of the jury, you understand that the letter is now in evidence, therefore it will be available for you when the time comes for you to read it. You will be entitled to look at all of it; there is nothing in it that anybody wants to keep away from you . . . It is not being kept away from you at all, and when the time comes, if you like, you can read it all, if it interests you.

(He had the curious habit of saying everything twice, or three times, or four times, varying the words slightly, so that half the time he wasn't saying anything except what he had just said already.)

After a discussion with the other counsel about how much of the famous letter to Irene should be read aloud, Croom-Johnson decided to begin at the beginning, to give the jury 'some sort of an indication as to what sort of a letter it is.' This was the letter:

No 880. Name: A. Rattenbury. Holloway Prison. 18.4.35.
Darling. Was glad to see you looking so nice, also your M. and F. I wrote you dozens of letters in my mind last night, and have nothing but an empty box on top this morning. Will you hand to Mrs Grieg (wardress at B.P.S.)* to give me before I go to Court a pair of tweezers, Yvette's rouge, things to do my nails with, and liquid polish, light colour. I think the perfume in small bottles would last longer, also that grey or fawn pair of slippers (same colour you were wearing), in case the brown suede are not O.K. and I can in that case change over. The brown shoes with laces would be best. On second thoughts perhaps the crocodile pair would be best. You might tell Mrs Grieg how much I appreciate her kindness, which has been most considerate. Oh, darling, I hardly know to write. My mind is frozen. When Manning advised me to write about nothing but clothes etc., it almost made one smile. I can hardly concentrate even on them. I think my macintosh would help. Also that red woollen dress the skirt needs a hook on or something, and if I haven't a red belt, you might get a wide one. Oh Lord, and to-morrow Good Friday and I dare not think of the children. I even pretend I haven't any here. If one thought for five minutes they'd go mad. I saw nothing in the papers yesterday except what was cut out; I seem to see nothing but the missing parts. Darling, will one ever be happy again? Friday will be like Sunday here. Of all days in the week Sunday is the worst. I have to control my mind like the devil not to think of little John. Yes, take him out on Sundays darling. C was awfully pleased to hear from you. I cannot understand my M. not doing anything, can you?† Messages of love are not much use to me, when I wanted her help with Long, etc. However, if I feel awfully sad being separated in such a ghastly way from everything one loves, S's feelings must take some weighing up, but he'll be the same and not allow himself to think. Should think his remorse at what he's brought down on my head, the children's etc. — smashed lives — would drive him a raving lunatic — a

* Bournemouth Police Station.

† Since this letter was written Alma's mother had sent her £400, according to Mrs Kingham.

frightful responsibility to hold in one person's hands. God deliver me from such a hellish responsibility. I couldn't have courage to bear *that pain*; my own is more than enough in a hundred lifetimes as it is. Two times have found my feelings very hard and bitter – Oh, my God, appallingly so – but have managed to drown these feelings and get one's heart soft again. Darling, God bless you, bless us all and get us out of this nightmare. My love to your M. and F. My love be with you always. Lozanne.

This letter, even in Croom-Johnson's droning voice, could hardly fail in its impact. He concluded his examination by asking Irene if the name 'Lozanne' was used in the house for Mrs Rattenbury: she said it wasn't, and she personally never called her Lozanne.

> THE JUDGE : Now that letter must be made an exhibit. (The letter was put in and marked Exhibit 43.)

O'Connor now had the congenial task of conducting the cross-examination of this thoroughly sympathetic and co-operative witness. He launched into it with considerable *élan*, to which Irene responded. It was soon evident that both had the same interest at heart – to save Alma. He began by trying to disprove Croom-Johnson's suggestion that she had wanted to get rid of Rattenbury :

As the letter shows, you were on terms of the greatest friendship with Mrs Rattenbury? –Yes.

You had been with her for four years, and the relations in the house were extremely pleasant between everybody, were they not? –Yes.

You were something more than a maid – a companion and help. And Stoner also was a member of the houshold? –Yes.

During the whole four years that you have belonged to that household, have Mrs Rattenbury's relations with her husband been perfectly friendly? –Yes.

With the exception of one trivial quarrel, have you ever known them to have a quarrel? –Just funny little affairs, but nothing.

Just funny little twopenny-ha'-penny affairs? –Yes.

You have known for some time, have you not, that the relations between Mrs Rattenbury and Stoner were those of a woman and her lover? –Yes.

There was no mystery about that either, was there? –No.

He next got her to confirm that Stoner was capable of violence :

And did Mrs Rattenbury tell you that her life had been threatened by Stoner more than once? –Yes.

Was there an occasion . . . (Here Casswell intervened.)

CASSWELL : My lord, I object. This apparently is evidence of something which was said to the lady by one of the accused.

THE JUDGE : Well?

CASSWELL : It does not appear to have been said in his presence, and in my submission it cannot be evidence against him.

THE JUDGE : I am not concerned with the object of learned counsel in bringing out something which, in my view, is clearly admissible in evidence for or against his client. I will tell the jury now if you like, but I have not a shadow of doubt they thoroughly understand it. Members of the jury, documents written by 'A' in the absence of 'B' are never evidence against 'B' merely because 'B' happens to be sitting in the dock and is being tried with 'A'. Statements made by 'A' under these circumstances are not admissible against 'B' for the same reason. Therefore when evidence of this sort is being given, whether for the prosecution or the defence, of some statement made by one of the persons in the absence of the other, you will understand that statement is evidence in regard to – I do not say for or against; it does not matter – that particular person who made the statement. It is not evidence against his or her co-defender. I hope that is very clear. I have very little doubt you have understood it already. I cannot fail to admit evidence merely because it is not evidence against one of the two accused.

Whether or not the judge's explanation had made this any clearer to the jury, O'Connor was permitted to continue his line of questioning :

. . . was there an occasion, in February, when you heard a quarrel going on between them? –Yes.

What time of the day or night was that? –At night, between eleven and twelve.

Where was the quarrel going on? –First, in Mrs Rattenbury's bedroom, and then they went along the landing to Stoner's bedroom.

Did you go out to see what was happening? –I went into Stoner's bedroom.

What did you find was happening? –Well, Stoner had hold of Mrs Rattenbury.

Of what part of Mrs Rattenbury did he have hold? –I could not definitely say.

Could you see if it was the throat or the arm? Was it a firm hold that he had of Mrs Rattenbury? –Yes.

Who separated them? –I separated them.

What was her state of mind on that occasion? –She was rather scared.

Used Stoner to carry a dagger about with him? –Yes.

What kind of length was it? –A blade about four inches.

He got Irene to confirm also that Stoner possessed an airpistol. Then he asked her about Alma's drinking habits – it seemed that about once a month she drank too much, but was not a consistent drinker. She was very highly strung, and any sudden or violent happening would throw her into a state of very great excitement. If Irene was to be believed, it was inconceivable that she should have come into her room on the night of the murder and had a perfectly normal chat if she knew the attack on Rattenbury had already taken place, as Mr Croom-Johnson had suggested. She was even 'a little bit excited' about the preparations for the trip to Bridport she had planned for the following day.

She told you she was going off with her husband to stay with Mr Jenks. Was there anything unusual about her? –No.

Did she look as though she had just had a great shock or heard something very terrible? –Nothing at all.

Did she look as though she had any knowledge at that time that her husband was down below struck with a blow on the head? –No.

It was not an unusual thing for her to come and have a chat with you before going to bed, was it? –No.

She often used to come, I suppose? –Very often.

For a chat with you about what was happening, and on this occasion they were going away the next day, and she told you it was not quite certain whether her husband was going to drive, or Stoner? –Yes.

Did she tell you whether she had been telephoning to Mr Jenks or not? –Yes. She told me she had telephoned.

And then subsequently she left you after five or ten minutes, or whatever it was, and went back, as far as you can make out, to her room? –Yes.

You said you heard someone going downstairs. Was it someone going very quickly? –It seemed to be, yes.

Somebody rushing downstairs? –Oh, in a hurry.

In a hurry. And then, almost immediately afterwards, the cry of 'Irene'? –Yes.

Were you down in the drawing-room within a few seconds of that cry? –Yes.

What was her condition then? –In a terrified state.

Was her condition then like the condition that you had seen a few moments previously in your bedroom? –Nothing at all like it.

Was she a changed woman? –A changed woman, absolutely.

Had she obviously had a sudden and terrifying experience? –Yes.

She had no slippers on, you have told us? –No.

And in her pyjamas which, you say, I imagine she wore about the house sometimes in the afternoon? –Yes.

She told you to telephone for the doctor? –Yes.

She told Stoner, after you had telephoned, to hurry up in the car to see if he could be fetched a little quicker? –Yes.

So that no moment should be wasted? –Yes.

Incidentally, Stoner had no collar on, had he? –I do not know.

What was she saying to her husband, or her unconscious husband, all the time? –Well, she was raving. You could not make out what she was saying – 'Oh, poor Ratz.'

It was dreadful, and you could not make out what she said, but she said, 'Oh poor Ratz.' Did you hear her say, 'What have they done to you?'? –'What has happened?'? I am asking now about the time when you came down and found her with her husband in the drawing-room? –Yes.

You understand that that is the time I am addressing your mind to? –Yes.

She was very impatient with you? –Yes.

What did she think you ought to have done quicker? –She was telling me to hurry – 'Can't somebody do something?'

How did she tolerate the time that elapsed between the telephoning for the doctor and the time he came? –Raving about the house.

Was she drinking? –Yes.

Drinking continuously or not? –She came out for some whisky, yes.

THE JUDGE : Was she drinking whisky continuously. –Well she kept going backwards and forwards for some.

Questions followed about where Stoner was during the time the doctors were attending the patient, then,

What was Mrs Rattenbury's condition when the police arrived? I think they arrived about two o'clock –Yes. She was still in a terrified state.

Was she playing the radio-gramophone? –No.

Did you hear that played at all during the night? –No.

Was she 'making up' to the police? –Yes.

Trying to kiss them? –Yes.

Did one of the police officers complain to you about trying to kiss them? –He did not complain. (*Laughter*) But I heard about it.

Well, he said something about it. What did he say? And if you remember who it was, tell me? –Well, he simply went out of the house, the police officer.

Did he say anything to you about it? –He said he was going to fetch another police officer.

Did he say why? –To stay in the house with him, I suppose. He did not say why.

Do you know why it was? –I do not know why, but I suppose it was because of Mrs Rattenbury.

Because of what you had seen – her trying to kiss him? –Yes.

After the police went away we know that Police-constable Bagwell came at first, and then Mr Mills, and then they went away again, did they not? –Yes.

And that left you and Mrs Rattenbury in the house? –Yes.

You did not see Stoner then, did you? –No.

What did she try to do when you and she were alone in the house? –She tried to rush out of doors. She went to different doors trying to get out, and I locked them and took the keys.

THE JUDGE : You mean the front door? –All the doors.

Cross-examination continued :

All the doors in the house, front and back. How did you keep her in? –By taking all the keys out, and sitting on her in the dining-room.

You put her down on the dining-room chair, and sat on her? –Yes.

When the police came back, did they begin to ask her questions? –Yes.

What was she talking to them about? Was she talking anything that you could understand? –At times you could make out what she was saying, but at others you could not . . .

THE JUDGE : There was a time, was there, when there were no police there and no doctors? –Yes.

A publicity photograph of 'Lozanne', the name Alma used as a songwriter

The Villa Madeira

Rear view of the Villa Madeira. Alma's room is on the left on the first floor

After Mr Rattenbury had been taken away? —Yes.

O'Connor asked:

If you can remember, for how long were you in this uncomfortable predicament – you alone with this lady in the house? —About ten minutes to a quarter of an hour.

That helps us a great deal. That means at the end of this ten minutes or quarter of an hour the police came back again? —Yes.

Who came back this time? —Two or three policemen, I think.

Was that the time when they came back the second time? Was it that time you were talking about when you told me a moment ago that you could not understand what she was saying? —Yes.

Did they begin to ask her questions? —Yes.

Just to make it perfectly clear, I will go back for a moment to this occasion when you took the keys out of the door. She was not trying to escape, was she? —No. She was trying to get out after the policeman.

She described how Dr O'Donnell returned from the nursing home and gave Alma an injection:

You knew he was going to give her an injection? —Yes.

In what condition was she before he took her upstairs? —In a terrible condition.

Did she stay upstairs? —No.

How long after he had taken her up did she come back again? —Not long.

Five minutes? —Yes.

Was she then talking to one of the police officers again? —Yes.

Did you hear Dr O'Donnell warn the police officers that she was not in a fit condition to make a statement? —Yes.

And did he take her up to bed again? —Yes.

Did you help her up that time? —I went upstairs, yes.

Could she get upstairs easily? —No.

Was she falling on the stairs? —She was nearly asleep on the stairs.

And did the police officer call out, 'Look out, she is nearly asleep'? —Yes.

And then she went to bed? —Yes.

O'Connor then passed to the events of a couple of hours later when Alma again opened her eyes:

. . . did the police ask you several times whether she was awake? –Once, or twice, I should say.

Did you go with one of the police officers to her room between six and half-past? –Yes.

That would be after she had only been in bed for a couple of hours, I suppose? –I don't know what time it was.

At any rate not more than three hours? –No.

Was that for the purpose of getting her up? –To see if she was awake.

Did she say anything? –Yes.

Could you make out what she was saying? –No, you could not exactly say what she was saying.

Did she say she wanted to be sick? –Yes.

Did she recognise you? –I do not know.

Did she appear to recognise you? –No.

Irene said she brought Alma some coffee – she couldn't hold the saucer, but could drink after a fashion. There were three men in her room. At about seven a police-matron arrived who said she had come to get her up. Alma staggered down to the bathroom, which was on the ground floor; she had to be helped. After her bath she told Irene she just wanted to go to sleep.

Would you by any stretch of imagination describe her condition at that time as normal? –By no means normal.

When she was going away finally to the police station, did she say anything to you about what you were to tell Stoner? –Yes.

Just try and recollect her exact words as she was being taken away to the police station. What did she say? –She whispered to me and said, 'Tell Stoner he must give me the mallet.'

Did Stoner on some occasion or other say anything to you about the mallet? Did he say anything about fingerprints? –Yes. I asked Stoner would there not be fingerprints on the mallet? He said no, he wore gloves.

THE JUDGE: Would you just ask her what time she is speaking of when she says Stoner made this observation to her? Was it some days afterwards?

O'CONNOR: That, I think, was a day or two later.

He continued his cross-examination:

Was it the next day, the Monday, or the Tuesday? –About the
gloves, you mean?

Yes? –It was on the Tuesday that happened . . .

THE JUDGE: What I really wanted to know was this: getting this
message on the morning of the 25th, the Monday, 'Tell Stoner he
must give me the mallet.' Did you tell Stoner that? –Yes . . .

What did he say when you gave him the message? –Well, I realised
when I asked him the police had already found the mallet . . .

THE JUDGE: I should still like to know from you what Stoner said
when you gave him Mrs Rattenbury's message, which was 'Tell
Stoner he must give me the mallet.'? –Well, he did not have a chance
to answer me, because I realised the police had got the mallet.

O'Connor continued:

You said that to Stoner? –Yes.

THE JUDGE: So that he did not answer? –No.

This piece of evidence was another unpleasant surprise for Casswell:
he wondered why the prosecutor had not made sure that it came
out when he was examining Irene instead of leaving it to be brought
out by O'Connor. 'To me,' he wrote, 'this clearly indicated that Irene
Riggs had not told the police of this vital statement which clearly
presented a picture of a harassed paramour endeavouring to protect
her murderous lover. And if she had not done so, why not?' He
continued, in his account of the trial:

Nor was this the only piece of incriminatory evidence that Irene Riggs
gave against my client . . . on the Monday morning again, according to
her, he had asked her: 'I suppose you know who did it? but when she
replied, 'Well?' he had said nothing further.

And this was not the end of her testimony – Terence O'Connor was
already sitting down, his cross-examination completed, when she added,
'There's something else on the Tuesday I remember. I asked Stoner why
he had done it.' There was a perceptible raising of the tension in court.
'Wait a minute,' interposed Mr Justice Humphreys. 'Do you want to put
any further questions, Mr O'Connor?'

O'Connor was not slow to pick up a chance like this. 'What was it?'
he asked. 'On the Tuesday I asked Stoner why he had done it,' replied
Irene firmly.

'What did he say?' asked O'Connor, presumably blessing his good fortune in having so wonderful a witness to cross-examine. 'He said because he had seen Mr Rattenbury living with Mrs Rattenbury in the afternoon,' said Irene Riggs.

And after two or three more short questions Terence O'Connor resumed his seat, well content, I have no doubt, with his cross-examination.

My cross-examination (Stoner's name followed Mrs Rattenbury's on the indictment, therefore I cross-examined after O'Connor) was long and detailed, but, all the same it was barren. Irene Riggs readily agreed that she was not pleased with the change in the situation when the teenage Stoner came between her and her mistress, but as to the basic facts she was unshakable. This domestic servant was one of the strongest witnesses I have ever cross-examined.[3]

He tried to counteract the favourable impression Irene had given of her mistress, asking whether she had not found it a very curious atmosphere indeed at the Villa Madeira, and got her to admit, 'It was just a little unusual.'

Had Mrs Rattenbury ever been on the stage, do you know? –Not to my knowledge.

Did she ever tell you she was a child impresario? –The concert stage.

Not, so far as you know, the actual stage? –No.

She used to do strange things, did she not, sometimes – walk about the garden late at night in her pyjamas? –No, I did not think it strange.

Did she sometimes stay up all night playing the gramophone? –Yes.

Did you think that was strange? –No, because I used to be with her.

All night long? –Yes.

He questioned her about her friendship with Alma before Stoner came, their visits to London together, and other places: then there was the trip to Oxford, but Stoner was there too.

Was it not almost as soon as that trip was over that Stoner came to live in the house, the Villa Madeira? –Yes.

Did you approve of that? –Well, it was not my duty to approve or disapprove. It just hurt me.

THE JUDGE: How did it hurt you? –Well, just because Mrs Rattenbury, shall we say, hurt my feelings.

Casswell continued :

> You were not pleased, were you, perhaps naturally having been a close friend of Mrs Rattenbury's for about four years, that suddenly this lad of seventeen should come in? –No.
>
> You were not pleased about it, were you? –Not very.

As his instructions were that Stoner's defence was to be that he was under the influence of cocaine and didn't know what he was doing, Casswell now slipped in the suggestion that Alma might be an addict, implying that she had influenced Stoner to be one also. He questioned Irene about a sudden attack Alma had had on one occasion that had prevented her from entertaining a guest to dinner, then :

> Let me see if I can suggest to you what these sort of attacks were – that suddenly she became very excited and used to run about a good deal? –Yes.
>
> And that would last for a bit of time, and then she perhaps would get drowsy and go to sleep? –She would always be in bed, yes.
>
> What I am suggesting is that every now and again she had sudden attacks and got very excited? –Yes.
>
> And ran about? –Yes.
>
> Just as if she had taken something? –Yes.
>
> And then at the end of the attack she would go to bed, would she not? –Yes.
>
> And that used to happen, say, two or three times a month, did it not? –Not quite so often as that.

Coming to the day of the murder, he again asked about Alma's pyjamas, and whether she had worn them that afternoon in her bedroom. Irene said that she had, and explained,

> Her pyjamas were a three-piece suit, rather a pyjama suit top and a long Yvonne three-quarter coat.
>
> Was that what she used to go about in? –Yes, frequently.
>
> It did not mean she was ready for bed? –Not necessarily.
>
> Could you tell us whether she had anything on underneath or not? –I could not say.

Next he tried to establish that the mallet had been borrowed for a quite ordinary purpose :

With regard to the question of the mallet, do you remember a Mrs Almond being there as a nursemaid? –Yes.

During her time, whatever it was, a canvas sun-shelter was put up, was it not? –I expect it would be.

That was about the 24th or 25th of September, and was it not a great nuisance keeping the pegs in? –They would slip out, yes.

At that time there was no mallet on the premises, was there? –No.

Mrs Rattenbury was the sort of lady who would put up a shelter in March, when others would not put it up till June? –No. She would only put it up on very hot days when the little boy could sleep out.

Was the 24th March quite a hot day? –I do not know; I can't remember.

You cannot remember that morning, perhaps, but you went out in the afternoon. I suggest it was one of the first hot days this year? –I do not know. I cannot remember.

Next he tried to lessen the impact of Irene's additional evidence – Alma's message to Stoner about the mallet –

You have told us, of course, something which is not evidence against Stoner, but which was brought out by my learned friend, Mr O'Connor, for some reason or other he himself knows, and that is, as Mrs Rattenbury went out of the door, when Stoner was not there, she whispered to you something about, 'Tell Stoner to give me the mallet.'? –Yes.

'He must give me the mallet?' –Yes.

And you say also she was not herself at the time? –Not quite herself, no.

She was going away to the police station, was she not? –Yes.

How could anyone bring a mallet to the police station? –I suppose she wanted it before she left.

She wanted it before she left, but it was not until she was being taken away by the police-matron and the police officer that she told you to tell him he must give her the mallet? –It was when the police were outside the room.

When the police-matron was outside the room? –When she was getting ready. She was not quite ready to go.

THE JUDGE: There was no policeman actually in charge of her at the moment? –No, nobody knew she said it to me.

Casswell continued:

Did you tell the police about it? –No.

Why not? –I did not remember it at the time I was giving my statement.

The judge wanted a more precise answer to Casswell's suggestion that Alma habitually behaved 'as if she had been taking something'. He asked Irene if she had ever known her to take drugs, things like cocaine, morphia, and heroin. She answered, 'Not to my knowledge.' After further questions to Irene which did not elicit any new information, the court adjourned.

The day's proceedings were reported under sensational headlines: LOZANNE FACES HER JUDGE. TRIED TO KISS POLICE, SAYS WOMAN WITNESS. A QUARREL AT MIDNIGHT. BOY CHAUFFEUR'S ORDEAL. 'HUSBAND IN THE WAY' COUNSEL SUBMITS. NIGHT WALKS CLAD ONLY IN PYJAMAS. 'THIS GUILTY PASSION': PROSECUTING COUNSEL. MRS RATTENBURY 'IN A TERRIFIED STATE'. LOZANNE WRITES FROM GAOL OF 'SMASHED LIVES'. SEPARATE TRIALS REFUSED.

CHAPTER SEVEN

Detectives and Doctors Disagree

The first important witness to be heard on the second day of the trial was Dr O'Donnell. He was inevitably a witness for the prosecution because he had been the first doctor to see Mr Rattenbury after he had been injured, and it was he who had reported the incident to the police: he was, however, essentially a witness for Alma's defence, believing in her innocence and being her friend. According to Mrs Kingham he was furious with the police for questioning Alma and taking statements from her when she was intoxicated, and after he had given her an injection of morphia.[1]

He was examined by Mr Anthony Hawke who had been instructed, together with Mr Croom-Johnson, by the Director of Public Prosecutions. He explained first that he had attended the family for two and a half years when, on 24th March at half-past eleven at night, he received a telephone call summoning him to the Villa Madeira. He found the front door open. He went straight through the hall to the room at the end of the passage where Mr Rattenbury was lying partially dressed upon his bed, a blood-stained towel round his head. He removed the towel but could not make a proper examination of the wound because of the quantity of blood, matted and clinging to his hair. The patient was unconscious with laboured breathing, his left eye was purple, very contused and swollen, his pulse was slow and irregular. It was a case, he thought, that required the immediate attention of a surgeon, so he telephoned a colleague, Mr Rooke, and said he was sending a taxi to fetch him. Mr Hawke asked:

. . . Mrs Rattenbury was there? –Yes.

What condition was she in? –Very excited and inclined to be intoxicated.

Had she any materials for becoming inclined to be intoxicated with her? –Yes.

88

What had she got? –She had a whisky and soda in a glass in her hand.

How was she dressed? –In her pyjamas without any shoes.

Had she anything over her pyjamas? –No.

Did you speak to her when you saw her? –I did.

What did you say? –I asked her what had happened.

What did she say? –She said, 'Look at him, look at the blood; somebody has finished him.'

. . . did you discuss with Mrs Rattenbury, or did she discuss with you, anything that had happened that evening before you arrived? –Yes. She told me that she and Mr Rattenbury had had a very happy evening, that they had arranged to go down to Dorset the following day, Monday, to stay with a Mr and Mrs Jenks, and that Mr Rattenbury was very happy to be going away on the Monday.

Did she draw your attention to anything in the room while she was talking to you? –She did. She tried to show me the book which was then on the piano in the sitting-room, and I told her that I did not wish to see it, that I had not time to bother about it. (He was then shown a book, Exhibit No. 6. He agreed that it was similar to the one he had seen.)

Continuing his account of what had passed, he said Alma told him she had been aroused by a cry or a noise, had run downstairs and found her husband lying back in his chair, with a pool of blood beside him on the carpet, and that his artificial teeth had fallen out. Shortly after twelve, Mr Rooke arrived, made a superficial examination of the patient, ordered an ambulance to take him to a nursing home, and went on ahead to prepare his instruments. Dr O'Donnell waited and went with the patient in the ambulance.

When Mr Rattenbury's head had been shaved in the operating theatre, Dr O'Donnell saw that the wounds were serious and that they had obviously been inflicted by external violence. He telephoned the police.

Later, at about 3.30 a.m., he returned to Manor Road in Mr Rattenbury's car which Stoner was driving. Alma was still in her pyjamas, but she had put a light dressing-gown or dressing-jacket over them, and she was wearing shoes or slippers. By this time she was very intoxicated. He sent her to bed and gave her an injection of half a grain of morphia. He went downstairs to the kitchen and talked to Miss Riggs and Stoner. After about five minutes he went into the sitting-room and found Alma there, talking with two police officers:

> Who was speaking? –Inspector Mills.
>   Who was he speaking to? –To Mrs Rattenbury.
>   What did he say? –He asked her, 'Do you suspect anybody?' Her reply was, 'Yes.' He asked, 'Whom do you suspect?' and she replied, 'I think his son did it.'
>   THE JUDGE: At this time she was, as I understand your evidence, unquestionably very much under the influence of drink? –Yes.
>   Actually intoxicated? –Actually intoxicated, and at this time she had had one half grain of morphia.

Mr Hawke continued the examination:

> Did Inspector Mills say anything when she said that? –Inspector Mills asked, 'What age is his son?' and her reply was 'Thirty-six years of age.' Inspector Mills asked her, 'Where is his son?' and she said, 'I do not know.'
>   Did you take any part in this conversation? –I did.
>   What did you say? –I asked Inspector Mills if he had cautioned this lady, and his reply was, 'No.' I then said, 'Look at her condition. She is full of whisky, and I have given her a large dose of morphia. She is not fit to make a statement to you or to anybody else.'
>   Did you then put her to bed? –I sent her up to bed.
>   And this time she stayed there, and you left the house? –I left the house after that.

Dr O'Donnell was then cross-examined by Alma's counsel, O'Connor. He asked him what time his last conversation with Inspector Mills took place. He answered that it was about four o'clock in the morning. He then asked about Alma's state of health, and he answered that she had chronic lung trouble: he had frequently examined her and had never seen any indication that she was a drug addict.

> THE JUDGE: When you gave her the hypodermic injection, did you notice any sign or indication of any description that she was in the habit of using a hypodermic syringe? –No.

Questioned about her relations with Mr Rattenbury, the doctor described the incident of 9th July 1934, when Alma had telephoned him at midnight to say her husband had left the house threatening suicide :

. . . I found Mrs Rattenbury very distressed. I found her with a black eye and a cut over her eye. I asked what was the matter and she told me that Mr Rattenbury had struck her. I dressed her eye and sent her to bed, and gave her a quarter of a grain of morphia to quieten her so that I might be able to get out to see if I could find Mr Rattenbury . . . I hunted about the cliffs myself with Miss Riggs and could not find him.

Was that the only occasion, except the night of the 24th, on which you have injected a drug into Mrs Rattenbury ? –Yes.

. . . speaking generally, how would you describe her temperament ? –Uneven.

Excitable ? –Yes, very.

As her medical attendant, and one who has had every opportunity of seeing her temperament at close quarters, do you think it would be possible for Mrs Rattenbury to take part in a crime of this description and then act perfectly peacefully and normally with her maid ? –I do not consider it possible.

Have you ever seen her in a condition as excited as she was on that night ? –No.

What were her habits as regards drink ? –Occasionally she had too much.

She was not a chronic drunkard, but had bouts ? –No. Occasionally.

Did she tell you that Stoner was her lover ? –She did.

What date was that ? –12th February 1934.

She had told him also of his violence to her, and of her worries about whether he was taking drugs, asking him to see Stoner and talk to him. The doctor had seen Stoner who admitted that he was taking cocaine but refused an offer of help to give it up.

He was then asked about Stoner's movements on the night of 24th March, how he was dressed, and so on – but he had been fully occupied with the patient and hadn't noticed Stoner particularly. As far as he could recall, he had a grey suit on, and no collar. Asked whether, during his visit, Alma and Stoner could have been at any time alone together, he said he thought not.

At the nursing home in the ante room of the operating theatre he had seen Inspector Mills who had remarked to him, 'I've been down to Manor Road. That woman's drunk.'

When he got back to the Villa Madeira at 3.30 a.m., he said, Alma was very excited. The radio-gramophone was playing and she was staggering about. There were four police officers in the house, and she was running among them from one to another. He tried to explain to her Rattenbury's serious condition, but she couldn't take it in. To stop the exhibition she was making of herself, he had given her the injection.

On the following day, at one o'clock in the afternoon, after her first appearance at the Magistrates' Court, he saw her at the police station : she could not walk, and had to be supported to bring her into the room where he was, a police-matron on one side and Inspector Carter on the other. When she tried to stand, she tottered and swayed about.

What were her reactions to light? –The only thing I noticed was that her pupils were contracted.

At that time, one o'clock in the afternoon, was she dazed? –Yes.

Was she in a fit condition to make a statement? –I do not consider so.

What do you say as to her fitness to make a statement at six, seven or eight o'clock that morning, previous to your examination? –I should not place any credence on a statement given under such circumstances.

By any stretch of imagination, from what you saw of her at 3.30 and at one o'clock the following day, would it be true to say that at six o'clock that morning she could have been normal? –I should say no.

Or at eight o'clock? –No.

Speaking generally, Mrs Rattenbury was devoted to her children, was she not? –Most devoted.

There was nothing at all out of keeping with her general attitude that she should desire to clean up the blood? –She said that night, 'Wash it up, wash it up. I cannot have little John frightened by the sight of blood.'

That seems to be the one thing she was quite clear about? –Yes.

It was now Casswell's turn to cross-examine on behalf of Stoner. He seemed anxious to establish that the doctor was not only a medical adviser but a friend to Alma, and that the jury should bear this in mind when assessing the value of his evidence. From his answers it was clear that O'Donnell did consider himself to be Alma's friend, but his visits to the Villa Madeira had nearly always been for professional reasons. He had visited her about a hundred times in the past two and a half years, and had charged half a guinea a time, a guinea if he had had to give her an anaesthetic :

So when she was upset or when she was cross she sent for you, did she? –If it was necessary she did so. If I may put it this way, on the occasions that I saw her it was necessary for me to do so.

Simply because of an upset or crossness? –Yes.

It was nearly all temperament, was it not? –No. Illness.

What illness? –The condition that I attended her for since 1932 was pulmonary tuberculosis.

Did you send her away anywhere for treatment? –I sent her to a nursing home.

When was that? –In 1932

For how long? –For a fortnight, for observation.

. . . was the result of that observation that she had tuberculosis or not? –That she had. I had her X-rayed, and the X-ray report definitely diagnosed the case.

What treatment did you order? –Open air.

Simply that? –Yes.

When you went round on those four occasions and anaesthetised her, what was that for? –Tubercular glands.

What? –Suppurating glands. I had Mr Rooke in consultation to operate.

Did you sometimes have to go round there in order to put her to bed in a state of excitement? –No, never, except the morning of the happening.

What about the occasion of the black eye. Had you forgotten that? –Yes, I had forgotten that . . .

THE JUDGE : Being a person suffering from tuberculosis, did you recommend any alcohol to her? –No, I did not.

Did you advise her about alcohol? –I tried to.

What was your advice? –My advice was to lead a quiet life, and not to drink.

At all? –Practically to give it up.

Casswell now concentrated on trying to demonstrate by implication that Stoner was a drug addict. He mentioned several textbooks on narcotics, which the doctor had not read. Then there were questions about 'the cocaine bug', an expression which the doctor had not heard used, but he said he supposed it referred to a condition of worms existing under the skin in chronic cases of cocainism :

> And is typical? –After prolonged taking and in large doses.
> What is it due to? –It is due to the abuse of cocaine.
> Is it due to a hallucination of touch? –It is due to nerve sensations from the abuse of cocaine.
> Do you suggest there is anything there under the skin? –No.
> THE JUDGE : I am not sure that I follow this. Is this what you have told us, that people who take cocaine in large quantities for a prolonged period may get a sensation as though there were worms under their skin? –Yes.
> And in fact there are no worms under their skin? –No.

Casswell referred to the doctor's talk with Stoner about drugs and asked what Stoner had said, where he got cocaine, where he got the money to buy it with, how much dealers charged for it, how much he took as a dose, and so on. The doctor said he only knew what Stoner had told him, that he took cocaine.

There were a few more questions about how Stoner had behaved on the night of the 24th : the doctor could only repeat that he had had no particular reason to observe him, he hadn't appeared to be agitated or apprehensive.

Still trying to give the impression that Alma took cocaine and had influenced Stoner to do so as well, Casswell concluded his cross-examination by commenting that she had awakened only two and a half hours after being given an injection of half a grain of morphia :

> Do you think, by any chance, she took some sort of drugs without your knowing it? –I do not think so. As a matter of fact she was averse to any treatment which she considered dope.
> Of course, the normal way to take cocaine is by snuffing, is it not? –So I understand.
> That would leave no mark? –No, unless you get a mark on the septum of the nose. You do get a perforation of the septum of the nose from cocaine taking.
> That would be on the inside of the nostril? –Yes.
> You would not notice it unless you were told about it? –No, unless you examined for it.

That was the end of Casswell's cross-examination of Dr O'Donnell. He had certainly done his best to carry out his instructions and at least created the suspicion that the accused were cocaine addicts whereas in fact there was no evidence that Stoner took drugs except his own statement, and none at all that Alma did.

There followed a brief re-examination of the doctor by Croom-Johnson who was looking for evidence to support his contention that it was Alma who struck the blows that killed her husband, and that her confessions to the police, though made under the influence of alcohol, were true.

Does what you have had to eat or drink before you are given morphia have any effect on the effect of the drug itself on the patient? –I do not think so.

Does the drug react on different constitutions in different ways? –Yes.

Is coffee a thing which might assist in getting rid, temporarily at all events, of the effect of the drug? –Coffee, walking about, and a hot bath.

. . . I am talking about the dose you actually gave? –Yes, it probably would have.

Coffee would assist by itself? –Yes.

Walking about would assist by itself? –Yes.

A hot bath would assist by itself? –Yes.

By 'assist', do you mean assist in causing the effect of the drug to disappear more quickly? –No.

What do you mean? –I mean it would keep them wakeful.

Is the effect of morphia, as a rule, to make you sleepy? –Yes.

What other effect does morphia have on the patient besides making the patient sleepy? –It makes them fuddled and muddled and not able to think properly.

Not able to tell a coherent story? –Yes.

You appreciate what I mean by a coherent story – I just want you to understand what I mean – a story which is coherent as a whole, not a story which is merely untrue? –Yes.

Unable to tell a coherent story? –The brain will not function properly.

So you would not expect anybody under the influence of morphia to be able to tell a coherent story at all? –No.

He seemed to be trying to make the point that Alma's story to the police was coherent, therefore she was not under the influence of morphia, therefore it was true – but the judge brushed it aside by asking O'Donnell :

> THE JUDGE : Would you like to place any reliance at all on any statement made by a person under the influence of morphia? –No, my lord.

Croom-Johnson wanted to know more about the occasion upon which the doctor had treated Alma for a black eye :

> . . . her husband had struck her? –Yes.
> Did she tell you anything more about the circumstances of the striking than that? –No.
> What sort of a man was Mr Rattenbury? Was he a quiet man? –A very charming, quiet man.
> THE JUDGE : Did you go into the matter any more than that when you were told this very charming quiet man had given his wife a black eye? –No.
> Did it surprise you? –It did.

The doctor said he had never seen any signs of violent disposition on the part of Mr Rattenbury. Croom-Johnson went back to the question of Stoner and the cocaine . . .

> Did you make any enquiry as to how often he had taken cocaine since he had discovered that it gave him a pleasant sensation? –No.
> THE JUDGE : Or as to how long it had been going on? –No, my lord.
> Does that mean that you did not gather from him whether it was a matter of a week or five years? –That is so. I did not ask him.

Croom-Johnson continued :

> You did not ask him? –I was only asked to find out what drug he was taking and to warn him about it.
> I gather you have no experience of people who are taking cocaine? –No.
> THE JUDGE : Surely your experience is enough, is it not, to know that it is important to find out whether a person has been taking it for a week or for five years? –He appeared perfectly normal to me that day. I had no reason to believe he was taking large doses of cocaine.

Counsel for the prosecution
Mr R. P. Croom-Johnson
KC

Mr Justice Humphreys

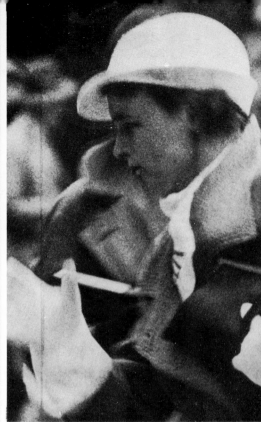

Alma's counsel, T. J. O'Connor KC

Irene Riggs

Police Constable Bagwell

Mr J. D. Casswell, Stoner's Counsel

Or that he had been taking it for some time? —I could not say that he had taken any from what I saw that day.

He said he had? —Yes, he told me he had.

Croom-Johnson's final question was about Alma's condition when she came downstairs again after having been put to bed and given an injection of morphia – was she less mistress of herself than when she went up? The doctor replied that she was less mistress of herself. The drug was taking effect.

The next witness for the prosecution was Alfred Basil Rooke, the surgeon who had been called in by Dr O'Donnell. After giving particulars about himself, he stated that when he saw the patient in the Villa Madeira he could not examine him properly because there was such a disturbance going on: Alma was pressing attentions upon her husband, trying to remove his clothing, calling for scissors to cut his shirt off, and talking incoherently.

THE JUDGE : She was in a very abnormal state, I suppose? —She was in a very abnormal state; but may I just add, the conditions appeared to me to be such that one would expect an abnormal state in a person of her temperament. I had seen her before.

Was she naturally an excitable woman? —Yes, and in conditions which justified great excitement.

Dr Rooke explained that he decided the only thing to do was to remove the patient at once to a nursing home. Here, free from interruption, he shaved Mr Rattenbury's hair, got the blood cleaned up, and found there were three wounds upon his head :

One wound was above the ear on the left-hand side. That one had irregular jagged edges. It would be, I should say, three to three and a half inches long. The bone was exposed in the deep parts of the wound, and there was an obvious depressed fracture of the skull. I was able to feel where the bone had been driven into the brain. The next wound would be approximately in the midline at the back of the head. That was a lacerated wound that reached down to the bone. I was unable to feel any fracture beneath it. The third one was similar to the second, situated a little further round to the right. I was not able to feel any fracture there.

Croom-Johnson asked:

I think you removed the largest piece of bone from the place where the depressed fracture was? –I first of all cleaned up the wound, excised the edges, and when I had sewn up all the wounds I turned the flap down to expose the skull beneath, because I knew there was a pretty extensive bone condition there.

Having examined the wounds, did you form an opinion as to how they were caused? –I formed the opinion that the injuries had been caused by three separate blows with some blunt instrument.

Did you form an opinion as to whether the blows had been struck from the front or from behind? –From behind.

(Dr Rooke was shown Exhibit No 7 – the mallet.)

Did you examine that mallet for the first time at the police station? –Yes.

How long after this examination at the nursing home? –I cannot say, but between my operation and Mr Rattenbury's death. I did not take a note of the exact date.

Somewhere between 25th March and the time when he died on Thursday, the 28th? –Yes.

Were the wounds that you saw, in your opinion, capable of being administered by such an instrument as that? –They were.

When you examined that mallet, did you observe anything particular about it? –I observed on one side of it some hairs and a fragment of dried skin.

Did you examine the hairs? –I noticed that they resembled Mr Rattenbury's hair in texture and in colour.

Did you observe anything about the eyelids of the patient that night? –I did. I observed that the left eye was completely bunged up, to such an extent that one was unable to separate the lids to examine the pupil beneath.

From your general examination, can you tell us how that condition was brought about? –Well, haemorrhage proceeding from behind forward into the orbit.

THE JUDGE: Not a separate blow? –No, it was simply the haemorrhage passing forward inside the skull into the orbit.

Dr Rooke was shown two photographs of Mr Rattenbury's skull. He indicated on them the part representing the true wound and the part he had enlarged for the purpose of getting fragments of bone from the brain.

The jury were handed the mallet for the purpose of feeling the weight of it. Then Croom-Johnson asked :

Are you able to say yourself what the cause of death was? –Yes. The cause of death was injury to the brain which produced oedema of the brain and death.

Dr Rooke was then cross-examined by O'Connor, who was concerned to show that Alma did not strike the blows :

It was a very formidable wound, was it not? –A very formidable wound.

And must have been caused by a blow delivered with such force that it caused a *contrecoup* on the other side of the brain? –Yes.

Which presupposes great violence on the left? –Not very great violence.

A considerable degree of violence? –Yes.

. . . you told us she had a highly excitable temperament. There was an answer of yours I did not quite catch, but I think it amounted to this, that her condition when you arrived at the house showed just that degree of reaction that you would have expected from somebody of her temperament in the circumstances? –It showed a degree that I thought was compatible with the ordinary reactions of a very highly-strung person.

To the horrible situation in which she found herself? –Exactly.

THE JUDGE : In association with alcohol? –Yes.

O'CONNOR : She was a perfect nuisance when you arrived? –She made an examination impossible.

Making utterly incoherent remarks, but nevertheless solicitous for her husband's welfare? –So solicitous that when I was making futile efforts to conduct my examination I said, 'If you want to kill him you are going the right way about it. Do let me get near him and attend to him.'

O'Connor tried to establish that Alma had been present all the time that Dr Rooke was there – he wanted to show that she had not, during that time, been in consultation with Stoner. Dr Rooke said he believed she was there all the time, for he could not recall being able to carry on his examination without disturbance. The tone of his evidence was, however, sympathetic to Alma.

A brief cross-examination followed by Casswell who did not dispute or criticise Mr Rooke's evidence except to maintain that the blows could have been struck by an assailant standing in front of Mr Rattenbury: this view would have made Alma's confession more believable than Stoner's, but Mr Rooke would not accept it, as the direction of the force was from behind.

Now members of the police force took the witness-stand in the order in which they had appeared at the Villa Madeira on the night of the 24th/25th March. The first was Constable Arthur Ernest Bagwell of the Hampshire Constabulary stationed at Bournemouth. He said that when he went to the Villa Madeira at about 2 a.m. he noticed that Mrs Rattenbury was under the influence of drink to a mild extent:

> When I got into the drawing-room I said to her, 'I have just come from the Strathallen Nursing Home where your husband has been taken this evening, where he is suffering from serious injuries. Can you furnish me with any particulars as regards how he came by them?' She said, 'At about 9 p.m. I was playing cards with my husband in the drawing-room, and I went to bed. About 10.30 I heard a yell. I came downstairs into the drawing-room and saw my husband sitting in the chair. I then sent for Dr O'Donnell. He was then taken away.'

It seemed that this businesslike constable had succeeded in getting a coherent statement from Alma when both the doctors and Miss Riggs had found her babbling and incoherent. He must have followed her doggedly around with his notebook and pieced together her 'statement' from disjointed phrases.

He said he was joined by Inspector Mills, and together they searched the premises, finding bloodstains on the carpet, a blood-stained collar in the dustbin, a jacket and waistcoat that had been washed in the bathroom, etc. Inspector Mills then returned to the nursing home, leaving Bagwell alone for about an hour with Alma and Irene. Pandemonium reigned. Alma was playing the gramophone and drinking. She tried to kiss Bagwell who nevertheless got another of her 'statements' down in his notebook : 'I know who done it.' He cautioned her, he said, but she went on : 'I did it with a mallet. Ratz has lived too long. It is hidden. No, my lover did it. It is urine on the chair. I would like to give you £10. No, I won't bribe you.'

Then Bagwell fled – according to Irene it was to escape Alma's attentions, according to himself it was because he couldn't go to either of the two lavatories in the house, because she was pestering him, and so he had to go outside for a natural purpose; also according to himself he told Alma he was going out to find another police officer, thinking that that would calm her a bit. He was outside, he said, for only about three minutes, spoke to the policeman on the beat and brought him back with him. At about 3.30 Inspector Mills returned :

He spoke to Mrs Rattenbury. He said, 'I have just come from the Strathallen Nursing Home where your husband has been taken seriously injured. Can you give me any particulars as to how it happened?'

Bagwell then described how he searched for the mallet, because Alma had said, 'It is hidden,' and how he found it outside the front door, hidden behind a box behind the trellis work.

(The mallet was brought to Bagwell.)

THE JUDGE : Have a look at it. There is a little hair on it now. Was there more when you found it? –Yes, my lord.

O'Connor, cross-examining, tried to show that it was unlikely Alma had hidden the mallet. He asked Bagwell to look at photograph No 2 in a book of photographs that was handed to him :

. . . in order to get to the place where the mallet was found you have to bend down and get under an overhanging tree? –Yes.

And the ground there looks pretty rough? –Yes.

Do you have to squeeze through a narrow passage? –Well, it is a bit narrow there, yes.

The gap between the trellis work and the wall is pretty narrow? –Yes.

It is not the sort of expedition that anybody would be likely to undertake in their bare feet, in their pyjamas? –The ground is quite even.

Do you think it is? –Yes.

Whoever went would have to crush in between the trellis work and the wall? –They would just have to bend down.

Having failed to get any help from Bagwell about the inaccessibility of the hiding place, he went on to the question of the blood-soaked collar, and asked, 'What did you do with it?' Bagwell didn't know what had happened to it except that it had been taken away, he thought by Inspector Mills. The judge, wondering what Alma's defender was getting at, intervened:

THE JUDGE: If you want it, you can have it, I suppose. The man who suffered those injuries would have blood on his neck I suppose?
O'CONNOR: I thought it was on the assumption that it was Mr Rattenbury's collar.
THE JUDGE: Nobody has suggested it belonged to your client.

O'Connor abandoned the question of the collar, and tried to establish that Alma's statements to the police had no value because she was drunk when she made them. This was certainly the view of the doctors, but not of the police. He asked Bagwell:

. . . was she very drunk? —Not when I first arrived on the scene.

She was very drunk later on, of course? —Well, you would not say very drunk, not incapably drunk.

She was not incapably drunk, according to you, at any time? —I should not say so.

Was she trying to kiss you? —Yes.

. . . do you know that Miss Riggs says that while you were outside she had to lock all the doors of the house to prevent Mrs Rattenbury trying to get out to find you? —The front door was never locked.

Then what Miss Riggs says about that is not true? —The front door was not locked.

She says that during that time she had to put her down into a chair and sit on her to prevent her breaking out of the house. Is that all untrue? —I could not say.

You heard no sound coming from the house? —No.

Was the gramophone playing? —She played one record while I was in the house.

You did not hear any of the kind of disturbance that I have been describing? —No.

And you say you were only out for a few minutes? —That is all.

I suggest to you, you were out a considerable time, and you came back with another officer? —I was never away from the house for more than three minutes.

Did you come back alone? –There was another officer. I happened to see him. That was the officer on the beat.

So you did bring another officer with you? –He just came to the door.

He was very evasive about having gone out and brought in another policeman: possibly he had had a telling off for leaving the villa. It had happened, he said, shortly before Inspector Mills returned.

Were Inspector Mills's questions asked before Dr O'Donnell arrived, or after? –Before Dr O'Donnell arrived.

Long before? –About ten minutes or a quarter of an hour before.

Then after Dr O'Donnell arrived and put her upstairs and gave her morphia, she was still talking to Inspector Mills at a later moment? –She came down immediately behind Dr O'Donnell.

Did you help to get her to bed? –No.

Did you see her helped to bed? –I believe Stoner carried her upstairs on one occasion.

Were you there the whole night? –Until about seven o'clock in the morning. I went immediately after the police-matron had taken over.

During the time that you were there, did you go into Mrs Rattenbury's bedroom to try to wake her? –No, not to try to wake her. I made a search under the bed while she was there.

While she was in the bed? –While she was in the bedroom.

Was she in bed? –No.

What time was that? –I cannot remember. I should say it may have been four o'clock, or something like that.

After Dr O'Donnell had given her morphia? –Yes.

Was she undressed, or lying on the bed, or what was she doing? –She was just in her pyjamas and a light dressing-gown.

What was she doing – Walking about? –Yes.

Was anybody else there? –Yes, Miss Riggs was there, and Stoner I believe.

Bagwell was again being evasive. He had just said that Alma came downstairs immediately after the doctor, when she had had her injection. Now his account was that she was walking about her room for ten minutes or a quarter of an hour after she had had it and the doctor had gone, during which time he, Bagwell, had searched under her bed.

Casswell's cross-examination consisted only of questions about the blood-stained collar which was now produced as Exhibit No 47.

Inspector William James Mills of the Hampshire Constabulary then stepped into the witness-box and was examined by Croom-Johnson. He said he went to the Villa Madeira at 2 a.m. on 25th March, and in answer to his question of 'What has happened?' Alma said, ' I was in bed when I heard someone groaning. I came downstairs and found my husband in the easy-chair. He was unconscious, and blood was flowing from his head.'

The inspector then told of his search of the premises with Bagwell, and mentioned that he noticed on a small table a book face downwards and open at page 296. At about 2.45 he went to the nursing home: outside it there was a motor car and Stoner was in the front seat, apparently asleep:

I returned to No 5 Manor Road at about half-past three, in the police car. When I got back to the house I saw the accused Rattenbury. She was in the hall. She was in a very agitated condition and under the influence of drink. I spoke to her.

THE JUDGE: Was she better or worse than she had been at two o'clock? –Slightly worse. I said to her, 'Your husband has been seriously wounded and is now in a critical condition.' She said, 'Will this be against me?' When she asked me that question, I cautioned her. I said, 'I caution you; you are not obliged to say anything unless you wish to do so, but whatever you do say will be taken down and may be given in evidence.

Croom-Johnson continued his questions:

Did she appear to understand? –Yes, I was satisfied she understood.

After you had cautioned her, did she speak to you again? –Yes, immediately.

What did she say? –She said, 'I did it. He gave me the book.'

Did you know what book she was referring to? –No.

What else did she say? –'He has lived too long. He said, "Dear, dear".'

Did those two sentences follow on one another? –Yes. 'I will tell you in the morning where the mallet is.'

Up to that time, had anybody mentioned a mallet in your hearing? –No one at all.

Did she say anything else? –Yes. 'Have you told the Coroner yet?

I shall make a better job of it next time. Irene does not know. I made a proper muddle of it. I thought I was strong enough.'

. . . When Dr O'Donnell came into the house, were you in the room then? –No, in the hall.

What happened next? –The accused Rattenbury rushed towards him when she heard his voice.

What did he do, if anything? –He went upstairs with her.

What happened after that? –Sometime afterwards, Dr O'Donnell came down again, and he then said, 'She is quiet; I have given her morphia.'

When did you next see Mrs Rattenbury? –About a minute after the doctor came into the drawing-room.

Did she come back into the drawing-room? –She did.

Did she speak to anybody? –Yes, immediately she said, 'I know who did it – his son.' I said, 'How old is he?' She replied, 'Thirty-two, but he is not here.'

At that time, in her presence, did Dr O'Donnell say something to you? –Yes.

What did he say? –He said, 'I have given her morphia. I do not think she is fit to make a statement.'

And then what happened? –With some difficulty we got her to bed.

What was the difficulty? –Well, it was like getting anyone to bed when they were under the influence of drink; they will not do what you want them to.

O'Connor, cross-examining Inspector Mills, wanted to know how long he had been in the house, after his return from the nursing home, before he told Alma about her husband being in a serious condition. He answered that it was about five minutes:

She was obviously very much worse then? –Slightly worse.

Very much worse, I suggest? –No.

That statement, you say, you made a note of? –That is right.

At the time, or the next day? –At the time.

Did you follow the statement up? –In what way?

She said, 'I will tell you in the morning where the mallet is.'

Did you ask her where it was? –No, I did not question her.

Why not? –I did not question her at all.

Did you not question her because you did not think she was in a fit condition to give intelligent answers? –No, not at all.

Why did you not? –I had taken that statement.

Was this the first you heard of the mallet? –That is right.

It was very important for O'Connor to establish if he could that Alma had no idea where the mallet was – it was the weak point in her 'confessions'; if she had committed the crime, she would have known. So he went on:

You knew this man had been very seriously injured with some heavy weapon, and here was this woman telling you, 'I will tell you in the morning where the mallet is.' I am suggesting the only reason why you did not follow that up was because you thought you could not place any reliance on her statement? –Not at all. I started searching for the mallet.

Why did you not ask her where it was? –I did not ask her.

That would have helped, if she knew? –Yes.

THE JUDGE: Do you really suggest, Mr O'Connor, if after a woman has said – believe it or not – that she was a party to a crime like this, the police officer would be justified in cross-examining her at all?

O'CONNOR: I accept your lordship's suggestion at once, and apologise for the question.

He continued to cross-examine:

I am not blaming you for not having pursued the point. How soon after that did O'Donnell arrive? –About ten minutes.

When did Dr O'Donnell first tell you that he had given her morphia? Was it immediately he came down and while Mrs Rattenbury was upstairs, or was it later? –That was the first time, and then he repeated it when she was making statements.

How long was she in the drawing-room with you before Dr O'Donnell joined you? –Dr O'Donnell was there first.

He says he was not? –He is mistaken.

Are you quite sure of that? –Absolutely.

I do not think you were in Court when he gave his evidence. He said, 'I was in the kitchen with Stoner and Miss Riggs and I came into the drawing-room and found Mrs Rattenbury talking to Inspector Mills.'? –That is wrong.

Your recollection is different from that? –Mine is correct.

You say he was in the room at the time when she came in? –Yes, but he had hardly finished saying to me, 'I have given her morphia,' when she rushed into the room and began making this statement about 'I know who did it – his son.'

And then you were checked from making any further enquiries by what Dr O'Donnell said to you? –Yes.

There was nothing else of importance in the cross-examination. Inspector Mills said he didn't go into Alma's bedroom while she was asleep – just looked in as a precautionary measure – and at about 4.30 a.m. Inspector Carter arrived and took charge.

Casswell's cross-examination was again brief. He asked Inspector Mills if he had had any conversation with Stoner. The inspector replied he had only asked him if he had seen a mallet about the place, and he answered no, he had never seen one. Between 4.30 and 7.30 Stoner had been walking about in all the rooms, sometimes in the drawing-room, sometimes in the kitchen and sometimes out in the hall. Mills had not asked him for a statement. During all that time Alma was in her bedroom.

The next witness for the prosecution was William Goldsworthy Carter. Examined by Croom-Johnson, he said he was a detective-inspector of the Hampshire Constabulary stationed at Bournemouth. He had arrived at the Villa Madeira at about 4.30 a.m. on 25th March. He stated:

I went into Mrs Rattenbury's bedroom first, the room on the first floor at the rear of the house, immediately over the drawing-room. Mrs Rattenbury was asleep. I also saw the accused Stoner and the maid Riggs. They were in the dining-room on the ground floor. I then went into the drawing-room. Later on I made an examination of the house and grounds. I was in Mrs Rattenbury's room when she woke up at 6 a.m. . . . I simply stayed there and watched her. I did not say anything at all. I said nothing at all for about ten minutes.

Then I called her maid, Riggs, and asked her to get her mistress some coffee. It was my idea. The coffee was brought and she was served with it. She had one cup, not quite the size of a breakfast cup. I sent for the police-matron, and she came about 7 a.m. After that, the accused Mrs Rattenbury had a bath . . .

While Alma was dressing he said he saw the accused Stoner in the kitchen and asked him if he could tell him anything concerning the affair that evening whereby Mr Rattenbury had received his injuries:

In response to that invitation he made a statement to me, and I wrote it down in my book as it was made . . . (Exhibit 39)

George Percy Stoner states : 'I am a chauffeur-handyman employed by Mr Rattenbury of 5 Manor Road, Bournemouth. I retired to my bedroom about 8.5 p.m. on Sunday, 4th March 1935, leaving Mr and Mrs Rattenbury and the boy John in the drawing-room. About 10.30 I was roused by Mrs Rattenbury shouting to me to come down. I came down into the drawing-room and saw Mr Rattenbury sitting in the armchair with blood running from his head. Mrs Rattenbury was crying and screaming, and said to me, 'Help me to get Ratz into bed, he has been hurt.' I then took the car and went to Dr O'Donnell's house. He had left before I got there. When I returned, I cleaned the blood from the floor on the instructions of Mrs Rattenbury. Mrs Rattenbury was sober and, as far as I know, she had not been drinking. When I went to bed she was in a normal condition. I have never seen a mallet on the premises. Until I was aroused, I heard no sounds of a quarrel or a noise of any kind. Since September 1934 I have been employed by Mr and Mrs Rattenbury. They have been on the best of terms. I said to her, 'How did this happen?' She said, 'I don't know.' Mr Rattenbury was fully dressed in the armchair and Mrs Rattenbury was dressed in pyjamas and bare feet.

It was about 7.30 a.m. when that statement was taken down by me from Stoner. At 8.15 I went into Mrs Rattenbury's bedroom . . . she was fully dressed with the exception of her coat and hat. She appeared to me to be definitely normal. I was in plain clothes. I told her who I was. I told her I was a police officer and cautioned her. She appeared to understand. After I had cautioned her, I charged her.

What did you say when you charged her? —I said to her, 'I charge you that you did, by wounding, do grievous bodily harm to one Francis Mawson Rattenbury in an attempt to murder him on Sunday, 24th March 1935.' At this time Mr Rattenbury was still alive. When I charged her she made a statement to me and I took it down as she made it.

Before we read what she said, did she speak coherently? —Yes, she spoke with deliberation.

Had you any difficulty in understanding what she was saying? —None whatever.

Did you ask her any question while she was speaking? —I did not. I put it down as she made the statement.

Could she see that you were writing down what she was saying? –Yes, I wrote it in front of her.

After you had written down what she said in your book, did you read it over to her? –I did.

When you read it over to her, did she ask you something? –Yes, she made a request to read it herself.

Thereupon, did you hand her the book? –I did. She read it for herself. She read it aloud. Afterwards she signed it. Exhibit 41 is a copy of the statement which she made.

Where did she sign it? –In the bedroom, sitting on the bed.

Where was the book when she signed? –She was holding the book in one hand and writing with the other. She was not resting it on anything. This is what she said:

> About 9 p.m. on Sunday, 24th March 1935, I was playing cards with my husband when he dared me to kill him as he wanted to die. I picked up the mallet. He then said, 'You have not got guts enough to do it.' I then hit him with the mallet. I hid the mallet outside the house. I would have shot him if I had a gun. Alma Rattenbury.

As far as you could tell, did she appear to understand what she was saying and doing? –She did. I have been twenty-three years a police officer, and I have been an inspector nearly five years. I have had a good deal of experience in the hearing of statements by persons, and the taking of statements.

You have told us that she read it aloud? –Yes.

Did she read it clearly? –She did.

Shortly after that statement was signed, did you leave the house with the accused Mrs Rattenbury? –Yes, I did.

When you were in the hall on the way out, did you see anybody? –Yes, the accused Stoner and the maid Riggs, at the bottom of the stairs.

Did Mrs Rattenbury say anything to them? –She did.

What did she say? –'Do not make fools of yourselves.' Stoner replied, 'You have got yourself into this mess by talking too much.' I then took her to Bournemouth Police Station. She did not say anything on the way. At the police station in the presence of Superintendent Deacon I cautioned her once again and charged her. I charged her on the same charge, the attempted murder of her husband.

Did she make any answer? –She said, 'That's right. I did it deliberately and would do it again.'

He then related that he went to Bournemouth Central Railway Station at about 10.30 p.m. on Thursday 28th March, met Stoner who was in the train arriving from London, and conveyed him to Bournemouth Police Station . . . The two photographs of Alma that were found on him were now Exhibit 42, her gold watch Exhibit 3, and her letter asking him to come to her Exhibit 4, the envelope Exhibit 5.

O'Connor rose to cross-examine. It was a matter of life and death for Alma that he should succeed in dispelling the impression made by this completely self-confident, inflexible and businesslike detective-inspector who had asserted that when she made and signed her confessions she was in a reasonable state of mind and well aware of what she was doing.

He first established that while Carter was in the Villa Madeira, between 4.30 a.m. and 7 a.m., there were three or four police officers constantly in the house. Then :

Had you ever seen this woman in your life before? –Never.

The first time in your life you ever saw her was when she was asleep when you arrived? –That is so.

You took a statement from her at 8.15? –Yes.

And you have told us that she was then normal? –I did.

Did you say at the Police Court that she was then quite normal? –I said she was normal, I know.

Did you say she was quite normal? –Possibly I did.

Was she quite normal? –Yes.

How can you judge whether a person you have never seen in your life before was quite normal? –I saw Mrs Rattenbury when she woke up at 6 a.m. and she was then not in a normal condition, but it was at 8.15 that I decided that she was in a normal condition, before I attempted to take a statement from her.

So that when you are talking about 'normal' you are not relating your normality to the moment you saw her at six o'clock when she woke up? –Yes.

She was different at 8.15 from what she was at six? –She was very greatly different.

You are not suggesting that it is a true test as to whether a person is normal whether they are slightly different two hours later? –With respect, with my experience as a police officer, I consider I am a good judge.

You considered this woman at 8.15 that morning was a quite normal woman? –Definitely yes.

Do you agree with Dr O'Donnell that no reliance could be placed on any statement taken from her at that time, 8.15? –No, I do not.

Do you know she had had half a grain of morphia? –I was told she had an injection of morphia. I did not enquire how much it was.

Why not? –It did not concern me.

Did it not concern you, if you were going to take a statement to know how much it was? –No, because if I had not been satisfied that she was normal I should not have taken a statement from her.

Was it not natural to know how much drug she had had in order to know whether she was normal or not? –To my mind, no.

Did you find out how much she had been drinking? –I was told she had been drinking. I was unable to find out, because there was none in the house.

Did you know why she had been given morphia? –I was told.

Because she was not in a fit condition, walking about the house, to be left undrugged? –I was told she was given morphia to quieten her.

So you knew she was so much under the influence of drink that she had to be drugged, and also that she had had a considerable dose of morphia? –Only what I was told. You will appreciate that.

Did she wake, as you put it, at six o'clock? –She did.

Did you waken her? –I did not.

Did the police constantly go in and out of the room between 4.30 and six to try and get this wretched woman awake? –No.

Miss Riggs was there? –She was in the house.

Did you send her up to the room several times to see if she was wide awake? –No.

Did you go in yourself? –I was in and out of the room continually.

Did you send any other constable up to the room to get her up? –No.

Did you want to get her up? –No. Soon after she woke up, she wanted to get up and dress and I would not allow her to.

Did you want to leave her asleep or get up? –I would not allow Mrs Rattenbury to get up and dress, because I knew as a police officer that if she attempted to dress I would have to leave the room. Therefore I would not leave her alone until I had sent for a police-matron.

Did you go into the room with Miss Riggs between six and half-past? –No. I was in the room at six o'clock when I sent for Miss Riggs.

What for? You had seen her asleep at half-past four. You knew she had had morphia. Did you expect her to wake up in an hour and a half? I had no idea when she would wake up. I was out to investigate the cause of the injuries received by Mr Rattenbury.

And to investigate by asking Mrs Rattenbury questions about them? —No, I was not putting any questions about them.

Had you any intention of asking her about them? —No.

Did you intend, from what you had heard, to arrest her? —I had definitely made up my mind to arrest Mrs Rattenbury.

And the quicker the better? —No. Otherwise I should have done that at six o'clock when she woke up first.

What? —Had I the intention, you said to me, with every respect, the quicker the better. I said, 'No, if I had been of that mind, the quicker the better, directly she woke up at six o'clock I should have arrested her then,' had I been of that mind, but I was not. Her condition at that time was not such as she could be charged, therefore I did not charge her at that time. I took the precaution of sending for coffee, sending her to have a bath, and waiting for her to be definitely normal before I charged her, and I asked her no question, I charged her immediately.

You sent her to have coffee and to have a bath so as to make some semblance that she was a reasonable woman? —So that she could understand the charge which I was going to put before her.

Did you hear her try to vomit? —She felt sick, that is correct, and I sent for a bowl. Soon after she woke she wanted to vomit.

Did you see that the wretched woman could not hold the coffee cup? —To the best of my recollection she did hold it. I will not swear that.

Did you see that the saucer was shaking in her hand? —No.

And that she could hardly drink? —No.

O'Connor now asked about her meeting at the police station on the following day with Dr O'Donnell, and here too the detective-inspector's account was entirely different from the doctor's:

She was unable to walk then? —No.

Then Dr O'Donnell told us that which was untrue? —If he said that.

Do you say she was able to walk? —She walked from the cells to the waiting-room several times that morning.

Was she swaying about when Dr O'Donnell examined her? —He did not examine her.

Did you notice whether her pupils were contracted at that time?
–No.

According to you, she was talking normally? –Yes.

And walking normally? –Definitely normal.

Perfectly normal? –I say she was quite normal because of the
matters she discussed with Dr O'Donnell, and she had previously seen
her solicitor and the maid Riggs.

Do you know that the medical officer at Holloway has reported
she was still under the influence of drugs three days later? –No.

Have you never heard that until this moment? –No. He never
reported it to me.

O'Connor kept on at him for some time – had she been able to walk
downstairs to her bath? Had she to be helped? Did she say she wanted
to sleep? Did she speak in a clear deliberate voice? The detective-
inspector continued to insist that she was in a perfectly normal condition
and had not at any time appeared to be under the influence of a drug –
nor had it been reported to him that Miss Riggs had complained about
there being three police officers in Alma's bedroom.

Casswell, cross-examining the detective-inspector, wanted to know
how much he had seen of Stoner before he took the statement from him
at 7.30 a.m. He answered he had seen quite a lot of him in the house
and about the grounds.

I was wondering whether anybody said to him, 'Did you hear a
quarrel downstairs?' or whether he volunteered it? –No. As a matter
of fact Stoner was asked a number of questions during the time I
took that statement. I did not ask him anything personally, but he was
asked a number of questions. He was asked about a quarrel and he
was asked if he had seen a mallet on the premises, and several other
questions.

He had been asked several questions before he made the statement?
–Yes, quite.

Which may account for things like this: 'I heard no sounds of a
quarrel or noise of any kind'? –Quite. He was asked questions of
that nature. At that time there was no suspicion of anything connected
with Stoner in this case.

Croom-Johnson then re-examined Detective-Inspector Carter in order
to stress the point that in his treatment of Alma he had only been doing
his duty.

The fourth police officer to be called was Sidney George Bright, detective-constable in the Hampshire Constabulary stationed at Bournemouth. Carter had taken him as his assistant to the Villa Madeira. The interesting question was whether he would give the same account of Alma's condition as his chief – and indeed he did so, almost word for word. He was asked whether he had been in Court while Carter was giving his evidence, and he replied that he had not.

The day's proceedings ended with an exhaustive examination into Alma's accounts arising from the evidence of the chief cashier of Barclay's Bank in Old Christchurch Road, Bournemouth. At its conclusion the judge asked the jury to compare her signatures on the cheques with her signature in Detective-Inspector Carter's book after her statement to him made at 8.15 a.m. on 25th March so that they might form an opinion of whether she was in a fit state to write or not on that occasion, and whether she knew what she was doing. Then the Court adjourned.

'UNFIT TO MAKE STATEMENT.' ALLEGED CONFESSION 'WORTHLESS'. 'SHE TRIED TO KISS ME.' POLICE DENY K.C.'S SUGGESTION. 'INTOXICATED' DOCTOR SAYS. WHEN MRS RATTENBURY WAS DRUGGED. STORY THAT STONER TOOK COCAINE.

CHAPTER EIGHT

'That Awful Night'

At the beginning of the third day's trial the Senior Home Office Analyst, Dr Roche Lynch, gave a detailed description of the mallet which, it was alleged, had been used in the murder : some pieces of hair and outer skin had been found adhering to it, and there was a blood stain. The hair, which had been torn out by the roots, bore a striking similarity to the hair found growing on Mr Rattenbury's head. A piece of skin with some hair, mounted in a special glass, was produced and labelled Exhibit No 49. A juror asked :

Would a person using this mallet in the way that has been described to us be liable to get blood upon their clothing? –I think if one single blow were struck it is quite likely no blood would be on the clothing of the assailant, but if more than one blow were struck it would be quite likely to get on to the clothing. On the other hand I have seen cases where blows of this sort had been struck where no blood got on the clothing.

THE JUDGE : Does it depend on whether the blood spurts out or not? –Spurts or splashes. After the first blow is struck blood wells on to the scalp, and when the second blow is struck it splashes that blood as well as spurts it.

CROOM-JOHNSON : . . . I have spoken to my learned friend, and what I am saying I am saying with his approval, and I expect with the approval of my learned friend, Mr Casswell. Of course, both of the accused persons in this case helped Mr Rattenbury to his bedroom when there was any amount of blood about, and it has not occurred to the prosecution accordingly that any deduction can possibly be drawn adversely to any of the accused on the question of blood being on their clothes.

Dr Lynch was asked whether he would be prepared to assist the Court on the subject of cocaine : he agreed to do so to the best of his ability. Thereupon Casswell put to him a long series of questions. In his replies, various effects of chronic cocaine poisoning were mentioned – hallucination of sight and hearing, insane jealousy, the 'cocaine bug', insomnia, loss of appetite etc.

Dr Hugh Arrowsmith Grierson, the senior medical officer of Brixton Prison, was called. He said he had kept Stoner under close observation there from 14th May : he had been normal in behaviour, rational in conversation, had taken his food, and slept normally. Casswell asked :

Did he tell you that he had been taking cocaine between slices of bread and butter ? –Slices of bread, not bread and butter.

And did he tell you that he took a double dose at about 4.30 on 24th March ? –He said he took two eggspoonfuls.

It has been suggested by Dr Lynch that two eggspoonfuls would be more than a fatal dose ? You would agree with that, I suppose ?

Dr Grierson agreed that it would be more than a fatal dose, if it were undiluted. Stoner had told him also that cocaine was a brownish powder with black specks in it, whereas it was, in fact, whitish, colourless; and if the dope pedlars had diluted it they would certainly have done so with some substance of the same colour.

Dr Edward Waller Mann, the medical officer of Dorchester Prison, said that Stoner was under constant observation there before he was sent to Brixton – that is, from 29th March till 14th May. During that time he had given no sign that he was a drug addict, or a cocaine addict who had been deprived of his drug. His behaviour was very good with nothing abnormal in it. He had apparently slept well and not returned any food.

Finally evidence was given by a succession of salesmen, most of them from Messrs Harrod's, from whom Alma and Stoner had made purchases in London – men's underwear, a blue suit, pyjamas, shirts, shoes – and a ring from Messrs Kirby & Bunn. The bills for these articles were produced and given exhibit numbers. The reception clerk of the Royal Palace Hotel produced a receipted bill, Exhibit 22, dated 22nd March 1935, and a page from the visitors' register, Exhibit 23.

The case for the prosecution being concluded, the judge asked the Clerk of the Court to read the original statements made by the accused :

THE CLERK OF THE COURT : In answer to the usual caution the accused Alma Rattenbury said, 'I am not guilty, and I wish to reserve my right to cross-examine and reserve my defence.' And the accused Stoner said, 'I plead not guilty and reserve my defence.'

The moment Casswell, and many others, had been waiting for arrived: Alma's name was called and she entered the witness-box.

When her counsel, Mr T. J. O'Connor, KC, uttered her name at the close of the case for the prosecution, few people in court seemed to realise Mrs Rattenbury was going into the witness-box, but when she left the dock the atmosphere became electrical.

Every eye followed the woman who had written songs under the name of 'Lozanne' as she moved slowly through the well of the court to the witness-box with a wardress behind her. She took the oath in a voice that could scarcely be heard, and her counsel exhorted her to speak up. Her voice then became firm, and at times charged with feeling. Although pale she came through the three-hours ordeal with complete composure (*News of the World*, 2nd June 1935)

Miss Tennyson Jesse's comment was, 'There was probably no one in England, and no one in court when the trial opened save Mrs Rattenbury, her solicitor and counsel, and Miss Riggs, who did not think Mrs Rattenbury was guilty of the crime of murder.'[1] Miss Jesse was present all through the trial to edit an account of it, and she was accompanied by Raymond Massey who looked back nostalgically to his kindergarten days at Havergall College and to 'the blurred mass of little girls', seeing one of them again 'in clear and tragic focus, thirty-two years later . . .'[2]

O'Connor began by asking Alma the routine questions about her previous marriages and her children, the youngest of whom, he reminded the court, would be six in June, then :

Since the birth of that child, did you and Mr Rattenbury live together as man and wife? –No.

Did you occupy separate rooms? –Yes.

On what terms were you with your husband? –Quite friendly.

No marital intimacy, but were you cordial? –Absolutely.

Was your married life happy? –Like that. (She made a gesture with her hands.)

We were told about a quarrel. Were quarrels between you and he frequent or not? –Not very frequent.

Were they severe when they occurred, or were they just trifling quarrels? –It all depended on whether Mr Rattenbury got in a temper or not. He did sometimes.

One occasion has been spoken about when you received a black eye? –Yes.

I think that was in July of 1934? –Yes.

What was the occasion of that quarrel? –He was queer, morbid, and there was the usual talk of committing suicide, so I asked him, seeing he was always frightening me that he was going to commit suicide, why he did not do it for a change.

Then how did the blow to your eye occur? –He lost his temper and hit me.

He asked if her husband was free with his money, and she answered 'Very close,' then corrected herself and said, 'not very generous'. She admitted that during all her married life she had been in the habit of telling him lies in order to get money from him – it saved rows. About Stoner, she said he had been engaged as a houseboy and chauffeur, mostly as a chauffeur, in September, and she had become his mistress in November.

Was that before or after he had come to live in? –Before.

We know after that, that he did come and live in the house? –Yes.

Just taking it quite generally, from that time until your husband's death, did relations take place between you and Stoner regularly? –Yes.

In his room, or in yours, or in both? –Yes.

One or the other. What attitude did your husband take towards this, if he knew it? –None whatsoever.

Did he know of it? –He must have known because he told me to live my own life quite a few years ago.

As I understand it, there was no occasion on which you told him about Stoner, but your husband knew about it? –No. I told him I had taken him at his word and was living my own life.

Oh, you told him that, did you? Can you tell me when that was? –No. I would say it was somewhere round about Christmas that I told him.

We have heard the evidence given by Riggs of quarrels between you and Stoner. Was your husband in the house when these quarrels went on? –Yes.

And I think she has told us that they occurred partly in your room and partly in Stoner's. Where would your husband be at that time? –In the drawing-room. He always sat there.

That is, immediately below your room? –Yes.

As the Villa Madeira was a very small house, it would appear from this evidence that Rattenbury could not have helped knowing what was going on; and it would appear further that he didn't mind – unless, as Miss Tennyson Jesse suggests, his increasing deafness and his habit of consuming the best part of a bottle of whisky every evening made him completely uninterested in what was going on over his head.

The next questions were on the subject of her quarrels with Stoner and although they had frightened her at the time, so much so that she consulted Dr O'Donnell about them, she now made light of them:

Was there an occasion in the early part of the year when there was a quarrel between you? –Stoner and myself?

Yes? –Yes.

An occasion when Riggs came into the room? –I cannot quite remember that, but I dare say that is so.

What can you remember of the quarrel? –Well, I wanted to sever the connection on account of the difference in age, if you understand, and Stoner said – well, he did not want to, and really that was all the quarrels were about.

What did he do on that occasion? –Nothing very much. He lost his temper, but it was not very –

Was not very serious? –No.

But Riggs came in? –As I say, I cannot quite remember that.

Had Stoner ever threatened your life? –Well, yes, but I did not take it very seriously.

Alma's ingenuous charm and sincerity were already beginning to make themselves felt. Miss Tennyson Jesse wrote:

She was an excellent witness. Her voice was low and rich. She gave a great impression of truthfulness, and she was astonishingly self-controlled. Only a nervous tick in the side of her face, which jerked perpetually, betrayed the tension of her mind.

About Stoner taking drugs, she said he had told her there was something the matter with his head and that he had to take medicine twice or three times a year. She couldn't understand it and had told Dr O'Donnell about it. She denied absolutely that she had ever given him money to buy drugs.

THE JUDGE: Do I understand the only time Stoner spoke to you about taking medicine was on this occasion when he said that two or three times a year he had to take medicine for his head? –No. He afterwards changed it and said he was taking drugs, and it was then I got Dr O'Donnell.

Asked by her counsel, she denied that she herself had ever taken drugs of any description.

Next she was questioned about her visit to London with Stoner just before the tragedy, and how she got the money for it:

I got that like I always have. I always got extra money from Mr Rattenbury about twice a year when I was overdrawn and I always had to, what I call, make up a different story each time to get it. I asked for, I think, more money that time than I had before, but I always got about £100 or £150 twice a year extra, at Christmas and in June, say.

What was the pretext on which you got more money than you usually got? –Having been ill, I still used that as an excuse.

You had been ill. You had several operations? –Yes; they were so recent that it gave me that for an excuse.

Gave you an excuse to tell a lie? ...

THE JUDGE: What was the lie you told him? –I said I was going to London to have an operation.

She was asked what she did with the money. Rather vague, as always, about her accounts, she explained that part of it had been used to pay off what was owing to the tradesmen in Bournemouth, and part of it had gone on the hotel bill, clothes for Stoner, the cinema, a ring for herself, etc.

Did you get back to Manor Road on Friday night, the 22nd? –Yes.

About half-past ten? –About that.

Was your husband in? –Yes, in bed.

Did you see him in his bedroom? –Yes, I said goodnight to him.

Did he ask anything about what had been happening? –No, he was always jolly late at night.

When you say he was 'jolly', I think he used to drink a little whisky at night? –Yes, always.

About how much? –Well, he drank quite a lot then.

And I think from time to time you have yourself given way to drink? –Yes.

As she described the following day, Saturday, it could not have been more ordinary: she went to the little boy's school and brought him back for the weekend. In the afternoon, with Stoner driving, she took him to see Christopher playing football. 'That evening,' she said, 'I think we played cards. I think it was just the same as any other night.'

It was evident that the Rattenburys at that time were leading a very humdrum life, except for Alma's affair with Stoner. The Sunday morning was not very different, except that Rattenbury was depressed about the flats in which he was interested: she tried to be very nice to him and took him out for a drive, and to the kennels to see her little dog's puppies. After lunch he went to sleep and she played with little John – it was the usual Sunday afternoon.

And did you have tea with your husband? –Yes, upstairs in my bedroom.

We know that your bedroom had got a balcony. Who brought tea to you? –Stoner.

That was the usual practice I think, was it not? –Yes.

Of course Riggs, we know, was out? –Yes.

He brought you tea. Now, can you tell me this: after Stoner had brought you your tea, what happened to the door? –The door was always open with a basket in between, but sometimes the basket would be moved. John might move it going back and forward, and it closed.

On this particular afternoon, was the door closed? –For a little while.

She said Rattenbury had brought a book upstairs, and during tea had read to her a page from it. 'He was quite depressed, and when he read that in the book he said he admired a person who could –'

THE JUDGE: You said he admired a person who could do – What? (She didn't answer.) What had the person done? –The person in the book said he had lived too long, and before he became doddering, as far as I could understand, he finished himself.

THE JUDGE: Committed suicide? –Committed suicide, yes.

O'Connor continued:

He said he admired a person who could do that? –Yes.

So he obviously at that time was very depressed and gloomy? –Exactly.

Now, what did you do in order to try and cheer him up? –Well, I suggested several things, but nothing seemed to cheer him up.

I want you to follow my question : what did you suggest in order to cheer him up? Did you suggest you should do anything or go anywhere? –Oh yes; I suggested we should first of all go to London, and he said no. Then I suggested Bridport.

You suggested going to Bridport? –Yes, and he said 'All right', to that.

Why did you suggest Bridport? –Because there was a business friend of Mr Rattenbury's there.

Is that Mr Jenks? –Yes.

Was Mr Jenks associated with him in any way about these flats he was worrying about? –Yes.

And he might have been in a position to help with regard to finance? –Yes.

Now, was anything decided as regards going to Bridport? –Yes, I telephoned to Mr Jenks and made arrangements to go.

She described how Stoner came in while she was telephoning in Mr Rattenbury's bedroom : he had what she thought was a revolver in his hand. He was very angry and said he would kill her if she went to Bridport :

Could you go on talking there without being overheard by your husband? –Yes, practically. One could have, because Mr Rattenbury did not really take very much notice.

Where did you go to continue the conversation? –In the dining-room.

And had Stoner got the revolver when you went to the dining-room? –Yes.

What did he say about your relations with your husband? –He accused me of living with Mr Rattenbury that afternoon with the bedroom door closed.

What did you say to him about that? –I assured him that I had not, and he must put the revolver away and not make an ass of himself.

Of course, the little boy was upstairs in the bedroom then? –Oh yes.

What did he say as regards how you were to behave in the future? ...

THE JUDGE : It is much better she should tell her story. You see, you are putting it into her mouth; it is really much better she should tell it.

O'Connor continued:

What did he say then? –Stoner?

Yes? –He told me I must never have the bedroom door closed again, and that if I went to Bridport he wouldn't drive. He was very annoyed at my going to Bridport. We had quite an unpleasant time about it, but afterwards I thought it was all right.

He said he would not drive to Bridport, and you were not to go there. Did he give any reason why you were not to go? –He did not want me to go with Mr Rattenbury.

Did he say why he did not want you to go with Mr Rattenbury to Bridport? –He was very jealous of Mr Rattenbury, unnecessarily so.

What did he say? That is what I want to know? –He thought I would have to share the same bedroom there.

When he said that, did you say anything to him about what the arrangements would be? –I assured him I would have a separate bedroom.

What effect did that seem to have on him? –I thought it was all right, but I suppose he could not have taken it seriously.

THE JUDGE: He seemed to believe you? –He seemed to believe me, yes.

And to be all right? –Yes.

She described how she got her husband's clothes ready for going to Bridport the next day, and left them for Irene or Stoner to pack. Then she gave John his bath and put him to bed at about a quarter to eight:

Now, having put the little boy to bed, what did you do? –Played cards with Mr Rattenbury and talked to him. He was quite jolly then.

Was the little dog Dinah in the house? –Yes, always.

Who used to let Dinah out at night? –Before I went to bed I used to let Dinah out.

I do not want to take it too quickly. What was the general rule? Who usually let Dinah out? –I usually let Dinah out.

Where was she usually let out? –Out of the drawing-room french window, and I closed her outside, and it was Mr Rattenbury's habit five minutes later to let her in, because if you did not close the door she would not stay out.

The little dog used to come probably and scratch to get let in? –Yes.

This night did you let Dinah out through the french window in the drawing-room? –Yes, the same as usual.

Can you tell me whether you closed it or not? –I would automatically close the door, and then I would say goodnight to Mr Rattenbury and go upstairs. He would go and let Dinah in five minutes later, and then she would come upstairs.

THE JUDGE: I do not know what the answer is to your question. You asked her whether she closed the window? –Yes.

O'Connor continued:

Do you remember closing the window that night? –I would have to, because she would not stay out unless I did close the door.

Can you give me any idea of the time you let Dinah out? –I went to bed exactly at 9.30.

After letting Dinah out, what did you say or do to your husband? –I did not see him any more. I went to bed.

The first thing that appeared to her to be slightly unusual was that Dinah came upstairs soon after she had been let out – showing that Rattenbury, or someone else, had opened the french windows. She didn't pay much attention to this at the time, and went on making her preparations for spending the following day and night at Bridport, and getting ready for bed. She was already wearing her three-piece pyjama suit, so all she had to do was to take off what she was wearing underneath it – her vest, brassiere, shoes and stockings – and put it on again.

When Irene came in, she went along to her room – as she very often did – for a chat, and told her about the plans for the following day. After about ten minutes she returned to her own room where Stoner joined her:

About how long after you had got back to bed? –That I am not certain about, because I did not look at the clock.

I mean, was it long; was it minutes, or what? –Well, I did think it was shortly afterwards, but after hearing the evidence here I have become rather confused in time: it seems later than I thought it was.

Had you seen Stoner till he came in? –Not all the evening.

Since the time you had seen him in the dining-room? –No, not all evening. Not that I remember.

What happened after Stoner came in? What did he look like? –I did not notice anything at the moment, but a little later I noticed he was a little bit queer.

What did he do? Did he get into bed or not? –Yes.

He did. How was he dressed? –In his pyjamas.

How long had he been in bed before you noticed what you were just going to describe? –Almost right away.

What was it? Tell your own story, Mrs Rattenbury. I do not want to lead you at all on this? –Well, he seemed agitated, and I said, 'What is the matter, darling?' and he said he was in trouble and could not tell me what it was, and I said, 'Oh, you must tell me,' and we went back and forth like that for two or three minutes, and he said no, that I could not bear it. I thought he was in some trouble outside, you know – his mother, or like that – and then I said I was strong enough to bear anything, and he told me he had hurt –

What did he say? Put it in direct language if you can. What did he say to you? –He told me that I was not going to Bridport the next day as he had hurt Ratz. It did not penetrate my head what he did say to me at all until I heard Ratz groan, and then my brain became alive and I jumped out of bed–

Yes? –And went downstairs.

Did you stop to put any clothes on, or slippers? –Oh no.

Did Stoner say anything about how he had done it? –He said he had hit him over the head with a mallet.

Anything more about the mallet? –That he had hidden it outside.

I think you told us that you rushed down to the drawing-room. What did you find there? –Mr Rattenbury sitting in the chair, and he –

I do not think you need trouble to describe exactly what you saw, but he was sitting in the chair? –I tried to rub his hands; they were cold. I tried to take his pulse, and I shook him to try and make him speak.

Did you call for help? –Not right away. I tried to speak to him, and then I saw this blood, and I went round the table, and I trod on his false teeth, and that made me hysterical, and I yelled – I cannot remember, only vaguely. I took a drink of whisky to stop myself being sick.

You yelled for whom? –Irene.

Did she come down? –Yes.

Was that the only drink of whisky you had? –No. I took one drink of whisky neat, and I was sick, and then I remember pouring out another one. I cannot remember drinking the next one. I tried to become insensible, to block out the picture.

Do you remember the police officers coming? –Absolutely not.

Do you remember sending for Dr. O'Donnell? –I cannot remember anything from putting a white towel round Mr Rattenbury's head and the vomiting, and treading on those –

THE JUDGE: Do you say you were sick after drinking the whisky? –Yes.

O'Connor continued:

Can you remember anything more about the events of that night? –No.

Do you remember the gramophone? –No.

Do you remember the police? –Absolutely not.

Mrs Rattenbury, did you murder your husband? –Oh, no.

Did you take any part whatsoever in planning it? –No.

Did you know a thing about it till Stoner spoke to you in your bed? –I would have prevented it if I had known half – a quarter of a minute before, naturally.

O'Connor sat down. Croom-Johnson proposed to the judge that this would be a convenient moment to adjourn for lunch.

So far, in the hands of her skilful and sympathetic counsel, Alma had acquitted herself well, but she now had to face cross-examination by Casswell who had no hope of saving Stoner except by casting the blame on her.

Long before the luncheon adjournment was over, the square, oak-walled courtroom was filled, while queues waited outside the door leading to the special privileged seats. There were clergymen in the queue, women of fashion and coloured students.

Inside the court, while the sunlight shone through the round glass ceiling, there was a hum of conversation as the spectators discussed the latest phases of the trial.

Behind the front row of counsel engaged in the case sat the women barristers, behind them rows of women in fashionable clothes with furs round their necks.

Suddenly a hush fell on the court, eyes were turned to the judge's door. With gloves and black cap in hand, Mr Justice Humphreys, gravely judicial in his scarlet robes and wig, entered the courtroom. A pause. A man and a woman appeared in the dock.

Mr Justice Humphreys leaned forward and said to counsel, 'You wish the witness to return to the box?'

Mrs Rattenbury, a well-built, dark-haired woman, was dressed entirely in blue with a fur around her shoulders. Her face was shaded by a wide-brimmed blue straw hat. She walked quickly to the witness-box, seeming to tremble a little. She stood in the box, clasping and unclasping the edge with her gloved hands. . . . Those seated nearest the box noticed a faint aroma of the perfume she was using.

Leaning slightly forward and occasionally resting on her elbows, Mrs Rattenbury looked straight at Mr Casswell, counsel for Stoner, as he questioned her for almost half an hour regarding her relations with the young chauffeur and her feelings towards him. She replied promptly in a low clear voice, now and then illustrating her words with her hands. (*Bournemouth Daily Echo, 29th May 1935*)

Casswell did not consider her to be a good witness. He wrote :

To me she appeared vague and unconvincing, at time almost inarticulate; to some questions she replied merely with a gesture of the hands. She made so profound an impression on me that at one time I thought – almost certainly mistakenly – that she was under the influence of a drug. Yet however vague and unsatisfactory the manner in which she gave her evidence, there was no doubt that its content was bitterly damning to my client's interests.

He did not believe at all in her claim to have no recollection of what had passed for so many hours, nor did he accept that she was innocent, but he felt himself to be at a disadvantage because of Stoner's attitude in wishing to take all the blame : he thought his loyalty

may have been a moving demonstration of the bonds of romantic passion, but it made the task of defending counsel extraordinarily difficult. It also meant that I was unable to cross-examine Mrs Rattenbury at all strongly. If I had done so Stoner was quite capable of interrupting me from the dock with a cry that I had got it all wrong, he was the murderer.[3]

He started his cross-examination, therefore, by assuring Alma that he was not suggesting she had anything whatever to do with what happened on 24th March, or that she had ever incited Stoner or knew he was going to do it. This caused quite a stir in the Court, for he was already tacitly admitting that Stoner had committed the murder, but he tried to show that in doing so he had been very much under Alma's influence. Meanwhile Stoner sat motionless in his corner of the dock, resting his chin on his hand :

Of course, in the first place, you engaged him to come in by the day, did you not? –Yes, to take little John to school; he was a day-boy starting in the pre-prep, and it took a long time to go in on a tram.

So he had to be there early enough to take John to school? –A quarter to eight.

Well then, you went to the Randolph Hotel at Oxford? At that time did you tell your husband you were going to Leeds? – I thought of going; we could not get any farther. I tried to go there.

And was it there that you first had connexion with Stoner? –No.

Was it before that, or after? –No, after. 22nd November.

22nd November was the first day, was it? –Yes.

How long after that visit to Oxford? –I do not know.

Was it you who suggested it, Mrs Rattenbury? –What? Going to Oxford?

No. Living with Stoner? –No, I think it was mutual.

Mutual? Because, you see, he was in the position of a servant, was he not? –Yes.

And quite a young man? –Yes.

Did you think that it might have a very deleterious effect on him? –No, I never would have started it if I had.

You did not think then? –No.

But you made things easy by having him in the house, did you not? –Sleeping in?

Yes. –Yes; he used to stay occasionally before then.

According to Miss Tennyson Jesse's eye-witness description, Alma was perfectly calm, but it was a frozen, not an indifferent calm. The judge too noticed something, for he now said :

THE JUDGE : If you want to sit down, you can do so? –I think I would sooner stand.

You can do so if you please. You will probably be there some time, and if at any time you want to sit down there is a chair available? –Thank you so much.

Casswell continued :

I suppose you told him that you and your husband had not been living as husband and wife? –It was obvious to anyone living there. They would know it.

He would know it? –Naturally.

Did you tell him you were looking for sympathy? –No, most decidedly not.

You were looking for that, were you not, from someone? –No, I certainly was not.

It was just an infatuation, was it not? –I think it was more than that.

You fell in love with him? –Absolutely.

Because Casswell had been instructed that Stoner's defence was that he had acted while under the influence of cocaine, he tried to get Alma's support for this, not very successfully :

Now tell me, when did you first come to the conclusion that he was taking drugs? (Croom-Johnson interpolated, 'She has not said he was.) –He told me about his head, I think, some time at the beginning of November, but not as if he were taking drugs.

She repeated what Stoner had said to her about taking medicine two or three times a year – he wouldn't tell her why, and assured her that at the end of two or three years he wouldn't have to take it at all. She added that if he had been an addict she couldn't have had him around with the children.

I understood you to say in evidence he said he was taking drugs? –Yes, later than that.

Did you believe him then when he said he was taking less and less? Did you take no further notice of it in November? –Well, I watched him, and he seemed quite normal.

How did you expect to find him abnormal? In what way? –Well, it's difficult to explain. His temperament – he seemed to be so absurdly jealous at times, and that made me worried.

He did not seem quite normal at times? –No.

Now, what I want to know is : did he grow worse while he was with you? –No.

Did he seem to change from when he first came? –No, I thought he was much better.

Alma was being transparently honest in not going out of her way to support the drug theory – she may not even have realised that it was Stoner's main line of defence. Casswell complained in his notes on the trial that she was so vague he was sure her half-hearted corroboration of Stoner's predilection for cocaine convinced no one. He went on :

Now, you told us that you never took drugs yourself? –No, absolutely not.

You are quite sure of that? –Positive.

From time to time we have heard that you used to get very excited at times and then get drowsy afterwards? –Well, all my life with Mr Rattenbury was so what we call monotonous that at times I used to take too many cocktails to liven up one's spirits – take them to excess, say, or wine.

And you say that was the result of cocktails? –Anything like that, wines or cocktails – not spirits, not like that night, hard liquor.

Did Stoner take them also? –No; he was very much upset. He did not like me taking them; in fact, I stopped taking them after he came.

This didn't suit Casswell at all. He had been trying to show how much she influenced Stoner, and here was an example of Stoner influencing her. He referred back to the time in February when she had consulted Dr O'Donnell about his behaviour :

He had become violent, as I understand, had he not? –Yes, I was frightfully upset about it.

And you came to the conclusion that he was violent because he had been taking drugs? –Yes. I would not say violent exactly – more agitated.

Agitated? –Yes. He said he had to go to London that morning early to get this drug, and I begged him not to go, but he had to go and when he went I was so upset – it was dreadful. I telephoned Dr O'Donnell to explain everything to him, and said could he help this boy, I could not stop him going to London, and I explained it all to Dr O'Donnell to see if he would help him.

Now, have you any doubt that that boy at that time had such a craving that he went to London, and nothing you said would stop him? –To be perfectly candid, I was not certain then, and I am not certain now. I cannot answer that and say yes or no. I do not know.

Asked if she had done anything more about it, she said no, because
Stoner was better from then onwards:

> I do not quite understand. You mean to say from that time onwards
> there were no more threats from him? –Not with the drugs.
>
> What with, then? –No, I'm afraid that is a misunderstanding.
> I do not think I used the word threat.
>
> I thought Miss Riggs said – I may have been wrong – that you
> complained to her on several occasions that Stoner had been
> threatening you? –No, I'm afraid that is rather an exaggeration, to
> say threatening.
>
> Not on several occasions? –No, he was never like that.
>
> More than once? –Yes, but just like I said before, I wanted to
> break the connexion, say on account of the difference in age, and
> that would agitate him; that is all – not threatening exactly.
>
> Just what you took to be ordinary temper, was it? –Yes. Upset.
> THE JUDGE: Did you know his age when he came to you? –I thought
> he was older.
>
> Did you ask? –Yes.
>
> What did he say? –I thought he was twenty-two when he first
> came, and afterwards he said he was nineteen.
>
> How did you come to think he was twenty-two? –Because that is
> what he said.
>
> He said so? –Yes.
>
> When did you learn that his real age was eighteen? –I think – I
> am not quite certain – on his birthday.
>
> When was that? –19th November.

Casswell wanted to know about the pistol she said Stoner had when he
came in on the night of the 24th.

> Had you seen that before? –No.
>
> What was it like? –I did not particularly look at it. I hear it was
> a toy pistol, so I dare say that is what it was.
>
> . . . you did not look at this thing at all? –No. It was a small
> revolver, you know, and he had it like this (*indicating*), and I told
> him to put the beastly thing away; it might go off.
>
> Did you think it was a real one then? –Yes.
>
> Did you say anything to anyone about it? –No, naturally not.
>
> What did he do with it? –Well, he put it in his pocket.

Do you mean to say you did not take any further steps about that? –No. Why should I?

Well, I do not know. You thought it was a real revolver he was brandishing about? –Yes, but I did not see Stoner again that night after I had sort of, what I call, pacified him.

But he brought the supper or high tea into the drawing-room? –Yes, but I could hardly get up and say, 'Give me that gun,' in front of Mr Rattenbury, could I?

. . . I see. And you thought all was well. Had you ever seen – I am not accusing you of anything – had you ever seen this mallet in the house before? –No, never.

Had you suggested somebody should get a mallet? –Oh, no.

Had you not? –No, absolutely no.

Finally Alma had to face the ordeal of cross-examination by the prosecuting counsel, Croom-Johnson, who suffered from none of the difficulties and embarrassments that beset Casswell. He was harder with her, and forced her to show more of her intimate life and thoughts than either of the other counsel had done. In his opening speech he had submitted that both the accused with one common object and one common design had set out to get rid of her husband – but no evidence had as yet been heard that suggested Alma had had any such intention : it remained to be seen whether he could bring it out in his cross-examination. There were, of course, her signed confessions of her guilt, but in order to have them accepted at their face value by the jury he would have to break down her defence of complete loss of memory regarding them. He had an annoying trick of raising his pencil and pointing it at Alma to emphasize his questions. He asked :

What was the point of the journey to London with this boy whose mistress you were . . . if, in fact you and he had been living together practically as man and wife since 22nd November 1934? –I tried to explain that just now; it was all for Mr Rattenbury's benefit.

Mr Rattenbury's benefit? –Because I said I was going to London to have an operation, and I had to leave home.

That was the story you told your husband, who is now dead? –Yes, that is the truth.

What was the point of going on the journey at all? –Because I could not stay in the house when he had given me the money for the operation. As I say, I might have gone to Cornwall, or anywhere.

I want to be fair with you. Before you asked for the money from your husband, had you made up your mind to go to London? –To go to London, yes, because you would naturally say London for an operation, you see.

With Stoner? –Yes.

And did you take care, in asking your husband for money, to ask him for enough to enable you to defray the expenses of the journey to London? –Well, no. When I asked for the £250, I thought it would save me the trouble of asking him again in June, and then I could get through until next Christmas without asking him again.

When you went to your husband, had you made up your mind to fit this boy out with clothes? –No, not like that.

Had you thought about it? –No. I was going to get a suit of clothes, but when I got there I sort of went ahead and shopped like that.

Had you thought of giving him clothing before you went to your husband for money? –No.

Your husband was a man who had retired? –For about twenty years or more.

And was living largely, if not wholly on his means? –Yes.

Had he got sufficient money? –I understood he was very well off.

You had little, or nothing? –Exactly, except what I made with my writing, and I had cheques from my mother.

Should I be doing you an injustice if I suggested you had little, or nothing? –Except odd money from my mother.

If you please, how much in the year? –I do not know. She would send me at Christmas £25 or £10 – something like that.

Stoner had nothing? –No.

Had the question of money between you and your husband been a matter about which you had differences of opinion in the past? –Oh, yes.

Am I putting it fairly when I suggest that you were in the habit of deceiving your husband in order to get what you regarded as sufficient money for your needs? –Absolutely.

Did you know that your husband's securities had fallen considerably in value? –No. He was always talking like that, so it was a case of the lamb calling wolf. If it was so one would not have believed him.

Did you tell him before you asked for the money, or at the time you asked for this £250, that you were going up to London to have an expensive operation? –Yes.

Did he tell you that it would be at a considerable sacrifice if he gave it to you? –Yes, but he always all his life talked like that, so that no one ever took him seriously on the point of money.

Madam, please do not tell me 'no one'; let us confine our attention to you and your husband. When you say that you did not take him seriously –? –No. Absolutely not.

About how much money did he let you have in the year? –I could not answer that.

Hundreds? –I suppose so.

They reckoned up between them that she had from him about £1,000 a year from which she paid the staff, the household bills, Mr Rattenbury's clothes and the children's, and their schooling; so she was always overdrawn, even with the additional payments.

Did you tell your husband that Stoner was going to stay at the same hotel with you? –I never mentioned it. It was not necessary to lie.

THE JUDGE : It was not? –It was not necessary to lie. Just nothing was said.

Croom-Johnson continued :

Did you ever tell your husband that you were buying clothes for Stoner? –I never told my husband I was buying clothes even for little John. Expenses were never brought up in my life with Mr Rattenbury.

These clothes you did buy for him, did you regard them as necessary? You used the words this morning, I observed, that he required clothes? –Yes, I considered so.

Silk pyjamas at 60/- a suit? –That might seem absurd, but that is my disposition.

During the time you were in London were you on the, what had become, ordinary intimate terms with Stoner? –The same as at home, yes.

What was the last occasion on which you were intimate with Stoner? –Saturday.

You have told us that on Sunday night Stoner came into your bedroom and got into bed with you? –Yes.

Was that something that happened frequently? –Oh, always.

Always? Were you fond of your little boy, John? –I love both my children.

Were you fond of John? –Naturally.

Did John sleep in the same room? –Yes, but in another bed at the other side of the room.

It is not a very large room? –No, but little John was always asleep.

Are you suggesting to members of the jury that you, a mother, fond of her little boy of six, were permitting this man to come into your bedroom with you, in the same room where your innocent child was asleep? –I did not consider that was dreadful. I did not consider it an intrigue with Stoner.

This passage probably did Alma's reputation more harm than anything else in the cross-examination. Even Miss Tennyson Jesse was shocked, until she reminded herself that lovers, married and unmarried, were doing the same thing all over the country and thinking nothing of it.

Until Stoner told you during that time and in that bed about the mallet, and about the hiding of the mallet, can you recollect any other occasion that evening when he had that opportunity? –No.

THE JUDGE: I am not sure that I follow that. Do you mean that, after you found your husband injured, during the whole of that night you were never alone with Stoner? –Yes.

Were you alone with Stoner that night at any time after you found your husband injured? –No. I cannot remember.

Croom-Johnson continued:

You told us this morning that you did not hear Irene Riggs come in? –No.

There is evidence in the case that after Irene Riggs came in, Stoner was out on the landing, looking over the bannisters? –Yes.

From the time he got into your bed to the time that you jumped out of bed and went downstairs to the drawing-room, did Stoner ever leave your bed? –I was in bed when Stoner came and got into bed. Do you mean, did he get out before me? No.

Did he remain in bed with you? –Yes.

From then continuously up till the time when you jumped out of bed and went downstairs? –Yes.

Did you hear Stoner speak to anybody outside the door or on the landing? –No.

Did you know that he was out there at all? –No.

How soon after you got downstairs that evening and, as you say, discovered your husband in the chair, did you call out for Irene Riggs? –I should say it would be about three minutes; it would not be very much more – two minutes.

She told us, according to my recollection, almost immediately? –Yes, I just had time to walk round.

Was there a great deal of blood when you got down there? –Yes.

On the carpet? –Yes.

Did you notice blood on his clothes and on his collar, which had obviously run down from his head? –Yes; it was his eye that I noticed.

Was it apparent to you when you got down there that he must have been bleeding for some time? –I never thought one thing or the other.

You saw blood and did not think. Now do you think from the blood that you saw that he must have been bleeding for some time? –There was just about *that* much, a spot about *that* big. (*Indicating*)

On the carpet? –On the carpet round.

Soaked in? –I do not really know.

The sight upset you, according to your evidence? –Naturally.

Then there was the business again of her taking whisky and being sick, and he came to the barrier of her loss of memory. He tried to break it down:

How long was that before the doctor came? –I cannot remember the doctor.

Cannot you remember the doctor coming at all? –I have pieced together from hearing here . . .

Are you telling members of the jury that from the time practically that you were sick and poured yourself out a glass of whisky your memory does not serve you at all? –I can, yes, a few things. I remember like an awful nightmare.

You remember, as I gather, placing a wet or a white towel – I am not sure which it was – round Mr Rattenbury's head? –Yes, and I remember rubbing his hands, and they were so cold.

Is he still in the chair in the drawing-room? –Yes, I wanted to get his teeth in; I thought he could talk and tell me what happened.

And according to you that is the last thing that you recollect? –I remember one or two things more.

Tell me the things you recollect on that night? –Nothing that night. It was a shock to me to hear . . .

Do you recollect Dr O'Donnell coming? –I cannot.

What? –No, I have tried so hard, even with piecing together from what I have heard, to remember, and I cannot.

Do you recollect the second doctor arriving? –No.

Dr O'Donnell was a friend of yours and your medical attendant? –Yes.

As a rule, a person calculated to soothe rather than excite you? –Yes.

You recollect nothing of Dr O'Donnell that night? –No. As I say, I have tried in the last two months very, very hard to remember with piecing together, and still I cannot.

Do you recollect a succession of police officers coming in? –No, I could not; not one man could I see in Bournemouth. I tried to remember.

You recollect nothing at all more that night until some time the next day? –Little John standing in the doorway and his little face. I remember that.

What time of day was that? –I do not know. I can remember getting into a car, but I do not know what car, and that child's face in the doorway.

Where do you recollect yourself as being when that happened? –I was getting into a car, but I cannot remember – I had to ask what car afterwards.

Do you recollect arriving at the police station? –No – completely nothing.

Do you recollect being charged at the police station? –No, my mind has gone.

Do you recollect being before the magistrates about eleven o'clock the next morning? –No.

Do you recollect two interviews with your solicitors that morning? –No.

In the course of which, I suggest, you gave them instructions? –No.

Do you recollect seeing Dr O'Donnell somewhere about one o'clock? –No.

What is the last thing you remember of Stoner that night? –I remember Stoner kissing me goodnight in my bedroom, and I cannot remember going downstairs to the car, but I remember little John at the door, and those are the only two things at the Villa Madeira I remember after that awful night.

After a series of questions about her drinking habits, and a suggestion that Stoner had never undressed that night – she insisted that he came to her in his pyjamas – Croom-Johnson asked her about the projected visit to Bridport:

Have you ever stayed with Mr and Mrs Jenks before? –Yes. . . .

How long before? –Oh, I could not tell you the month we were there.

Before Stoner had come to the house, or afterwards? –Oh yes, before Stoner came.

Are you suggesting to members of the jury that you wanted to go to Bridport? –That I wanted?

That you wanted to go to Bridport? –No, not I. I wanted to cheer Mr Rattenbury up to make a change for him, and he did not want to go to London, so I suggested Bridport.

Did it occur to you that if you went to Bridport Mr Rattenbury might want to treat you as his wife? –No. If I had thought it was going to happen like that, I never would have suggested going.

It never occurred to you? –No.

You know exactly what I mean by saying treat you as his wife? –Yes, exactly.

When had you last been intimate with your husband? –About six years ago.

How old is little John? –Yes . . . he is six and a half in June.

Are you fond of him? –Naturally.

What? –Yes.

Your husband? –No. Did you ask . . .

Were you fond of your husband? –I did not love him, no. I was more of a companion than anything.

If he had wanted his rights as a husband, would you have been ready to grant them to him? –If he had wanted what? – oh no. I do not think so.

In March of 1935? –Oh no, I do not think so. Decidedly not.

Were you fond of this boy? –I loved him.

Croom-Johnson suggested that her visit to Irene's bedroom on the night of the murder was made in the knowledge of what had happened, and to make sure that Irene had not discovered her injured husband – but

Alma seemed not to understand him. So far he had not succeeded in penetrating her defence of complete loss of memory. He tried again, taking her statements one after the other, line by line, do you recollect this? do you recollect that? what did you mean when you said? . . . It was useless. The first thing she remembered was writing out two cheques on the morning of Monday 25th March at the police station. When he had concluded his cross-examination, the judge began questioning her:

THE JUDGE: I want to understand your state of mind on the 24th and the early morning of the 25th. According to what you are presenting to the jury, do you say that you have a perfectly clear recollection of what Stoner said to you when you were in bed? –I think so.

Well, have you any doubt about it? –No.

You say no? –Absolutely.

You remember even the trivial detail that he mentioned to you, that he had hidden the mallet? –Yes.

You are sure about that? –Yes.

And you are sure that is when you learned that he had hidden the mallet? –Absolutely. I never spoke to Stoner again.

Well then, the next morning we have evidence that you said to Irene Riggs, 'Tell Stoner that he must give me the mallet.' Did you say that? –I presume I did.

Do you mean you do not remember? –Absolutely not.

You must have remembered at that time all about it, must you not, or you could not have said that? –I wish I . . .

Do you really mean that you have no recollection of any conversation you had with anybody? –No.

The whole of the time? –No. I felt as if I were the one who had been hit over the head.

But you remember quite well what was said to you, and every word that was said to you by Stoner just before? –Oh yes.

In bed? –Naturally.

You say naturally? –Well, I had not had that dreadful shock then. We were quite happy; I was quite happy then. Life was different.

Now, it is quite clear that your evidence to the jury is that you do not remember even seeing a police officer that night? –No. I saw them all for the first time in Bournemouth.

You do not remember Dr O'Donnell coming? –No.

Did you have anything except whisky that night, except the morphia the doctor gave you hours later? –No.

Nothing else? –No.

Very well. Now, there is another matter I want to understand. You say you did not hear Miss Riggs come in? –No, I never did. She was very quiet.

She may have come in very quietly? –She always did.

Did you hear, while you lay in bed and before Stoner came into the bedroom, Miss Riggs and Stoner talking just outside your bedroom door? –No, I heard nothing.

Did you hear a word of that? –Absolutely not.

You were not asleep: can you explain why? –Well, it would not be very easy. My bed is over towards the window, and if they were out on the landing and my door was closed, and they would not talk in a loud voice, naturally I do not think anybody could hear it there.

We are told one of them, Stoner, was upstairs outside your room calling over the bannisters to Miss Riggs who was down below, and she answered him, or she called to him and he answered? –They are very soft-spoken.

You did not hear a word of that? –No, absolutely.

Did you hear your husband in the drawing-room groaning? –You could hear every noise in my bedroom from the drawing-room quite distinctly.

When Stoner told you he had done this thing, did you believe him? –No.

When you found your husband, did you believe him? –Well, I had to believe him then.

You did? –I hardly knew what to think.

Had you any doubt at all when Stoner told you that he had hit your husband on the head with the mallet, and you went downstairs and found your husband had been hit on the head, that what Stoner said was true? –Well, one would naturally think so, would you not?

I do not know. You are here to answer my questions. I would like to have a plain answer from you: had you any doubt that what Stoner said to you was true? –I did think it was.

Did you tell anybody of that? –No. Do you mean at the time?

Did you tell anybody that Stoner had done this to your husband and you knew it? –Oh no, unless I said something that night that I do not remember.

When did you first tell that to anybody? –I think my solicitor.

You told your solicitor? –I told him that, yes.

'And that was it,' Casswell commented.

Both to Croom-Johnson in cross-examination and the judge in his questionings, she preserved this impenetrable barrier of loss of memory. . . . When each of her various incriminating statements was put to her the answer was the same: 'Did I say that? I can give no explanation. I cannot have known what I was saying.' And the hands would wave forlornly.

In a brief re-examination, O'Connor read for the benefit of the jury an extract from a report by Dr Morton, Governor of Holloway Prison:

'She was received into my custody on the evening of 25th March, and I saw her early next morning for the first time. She was very depressed and seemed confused and kept repeating the same sentence over and over again. On the 28th March she was somewhat better and appeared to have forgotten what she had said and how she had behaved the previous days since her reception.'

He asked Alma, 'Does that correspond with what you recollect about your own mental condition during that time?'
She answered, 'Absolutely.'
Casswell wrote:

This was a clever stroke on O'Connor's part. The Prison Governor was ill and could not be called, so by adopting this tactic he was able to get before the jury something that was not really evidence. If the Governor had been present in court one would have wanted to cross-examine him fairly closely as to whether a temporary loss of memory could last from approximately 10.30 p.m. on Sunday until the following Wednesday. Even though she had received an extreme shock and been injected with a considerable amount of morphia, surely the effect would have worn off long before then?[4]

*

MRS RATTENBURY'S LONG ORDEAL IN THE BOX. MORE THAN INFATU-ATED. MRS RATTENBURY SAYS, 'I FELL IN LOVE.' STONER'S VISITS TO HER BEDROOM. HAIRS ON THE MALLET. MRS RATTENBURY AND 'THAT AWFUL NIGHT.'

During the whole trial this boy of eighteen had been like a graven image. In his neat grey suit, with his fair hair brushed back, his long fair eyelashes, and his frank open face, he looked what his counsel had described him as, 'an English boy.'

Throughout the long days he sat with his elbow on the corner of the dock with eyes half closed, watching counsel and the judge as they asked questions, but with apparently no interest in the witnesses, and least of all in the woman in the dock with him .

Only once did he show any emotion and that was when Mrs Rattenbury, in her deep musical voice, tense with anguish, fighting often for words that would not come and with her mobile mouth twitching with nervous strain, was laying bare her soul from the witness-box.

As she told intimate details of their illicit passion he fidgeted and became restless, and when, leaning over the box with hands outstretched, she barely breathed the words, 'I loved him', he showed the only signs of emotion he gave throughout. (*News of the World, 2nd June 1935*)

CHAPTER NINE

In Defence of Stoner

When the hearing was resumed on the fourth day of the trial, O'Connor obtained the judge's permission to recall Mr Rooke, the surgeon who had operated on Rattenbury after he had received his injuries: he wished to question him on the effects of morphia on the memory.

Mr Rooke went into the witness-box, and said that on a number of occasions he had given morphia to his patients and found that when he spoke to them they answered intelligently, but the next day they remembered nothing of what they had said; their memory had gone – which was precisely the effect it had evidently had on Alma. O'Connor asked:

Has the recollection of what occurred before come back to them at a later date? –I have known it last as long as two days.

Do you mean that the recollection of events of two days has been blotted out? –Has been lost completely.

Lost permanently? –Permanently.

As regards half a grain of morphia, is that a large dose? –The cases of which I speak have had a quarter.

Croom-Johnson asked:

In these cases, when you have asked questions, have the questions been coherently answered? –Coherently and intelligently.

Do they lose memory for events during the time the drug is operating? –Yes.

How far back does that go? Do they lose memory for events before the drug is administered or not? –In my experience they have not had a retrospective loss of memory. It has been after the time that the drug has acted.

So that the memory of events up to the time when the drug is administered remains? –It does.

It was now Casswell's turn to call the evidence on behalf of Stoner. Before he did so, he asked the judge if he might put to the jury one or two points he had inadvertently omitted.

THE JUDGE : I shall not stop you in a case like this.

CASSWELL : Members of the jury, I must apologise for troubling you once more before I call my evidence, but I am afraid I did not quite put before you the position in a case of murder. There was a recent decision in the House of Lords in which the Lord Chancellor laid this down . . .

The judge considered that directives to the jury on points of law were entirely his province, so he interrupted :

THE JUDGE : You are now going to talk of the law to the jury, are you?

CASSWELL : Just to show the jury what is the issue they have to try. (He turned again to the jury.) . . . when dealing with a murder case, the Crown must prove (a) death, as the result of a voluntary act of the accused, and (b) malice of the accused. It may prove malice either expressly or by implication. Malice is the intention which is in the mind of the person who does the act; and the malice which is necessary in the case of murder – speaking subject to my lord's correction – is the intention either to kill or to do grievous bodily harm.

He went on to explain that even if malice was proved, it was still possible for the accused to say in his defence, 'I did the act, but I had not sufficient intent owing to disease of the mind,' – which was the way, he said, in which lawyers speak of insanity or of drunkenness or of taking drugs – 'which rendered me in such a state that I was incapable of forming that design.' The case to which he was referring was that of *Rex v. Woolmington* in which, only a month ago, he and O'Connor together had successfully appealed to the House of Lords against a conviction for murder. He now put forward the same defence for Stoner :

On his behalf you have now heard the evidence of Mrs Rattenbury, and on his behalf I accept and endorse the whole of her explanation of the facts and matters which happened leading up to the day of 24th March, and what happened after that day. It necessarily follows that she, in my submission, did not commit this act and had nothing to do with it, and the accused does not deny, in fact admits, that it was his hand that struck the blow. In those circumstances, although the onus is on the prosecution to show you that it was his hand that struck the blow, you will probably have no difficulty in coming to that conclusion. The onus, therefore, remains upon the defence to show you that when he struck the blow he was, by reason, as I shall submit to you, of his addiction to cocaine, incapable of forming the necessary intent, that is, the intent to kill or the intent to cause grievous bodily harm . . . but had the intent merely to prevent the trip to Bridport.

He now called the evidence for Stoner – firstly to show his exemplary character before he met Alma, and secondly to show that he was a drug addict, which rested solely on his alleged statements to Alma and then to Dr O'Donnell.

> Stoner in fact did not go into the witness-box. His counsel said it would not help the boy at all to have him in the box, because he was under the influence of a drug at the time of the events on which he was charged.
> Stoner, however, very nearly entered the box, by an extraordinary accident. His counsel was calling a witness. He said, 'I call Mr Stoner.'
> The prisoner Stoner at once stood up. The dock door was opened. He stepped down into the well of the court accompanied by a warder. He had taken a dozen steps when a buzz of talk was heard at the solicitor's table. Suddenly the warder cried, 'Wait!' took the prisoner by the arm, conducted him back to the dock, and shut the door on him.
> It was not the boy who was wanted to give evidence. It was his father.
> (*Daily Express, 31st May, 1935*)

George Stoner described himself as a bricklayer of 104 Redhill Terrace, Bournemouth; he was the father of the accused who was his only child. He gave a simple account of himself and his family: after being demobbed from the Machine Gun Corps he had gone about the country from place to place wherever there was work, and consequently young Stoner, born in 1916 while he was on active service, had frequently been moved from one school to another or stayed with his grandparents. He left school when he was fourteen.

One could not wish for a better boy. He had just a few friends round about, not very many. He was not a boy to go out at all; he was rather keen on staying in – rather reserved, I mean. If he had friends he would have them rather younger than himself and he was a champion for those boys, because if they were oppressed he would help them out. That was his character right up until, unfortunately, he went out to work. I noticed a difference in his appearance after he went to the Rattenburys. He was a little while with a motor firm before he went to the Rattenburys, but this was really his first time out. My wife and I spoke about the difference in his appearance and demeanour frequently. He became pale. I put it down to the fact that perhaps he might have been indoors too much, but after looking at him as he lay in a chair sometimes (he went to sleep), we used to say that he was sunken in the eyes and rather drawn.

Casswell asked :

It has been suggested by some witnesses that your son said he found cocaine in your house, and that that first started him. Have you ever had cocaine yourself ? –No, never.

As far as you know, has there ever been any in your house? –There has been no cocaine, or morphia, or any drug of any description in my house.

Croom-Johnson asked :

You said the boy got to look very pale. Can you say you noticed any particular time when that commenced? –Towards the latter part of November and the beginning of December I noticed he was getting pale, but I first noticed his drawn appearance about Christmas.

You did not know that this boy of eighteen was living on terms of sexual intimacy with a woman twice his age? –He would not have remained there if I had known it.

Then Stoner's mother made a brief appearance, Olivia Matilda Stoner. She struggled hard to restrain her emotion while she explained :

I am the wife of the last witness and the mother of the accused, George Percy Stoner. I saw my son on Sunday, 24th March in the afternoon. I was lying down when he came in. I think it would be about three or soon after. I do not know how long he stayed. I should say it was just before half-past four when he left.

Casswell asked:

Was he talking to you during that time? –Well, a little. I cannot remember what he said.

Did you notice anything peculiar about him? –No, nothing more than he usually is when he comes in.

The prosecutor said, 'I have no questions,' and she was allowed to go.

The man, tall, soldierly; the woman, frail, in tears. At the Old Bailey yesterday they faced the most tragic moments of their lives, called as witnesses in the case in which their son is accused of murder.

They were the parents of George Percy Stoner, the boy chauffeur, whose trial with Alma Victoria Rattenbury – Lozanne, the song writer – on a charge of killing Mrs Rattenbury's husband, draws towards its close.

In the dock the pale, fair-haired lad watched them, heard his father tell in quiet clear tones, of his weakness in childhood and then say, 'You couldn't wish for a better boy.'

Soon the father left the box and, passing the dock, he smiled. His smile bore a message of affection and encouragement to his son.

Then the mother. Only for a little time was she in the box, her faltering sentences almost inaudible.

To every mother her son remains a baby all his life, and what must that poor woman have felt like! I had a lump in my throat, and my heart ached as she answered the few questions that were put to her.

She was crying when she stepped from the witness-box. With lowered head she walked past the dock without a glance at her accused boy.
(*Daily Mirror, 31st May 1935*)

The next witness to be called was Dr Lionel Alex Weatherly, a most unimposing little man in spectacles who told the judge he was very deaf. He listened through an ear-trumpet to everything that was said to him. He reeled off a most imposing list of his credentials: Doctor of Medicine of Aberdeen, Member of the Royal College of Surgeons, ex-President of the Society of Nervous and Mental Diseases, President of the section of Psychology and Neurology at the annual meeting of the British Medical Association in 1934 etc., with sixty-two years experience as a medical man. He had done no general practice since 1886, but had lived among mental cases practically all his medical life.

He said he had had an interview with Stoner at Dorchester Prison
and noticed a very definite dilatation of both pupils which did not
react either to natural or electric light . . .

That is undoubtedly consistent with the taking of cocaine . . . I came
to a very definite conclusion that he was a cocaine addict. I could
only form a conclusion of how long he had been an addict from
what he told me himself.

Stoner had described to him 'very fairly, feasibly and accurately' the
symptoms of cocaine poisoning – hallucinations of touch, the feeling of
a rash moving about beneath the skin, and so on. These hallucinations
could and did occur, Dr Weatherly said, the exalting effect followed
by great irritability and hallucinations that insects were crawling all
over the bedclothes. It was in accordance with the findings of the latest
authority on cocainism, Dr Meyer of Zurich. He concluded :

I understand that Stoner carried a dagger about with him for a time.
That is one of the common symptoms of cocainism. A cocaine drug
addict has besides the hallucinations of which I have spoken, very
definite delusions of persecution, and they often carry weapons about
with them either to protect themselves or otherwise. I have followed
the evidence which has been given in this case. I have heard the
evidence given by Mrs Rattenbury of the occurrences from 4.30
onwards in the Villa Madeira. Her description of what Stoner did
on that occasion, his sudden threat to her with a revolver, and his
sudden turn of violence and threats when she was telephoning, are
consistent with his having taken a dose of cocaine that afternoon.
THE JUDGE : Are they also consistent with his not having taken a
dose of cocaine, but being very angry and very jealous of his mistress?
–I doubt it.

Casswell asked him :

We have heard from Mrs Rattenbury that he accused her of having
connexion with her husband when the door was closed although the
young son John was there in the afternoon? –I consider that entirely
a hallucination of hearing arising out of cocainism, and this insane,
unreasonable jealousy.
    You have heard that the blow struck in this case was struck by
that big mallet, and you have heard the other evidence about where

the mallet was put. Is that consistent or not with the effects of a dose of cocaine? . . .

THE JUDGE : What on earth does that question mean? I do not know.

DR WEATHERLY : I think any assault would be consistent with the after effects of cocaine if those effects had created an abnormal and unreasonable, and insane, jealousy. I heard Dr Grierson say that this lad told him he had taken what he described as two eggspoonfuls of cocaine between bread at 4.30 that afternoon.

Casswell asked if the fact that Stoner went to sleep in the car outside the Strathallen Nursing Home could have been the comatose state after the exciting effect of cocaine – the judge again intervened and said, 'If you found a chauffeur going to sleep when he has been kept up to half-past two in the morning waiting for his employer –?' Casswell gave up, disappointed to find Dr Weatherly was impressing neither judge nor jury. Dr Weatherly however, was quite unabashed.

O'Connor had no questions, so Croom-Johnson began his cross-examination :

Have you known people get very, very jealous who were not drug addicts and not suffering from acute alcoholism? –I have only had my experience that I have told you of, of cases of definite cocaine addictism. I told you of one case with the hallucination of sight. May I tell you of another case that I have had?

THE JUDGE : No. Try and answer the question. I am sure you can answer it. Do you know, after sixty-two years as a medical man, that some people get very jealous without cocaine or drink having anything to do with it? –Of course. (*There was some laughter which the judge rebuked.*)

The cross-examination continued. Croom-Johnson tried to get Dr Weatherly to say that the one definite symptom of cocaine addiction he said he had observed in Stoner – that the pupils of his eyes did not react to light – might have been due to other causes, neurasthenia, nerve shock, or alcohol : he would not agree, but at last conceded that the effect was sometimes observed in a patient who was anaemic or very run down. The effects of cocaine addiction were then discussed in a long series of questions and answers, but it was not apparent that much, or any of it, could be applied to Stoner's case.

A second authority was then called and examined by Casswell – Dr Robert Gillespie of 6 Chester Terrace, Regent's Park. He was a more

formidable character than Dr Weatherly. His credentials were that he
was a Doctor of Medicine of Glasgow University, a Fellow of the Royal
College of Physicians, held a Diploma of Psychological Medicine and
was on the staff of Guy's Hospital. He too had had an interview with
Stoner but had noticed nothing relevant except that he was very tense
and anxious, which was only to be expected under the circumstances.
He was asked to describe the symptoms you look for in a cocaine addict.
He said it was extremely difficult to discover whether a person was a
cocaine addict or not:

> One looks for inexplicable oscillations of mood, that is to say at one
> time they are elated and at another time depressed without ascertain-
> able reason, and with the elation there goes a mental and physical
> activity which is quite different from the lethargy and tiredness and
> depression of other times; and later on, as the addiction persists,
> it begins to have more profound physical and mental effects. Sleep
> and appetite are interfered with so that they lose weight. They
> become pale and emaciated, ultimately, and mental symptoms are
> more likely to appear than with a more healthy mind in the direction
> of hallucinations, morbid jealousy and impulsive acts.

There was some difficulty in defining the word 'addict' to the judge's
satisfaction, and then Casswell tried to apply these symptoms to the case
of Stoner:

> What is the effect of cocaine on the sexual male? –In the male it
> produces a very definite morbid jealousy, rather akin to the morbid
> jealousy of alcoholism which, for example, is described by another
> authority in this country, the late Dr Sullivan.
>   Supposing a person to be under the domination of that morbid
> jealousy, is he likely to misinterpret what goes on around him?
> –Extremely likely.
> THE JUDGE: Is not that true of all jealousy? –Yes, but I should have
> thought it was more likely to happen with a diseased jealousy.
> THE JUDGE: Have you ever read the play of *Othello*? –I have, a
> long time ago.

Casswell wanted to know whether, when acts of violence were being
committed by a cocaine addict his mind is clear and capable of forming
an intent. Dr Gillespie replied that consciousness was often clear – that
is, from a medical point of view – but it was very different from being

able to come to a balance of judgement, from being able to weigh the pros and cons of a situation.

Is a person at the moment of that act of violence likely to think much of the consequences, do you think? –I should think not.

THE JUDGE: Can you answer that? –Perhaps I ought to put it this way, and say that he would be less likely to think of the consequences than a person who was not under the influence of cocaine.

Again Casswell was disappointed: neither of his witnesses would commit himself to a definite assertion that Stoner was, or even appeared to be, a cocaine-addict. Dr Gillespie was cross-examined by Croom-Johnson:

Unfortunately a great number of people in this world do not think beforehand of the consequences of their acts. Do you agree? –I agree.

Perfectly healthy people? –Yes.

And perfectly normal people? –It depends on how you use the word normal, but I suppose in ordinary language it would be so.

You were asked a moment or two ago what effect the taking of cocaine had on the sexual life, as I understood the question, of the patient. Does it have any effect on the sexual power? Is one of the effects of taking cocaine in the male that it very speedily produces impotence? –Yes.

Tell me something from a rather different point of view. Is regular sexual intercourse with a member of the opposite sex by a boy of about eighteen onwards likely to do him good or harm? –I should think that is a very difficult question to answer. I should not say that it did him good, if you are thinking of it from a moral point of view.

No, I am not talking from a moral point of view, I am talking to you as a doctor. Is it likely to cause him to look pale? –I should not think that necessarily it would.

Would you think it likely? –It depends on the frequency with which it occurred.

Frequently is my question? –It depends on what you mean by frequently.

Do you think one would be likely to look sleepy, or have the appearance . . .

THE JUDGE: I think you might take it in this way. To speak quite plainly, the learned counsel means as frequently as the nature of the woman would permit? —I think in that case, unless he was very worried about it, I should think it might not have any physical effect but it would obviously depend on the constitution.

Croom-Johnson solemnly persisted:

Take the ordinary case, the ordinary boy, not somebody very strong, talking about the ordinary English youth of eighteen, do you really find yourself in any difficulty in answering the question? —I find difficulty in answering the question as I believe you expect it to be answered . . .

So the argument went on and on, Croom-Johnson trying to put Stoner's alleged tiredness and paleness down to his sexual relations with Alma, and Dr Gillespie refusing to commit himself. At last they went on to discuss at length the effect on an addict of his supply of cocaine being cut off. After listening patiently for some time, the judge concluded as follows,

THE JUDGE: Do you know in your experience any such case as this: a cocaine addict suddenly cut off from any supply, given no drug of any sort or kind to take the place of cocaine, and from the day that the supply is cut off, for a period of two months, has been a person who can properly be described in this way: throughout rational, sleeping well, taking his food well, and been perfectly healthy? —I should be surprised, except on this one condition, that the doses had a considerable space between each of them. Then I should not be quite so surprised.

A juror asked for how long after a dose of cocaine would distension of the pupil continue. Dr Gillespie replied, 'Quantities of cocaine have been found in the pupil as long as twenty-one hours after the drug has been taken, but how long after that it might in certain cases be observable, I do not know.'

That concluded the evidence for Stoner. Casswell later commented:

For the reasons which I have already stated, the defence of George Stoner was one of exceptional difficulty, and I did not even enjoy the saving grace of having the final speech for the defence before the prosecuting counsel gave his closing speech. Because of the order of the two defendants' names on the indictment, I had to address the jury on

Stoner's behalf before both Croom-Johnson for the Crown and O'Connor
for Mrs Rattenbury. I did what I could, but with so preposterous a
defence as that with which I was saddled, it was very difficult to make
a really persuasive speech. I pinned my hopes on drumming home to
the ten men and two women of the jury, that if they were so minded,
they could find Stoner guilty of manslaughter instead of the ultimate
crime of murder.[1]

He began his closing speech :

May it please your lordship. Members of the jury, you have now
heard the evidence against and for the defendant Stoner. I think I
have made it clear that he does not deny that it was his hand that
struck the blows. What he does deny is that his mind was in such
a state at that time that he was responsible for striking those blows.
That is the question which I wish to discuss at no great length with
you today. I am not going to try to persuade you against your will.
I simply want to talk to you as business men and women. Is it not
clear that what I have proved before you shows that this cannot have
been the act of a sane boy?

Is it not clear that the taking of drugs, a fact spoken of by other
witnesses besides the witnesses for the defence, an issue raised as
soon as these proceedings were commenced, is the true answer to
the question you have to decide?

When one is dealing with the question of intent, it is a fact which
you, as a jury, are called upon to find : aye, or no, did this boy
have the requisite intent to commit this terrible crime? Or did he
have some sort of an intent merely to do something very different?
It is his mind that you have to enquire into, and it is very difficult
because none of us can get into a man's mind and see what was
there. Few of us are sufficiently skilled in language to describe,
perhaps, our own intent or our own state of mind, especially at such
a time as we are dealing with, when we were under the influence of
a drug . . .

How are we to find out what was the state of Stoner's mind on
that day, that all-important day, and how are we to find out what
were the motives that actuated him when he did this act?

In my submission to you, it could help you very little indeed to
have Stoner in the box. Since the year 1898 the defendant is entitled
to go into the box if he wishes, but in my submission that would not
have helped you at all. He was under the influence of a drug at the
time, and what he could say, and what he would know now, would

be of little assistance to you. Moreover he is a man with a shadow over him. He stands there in the terrible position of a man accused of the gravest crime in our calendar. So the evidence I have put before you, and the evidence which I wish to recall to you as shortly as possible, is the evidence which I can get from other people. You want to know the history of the man. You want to know all you can about things that bear on the matter, and especially things which happened before 24th March, before anybody heard of the crime, before any crime had been contemplated, so that you may have what is the best possible evidence. It is evidence uninfluenced by emotionalism, evidence uninfluenced by anybody wishing to pervert what really happened. When you have looked at that, I shall ask you to say that this crime is, in my submission, almost inexplicable in a young Englishman . . . Is it the sort of thing that one expects in a lad of seventeen or eighteen, and an English lad? I want you to ask yourselves that. If you come to the conclusion that it is not the sort of thing one expects, then we must look for a reason.

Was there any reason which made this lad do something that was so inconsistent with his nature? It is a very, very cruel act which the prosecution are asking you to say he committed deliberately, a dreadful act. An old man, apparently asleep, is hit on the side of his head with a heavy mallet and with no sort of urging motive of theft, no motive of revenge, no evidence telling of previous quarrelling or dislike. The evidence before you is that they got on extremely well together. I am perfectly certain that before you are going to accept the suggestion of the prosecution you are going to look into it very, very carefully indeed, to see whether any reason has been given as to why this inoffensive, straightforward, honest English boy committed so terrible a crime.

He now raised the question of motive, for it was a curious thing about this case that there appeared to be no adequate motive for the crime. He explained that there was no necessity for the prosecution to prove motive, but that it was often a very important thing for the jury.

If you heard that a friend of yours who had led an excellent life and held a wonderful character was suddenly accused of a crime like this, you would say, 'Why, there must have been some very strong reason, if he was sane, to make him do a thing like that.' Therefore, from the jury's point of view, I sometimes think that motive is the most important element of all. What could be the motive in this case?

The motive suggested by the prosecution is this – it was put very forcibly by my learned friend, and very fairly, as he always does – 'They wanted to get him out of the way.' Whose way was he in? Here was a lad who probably had to look at every sixpence before this first job of his; there was nothing to keep him from what has been termed an adulterous intercourse; everything was ready for him, everything was there. As far as we know, Mr Rattenbury knew all about it as Mrs Rattenbury said, and he did not care; or else he was in entire ignorance, and there is no evidence at all before you that here was a man in the way whom somebody wanted to get out of the way. Why should they need to get him out of the way? In order to live together? As I have pointed out to you already, any sane persons who wanted to get somebody out of the way in order to enjoy life and possess his money would at any rate take some proper precaution to see that he was put out of the way in some fashion which would not at once fix the guilt on one or other of them. I ask you to disregard this as a motive altogether. What other motive was there? There was no trace of quarrelling and no trace of ill-feeling between these two people. There was, of course, no sign of theft. In my submission the only motive that can be assigned here is a motive which was entirely insufficient for this crime. It was simply the motive to prevent the trip to Bridport.

He described it as the clumsiest crime that could possibly be imagined, particularly in fetching the mallet from some distance away where it was bound to leave a trail as the police would discover its owner :

Then there was no chance of an alibi. Two people in the house, and a boy – the man who committed this crime. How on earth was he going to fix the responsibility on anybody else? How was he going to come to the Court with evidence to say, 'I was miles away at the time'?

He pointed out that Stoner had plenty of opportunity to escape that night, but he never made any preparations, and never went. By using the heavy mallet it was obvious that suicide must be ruled out, neither could it be suggested that it was an accident.

In my submission to you, all of these considerations prove and inevitably prove, that this was an act on impulse, the act of somebody who did not plan it beforehand, who made no necessary provision for the future, but acted under an impulse, as I suggest to you, an uncontrollable impulse.

He warned the jury that controllable impulse was not a defence and must not be accepted as such : he would have to go further and prove to them also the absence of the necessary intent, that the doer was so confused, or so diseased in mind, as either not to understand what he was doing or that what he was doing was wrong; or else that he had not sufficient intent to constitute the crime of murder :

Let us consider the history of the lad based entirely on the evidence that you have heard in this Court . . . Juries in this country are supposed to have terrific memories. You have been here three days already. You are not supplied with notepaper or anything like that; you are supposed to carry it all in your head. So may I remind you of a few things which you may have forgotten?

He recalled that Stoner had an excellent character, was no trouble to anybody, was inoffensive, not pugnacious, didn't run about with girls or with gangs of lads, had no vices. He was born while his father was abroad on active service and developed late, not walking till he was three :

His education seems to have been about three years. I shall ask you to remember that when we come to consider the way in which he got, as I am going to suggest, under the domination of Mrs Rattenbury and became infatuated with her . . . I think you will come to the conclusion that there could not have been a worse environment for any lad of that age than the one in which he found himself. It would be very difficult to find one. It was a household where the husband and wife were not living together, and had not been living together for some time. It was a household where Irene Riggs was employed, and you will have but little doubt, having listened to her evidence, that she became, and was, jealous of this new helper in the house.

It was a household where there was a most extraordinary woman, unbalanced, hysterical and apt to fly into fits of excitement, to send for a doctor, to be given anaesthetics and be put to bed; the very reverse in character to the lad who suddenly found himself in her house, because, to use her own words, in order to get the money she required, she said she had lied all through her married life – a most unfortunate atmosphere.

I do not want to dwell on this side of the question. I want to make it quite clear that I am not asserting for one moment that this woman had anything to do with what happened at the Villa Madeira on 24th March, but I do say that when the lad found himself in that sort of society it may be that atmosphere which led him to the first dose of drugs, and it may be that life which increased the effect of the drugs and weakened his resistance.

Again and again we find Casswell being hampered in his defence by having to introduce the theme of drugs. Since it had come out in evidence that Stoner had described cocaine to Dr Grierson, Medical Officer of Brixton Prison, as 'brown with dark specks in it', it is hardly possible that anyone could believe he had ever taken it, or even seen it. In order to follow this line, Casswell had to paint an unsympathetic portrait of Alma, but he seemed to be apologising to her for it :

. . . in November we find that he is saying to Mrs Rattenbury – and I ask you to accept almost in entirety the evidence of Mrs Rattenbury because I invite you to say that it fits in with the facts as we know them from the evidence of the prosecution – this, at least, you will say, that she has been frank with you in many ways when it was perhaps not necessary for her to be so. I ask you to accept what she says, that in November he told her he had to take something for his head, some medicine to make his head normal, and that afterwards he told her that it was a drug . . . I think you may be quite certain of this, that the drug-taking started in November, or thereabouts.

He talked of what the prosecutor had called 'an adulterous intercourse', and commented that no doubt it was, from the point of view of the elder party to it, but not in the case of the boy :

I ask you, gentlemen of the jury, to look back, if you can, to the days when you were seventeen or eighteen, and try to put yourself in the position of that boy who was a servant in the house, the house of a lady who is well known, a writer of music under the name of Lozanne, a lady who provides him with more money than he ever had before, and finally offers herself to him . . . Do you remember, perhaps, the glamour of those days in the late teens – I feel sure that some of you do – the glamour of a woman for a young man? When a woman offers herself to a man who owes his livelihood to her, are you going to stress in any way the question of 'adulterous intercourse' between them? I am sure you will come to the conclusion that he never looked at it from that point of view. You will not take that into consideration against him.

He recapitulated the evidence about the lad's paleness and the suggestions that this was due to his intimacy with Alma, and he asked the jury to conclude that it was simply one more symptom of drug addiction:

But stronger still, you get the evidence of what happened with Dr O'Donnell, about 12th February I think it was. By that time not only was the lad taking some drug, but he was getting violent and Mrs Rattenbury was getting frightened about him; so nervous and so frightened about it, apparently, that she goes to a doctor and says that her lover has become an addict to some sort of drug and she wants him to find out what: and not only that, but this chauffeur at £1 a week has gone to London for the special purpose of obtaining drugs. You have Dr O'Donnell's evidence and Mrs Rattenbury's evidence. Is it not clear what happened? When Dr O'Donnell sees him the next day, and asks him about it, and asks him what he has been taking, he says, 'Cocaine. That is what I tried to get yesterday, but I could not get it.'

Have you any doubt that this lad was taking cocaine? He was sent to the doctor because the woman was frightened of him. Irene Riggs said complaints were made on three or four occasions of these attacks, and Mrs Rattenbury was saying that the lad was threatening her life – this lad who up to September had an exemplary character from everybody. What had changed him? What had turned him into a lad who rushes up to town, a lad who is getting so dangerous that Mrs Rattenbury sends him to her doctor? Why was it? Was it not addiction to cocaine? Was it not something that was taken into the system which was altering the character of the boy so much? I suggest to you there cannot be any doubt about it.

He said it was unfortunate that the doctor did not tell him to find another job, to 'get out of this hysterical household with people up all night, and all the rest of it; cocktails, drinking to excess, people having to be put to bed, and that sort of thing.'

Mrs Rattenbury said that after that talk the boy became less troublesome. At any rate we know that she took him up to London, and she raised quite a lot of money, and spent quite a lot of it on this journey to London, the buying of clothes, and all the rest of it.

Everything seems to be quite normal on the Saturday, and on the Sunday the boy goes round to see his mother, apparently in a quite normal condition, at half-past three and he does not leave her until about half-past four. At half-past four he goes back to the Villa Madeira, and there he serves tea, it was part of his duty; and there, in that room upstairs, for some reason or other, the door which is usually left open is closed. Now, the boy has told Dr Grierson that he took a double dose of cocaine that afternoon at half-past four. In my submission you cannot have a single doubt that that is true, although none of you know, or will ever know, how much cocaine was in those two spoonfuls, but I think you will come to the conclusion that it was a pretty severe dose.

What happened then? We know nothing more about him until we find him downstairs. When Mrs Rattenbury is telephoning to Bridport, the boy has entirely changed, the boy who was quite normal when he went round to his mother, and when he took the tea up, so that nobody noticed anything. What had happened? What had happened to make him suddenly violent? Threatening with a revolver, saying, 'I am going to shoot you if you go to Bridport'?

It is suggested that that is the jealousy of a normal man. Do you think it is? In my submission it is not, and it is not the kind of thing you expect to find in an English boy of eighteen. But there it is, this sudden change, the lad bringing out the revolver – I do not care if it is a revolver or a toy revolver – and threatening to shoot her if she goes to Bridport; and saying, moreover, 'You had connexion with Mr Rattenbury, I heard it going on. What do you mean by that? You told me I was your lover. You told me you had never lived with him for the last seven years, and that is why you wanted me. What do you mean by it?'

It was all hallucination. What caused it? Is it not quite clear that is the hallucination that Dr Weatherly and Dr Gillespie have spoken of, the hallucination that follows intoxication and cocaine. I ask you to believe that he had taken that double dose a few minutes before he listened outside the door, that he was under the influence of the drug at that time, and hence you get this unreasonable fury, this insane and unfounded jealousy.

For a time she thinks she has quietened him, but there it is, still on his mind. Away he goes and gets that mallet and commits this insane act; and I ask you to say that it is not the act of a normal boy, but that it is the act of somebody acting under the impulse of that insane hallucination, that insane jealousy which, as Dr Weatherly has said to you, may so affect his reason that he does not think of the consequences, and does not form an intent. That is the whole question: what was the state of that boy's mind, a boy who was normal at half-past four; and who was doing these extraordinary things at six. What was the state of his mind? Are you going to say, in view of all that evidence, 'this was a normal boy'? Are you going to say that he knew what he was doing when he did this awful thing?

He emphasized to the jury that even if they thought he knew what he was doing and knew it was wrong, they still had to consider whether he had formed the intent to do Rattenbury grievous bodily harm, or to kill him:

I suggest to you that the truth came out for the first time in a most illuminating expression used by Mrs Rattenbury: 'He came up to me, agitated, distressed, and he said . . .' What did he say? "There is something I cannot tell you about; you will not be able to bear it." 'Oh yes, I can bear anything.' What was it, then? "You won't be going to Bridport tomorrow." ' And later on she said – I took down her exact words – 'He gave me the impression that he had hurt Ratz to stop us going to Bridport.' In my submission, that is the truth of this. In his insane mind he had threatened her with the revolver: 'She is telephoning to somebody. What must I do? Something to stop that visit to Bridport.' In my submission to you, that was the only intent in that poor lad's mind at nine o'clock at the Villa Madeira.

He suggested Stoner was still under the influence of a drug when he went to sleep in the car outside the nursing-home at 2.30 a.m. on the Monday, and then he turned to the various statements he had made, the first being at seven-thirty that morning – obviously untrue:

I ask you not to hold that against him too strongly. It may be that just at that time he was waking up to the terrible danger that hung over his head. By that time he had no means of knowing that the police were suspecting Mrs Rattenbury. There is no evidence that he was ever present when those various statements were made by her. The first that he knows they are going to arrest her is probably when the police-matron is there, and they fetch her out of her bedroom and take her away. Then you get this: Mr Rattenbury is still alive. You have got this boy in this awful position: 'They have arrested Mrs Rattenbury. I know she did not do it. What am I to do?' He is deprived of the solace, the drug. He gets very, very drunk on the Wednesday night, and he tells Miss Riggs, 'I have put her in prison. I am going to see her, and I am going to give myself up.' He did intend to give himself up, but he was arrested as he came back . . .

He recalled Stoner's confession in the police station on the following day, 'I hit him and then came upstairs and told Mrs Rattenbury . . .' It was quite clear he wanted to tell the truth and that he wanted to get her out of difficulty. What he said then agreed perfectly with her evidence, and was an additional reason for believing that her account of what happened was true. He concluded:

I ask you, and I ask you on the facts that I have placed before you, on the evidence that I have been able to call before you, the evidence of two very eminent mental specialists who have come here to assist you to the best of their ability. They have not come here with the idea of deceiving you, they have come here with the result of their great learning, and their great experience on this one topic, hoping to assist you. I suggest that their evidence is of the greatest possible assistance to you, that it shows beyond reasonable doubt that that boy was under a heavy dose of cocaine that afternoon, and was still under its influence when the act was committed.

Therefore I ask you to say – there are three alternatives here – you may find either that this boy deliberately and of malice aforethought was guilty of murder; that is one. Or you may say, as I ask you to say, the evidence before us is sufficient to satisfy us, not only from the nature of the act but from what we have heard elsewhere, that the boy was not in his right mind when he did this act, and did not really understand what he was doing at all.

If you felt that he did not understand what he was doing, then, of course, your verdict would be guilty but insane.

If you feel you are bound to find that he knew something about what he was doing, then I ask you to say I have proved facts sufficient to satisfy you that he did not form the intent of doing grievous bodily harm to Mr Rattenbury, in which case your verdict would be manslaughter. I say to you as reasonable men and women that the verdict which you ought to find is one of these two; either he is guilty but insane, or he was guilty of manslaughter, and of manslaughter only, and not of murder.

At the end of this speech there was a short adjournment.

EXTRAORDINARY HOUSEHOLD. 'DEFINITELY AN ADDICT.' 'INSANE JEALOUSY.' TIRED MOTHER IN THE BOX. FATHER SMILES TO LOZANNE'S BOY LOVER. THE MOTHER'S BOWED HEAD. HER TEARS.

Mr George Stoner, Bournemouth bricklayer, a spare little man with greying hair, passed within a yard of his son, smiled through his tortoise-shell glasses to the boy in the dock, who never looked in his direction, and told the story of the respectable household in which the only child was born a war baby when the father was on service in the Machine Gun Corps.

Next came the mother, while a kindly policeman placed the father where he could watch his wife. The mother, worn and tired, clutched a moist handkerchief.

The mother passed within a yard of the son to join the father. Just two respectable parents passing and repassing in the grim chamber of the Old Bailey while their son did not look at them but gazed steadfastly at the sword of justice suspended over the judge's head. (*Daily Express, 31st May 1935*)

When the court rose and Mrs Rattenbury was being escorted down the stairs from the dock, she became faint and stumbled. The two wardresses caught her before she fell and supported her. (*Daily Mirror, 31st May 1935*)

When the evening papers were on sale, posters were displayed announcing, 'STONER'S COUNSEL SAYS HE COMMITTED THE CRIME.'

CHAPTER TEN

A Woman Taken in Adultery

When the case was resumed, Croom-Johnson replied for the Crown. He invited the jury in his closing speech, as he had in his opening, to find both the accused guilty. 'He put to them,' Casswell commented, 'the, to me, quite incredible suggestion that what had happened was that, in pursuance of a prearranged plan, Stoner had fetched the mallet and given it to Alma who had then herself struck the fatal blows.'

When he began he gave the impression of being quiet, lucid and businesslike, but his long sentences became more and more involved as he went on:

May it please your lordship and members of the jury, those of us who come into the Criminal Courts have very often very unpleasant, extremely disagreeable, but necessary duties to perform. My sole duty on behalf of the prosecution here is to put certain considerations to you with, I hope, complete fairness to each of the accused persons, but I should be lacking in my duty were I not to submit to you, as I shall have occasion to do before I sit down, where, in the submission of the prosecution, the facts proved in this case irresistibly should lead you.

If, as I said when I addressed you last, you have a doubt, a reasonable doubt about either one of these two persons as to whether he or she is guilty or not, it will not only be your duty but, I hope and believe it will be your pleasure to give effect to that doubt by acquittal.

May I say one other thing about the circumstances in which this case is being conducted? You have had to listen, unfortunately, for some days now to a story which to most of you I hope is unusual, but it is a story of immorality and vice. The only use which anybody would care to make of those facts is this: that in view of that state of affairs existing, does it throw any light one way or another on the facts and circumstances which you are engaged in investigating. From the point of view of your verdict, the fact that the two persons are persons who have been guilty of immorality in circumstances which you may deplore, has nothing to do with the case, but from the point of view of enabling you to judge of the truth of the evidence of Mrs Rattenbury, those facts may be all important.

It has rather been suggested to you that this is a case in which two persons, this woman whom probably you may think is a woman of experience, and this inexperienced boy, had arrived at a time when they were obtaining out of their illicit intercourse sufficient satisfaction to leave them no motive for getting rid of the husband in the case. It is a little difficult, you may think, to square that with the fact that only less than a week before that fatal Sunday, these two people for some reason or other had gone away together on an excursion to London where they were going to stay at the same hotel, and you may possibly think that suggests that the opportunities which were available to them at the Villa Madeira were not sufficient for their purpose.

On the other hand you have been told that they went away after the husband had been deceived, after he had been told by the prisoner Rattenbury a lie – a particularly mean lie, you may think. That also may suggest that they were anxious to get away from the Villa Madeira where the husband was living.

In addition you have been told that there was trouble about money, and that there had been quarrels about money, and if motive is to assist you at all in this case you may think that there is ample evidence available with regard to motive.

This unpleasant insinuation that Alma had a financial motive to murder Rattenbury was entirely without justification. She must have known the terms of his will, for his and hers were made at the same time, before they left British Columbia. He left his money to the children : Alma was to get only her allowance, and his car if he happened to own one at the time of his death.

On the subject of motive, I may perhaps say this to you, to approach it, as I am sure you will desire to do, with great caution. Motive in a case of this sort by itself proves nothing. The fact that somebody stands to gain or lose in one way or another by the death of an individual is not the remotest evidence of a desire to murder that individual; but when you come to sum up the evidence, when you come to look and see what the facts properly amount to, you may then think that motive may assist you in judging of those facts.

He proceeded to flatter the jury, their knowledge of human motives, their common sense point of view of ordinary responsible citizens – and could they have any doubt in their minds that Stoner, throughout that unhappy story, was dominated by Mrs Rattenbury? He suggested that that was the key to the solution of the problem which they were engaged in solving :

You are the judges – having seen her demeanour in the witness-box, having heard what she has had to say – as to whether what she has told you is the truth or is not the truth; but I must point out to you that she is a woman who, upon her own statement and, indeed, upon her own conduct, has for some years been engaged in lying to her husband about money matters and with regard to her daily life . . .

She has told you that her memory is a complete blank with regard to everything but the most trifling details in the events of that dreadful night after the time when she put a towel round Mr Rattenbury's head.

He reminded the jury that it was only very much later, at 3.30 in the morning, that she was given morphia, and in the meantime she had said and done a great many things. He recalled Dr Gillespie's evidence that people who are given morphia do sometimes lose their memory, but not of events which precede the dose. He asked, what was Mrs Rattenbury's condition when she made her incriminating statements to Constable Bagwell, who arrived on the scene at two o'clock in the morning?

She had had a glass of neat whisky; she had thrown it up, had been sick, and therefore that glass of neat whisky, you may think, could not have affected her mind at all, could not have affected any question of memory, or any question as to her being completely mistress of herself. She tells you – and you must judge whether it is likely that a woman who had been sick once after taking a dose of whisky could succeed within the next hour in taking other doses of whisky which she could keep down. You will judge of that from your own experience. I suggest to you that, although later on she was undoubtedly seen drinking whisky and soda, there is no real justification for saying that she was in such a condition before morphia was administered that she ought not to remember what took place.

He recapitulated her statements – 'I did it with a mallet . . .' 'He has lived too long . . .' 'He said "Dear, dear." ' This, Croom-Johnson suggested, sounded like the words of the victim when the blows were struck. 'Have you told the Coroner . . . ?' – nothing improbable, they might think, about making that enquiry. Then, 'I made a muddle of it.' they should remember that Mr Rattenbury was not killed outright; and finally, 'I thought I was strong enough . . .'

> Mr Croom-Johnson paused. He is a small man, very persuasive, very tenacious. As he pleads his case, his searching black eyes never for a moment leave the eyes of the jury. 'I thought I was strong enough,' he quoted from the woman's statement. 'Strong enough for what?' he asked.
>
> Mr Croom-Johnson urged the jury to reject the woman's defence that her mind was a blank on all these statements. (*Daily Express, 31st May 1935*)

He pointed out that she made these statements before she was given morphia. Later, when she was saying, 'I know who did it, his son,' and things of that sort, the doctor decided she was not fit to make a statement and gave her an injection :

> Are you satisfied that she made the statements which they say she made, and to which the only answer made by her is not 'I did not make them,' but 'I have no recollection at all of any of the events of that period'? Dr O'Donnell, it is true, says that up till six o'clock the next morning, and even at 8.15 the next morning, he himself would not give credence to statements made by her at those times. If you think, from what you know of the facts, there is anything which should induce you to disregard those statements, then, in pursuance of your duty, you will do so, but recollect, Dr O'Donnell did not see her at six o'clock or at 8.15. He had gone . . .

This was an inaccurate statement by Croom-Johnson. Dr O'Donnell had seen her even later than 8.15 – four hours later – and had found her to be still under the effects of the drug.

He then reminded the jury they had been told that walking about, coffee, and a bath, would assist in sweeping away for some short time the effects of the drug. This again was inaccurate: Dr O'Donnell, in answer to Croom-Johnson's own questions, had expressly stated that these measures would not assist in making the effect of the drug disappear, but would keep the patient wakeful. The prosecuting counsel was trying to make out a case against the accused in accordance with a theory of his own:

She tells you that she cannot recollect, and the suggestion was that she was ill and unable to do anything. She had a bath, she came downstairs and she had coffee; and if you believe the evidence of the police officers – and there is no suggestion, so far as I have listened to the case, that you should not – when that book that the detective-inspector produced, a man of responsibility, a man of position in the force in which he serves, was read out to her by him, she not only asked to see the book but read it out herself, and there is her signature to the statement in it . . .

Here Croom-Johnson omitted one very important consideration – that the detective-inspector knew nothing of the effects of morphia, and did not profess to, and that the doctors did not agree with his assessment of Alma's condition.

Continuing, he said it was his duty on behalf of the prosecution to suggest to them that what she said during that night was the truth, the result of remorse after committing the crime, and that when she put her signature to that statement she was signing that which was true:

Cne other piece of evidence which it is my duty to submit to you is of the greatest importance in the case: it is that at the moment when she is going off to the police station, with Stoner and Riggs in the hall, she speaks to them: 'Don't make fools of yourselves,' and Stoner says to her, 'You have got yourself into this mess by too much talking.' Does it suggest to your minds that Stoner and she had had a common object that night; that Stoner was the person who had gone away to fetch the mallet, and that she, thinking she was strong enough, had aimed the blow or blows at her husband's head but made a muddle of it? . . . that Stoner was a person who was likely, to say the least of it, to be acting under her domination. These are the essential facts of the case so far as Mrs Rattenbury is concerned.

The case against Stoner he considered simplicity itself: according to

Mrs Rattenbury he plainly understood what he had done, had done it deliberately, and had done it with the object of preventing the journey to Bridport :

> Yet for some reason or other he remains quiet and sees her go to jail, and it is not until some little time afterwards, when he makes first of all his statement to Irene Riggs, and later on when he makes his statement to the police officer, that you get any statement incriminating him :

He reminded the jury that it was only after Stoner's arrest that he had made the full statement which his learned friend, Mr Casswell, had suggested to them was a true statement, but he coupled this suggestion with the theory that the circumstances were so extraordinary that Stoner could not have realised what he was doing, and that the proper verdict would be guilty but insane :

> The evidence to which you have listened as to what this boy really did and said, whether you get it from Mrs Rattenbury, if you accept that story, or what he said to the police officer when he made his statement, or what he said to Mrs Rattenbury at the door . . . If you contrast all these facts with the theories of the learned medical gentlemen who have come here, I am bound to submit to you they indicate a person who was quite understanding the position, and a person in the possession of all his ordinary faculties . . .
>
> It is suggested to you that you ought to give effect to this theory so far as the boy is concerned, because you could not expect that an ordinary English boy of eighteen would do these things if he was in possession of his senses. Unfortunately you may think in this case that what looked at one time to be not merely an ordinary English boy of eighteen, but an English boy of irreproachable character and manifestly, having seen his parents, of good upbringing, that this boy has done a great many things which possibly all of you would not expect a boy of those antecedents to do. It is no good trying to suggest otherwise to you . . . Cases that get into these Courts are not the ordinary cases of ordinary decent English life; we are dealing with exceptional circumstances and exceptional cases. It is no good inviting people to come to a conclusion, 'Guilty but insane,' because they may not expect things of this sort to happen.
>
> His lordship will direct you as to the effect of a statement made by Stoner's own counsel that he accepted the position that Stoner

is guilty. I mean as to what that position is so far as it affects the case for the prosecution against Mrs Rattenbury....

THE JUDGE: I think I ought to say at once that I shall tell the jury that they ought to put out of their minds entirely that statement, not only as against Mrs Rattenbury but also against Stoner. They have to decide the case upon evidence and not upon any *quasi*-admissions which counsel may think it desirable to make from his point of view. Stoner is the only man who can say, 'I am guilty.' His counsel cannot say that.

CROOM-JOHNSON: If your lordship pleases. I anticipated that that would be the direction your lordship would give.

He went on with his speech:

Now, members of the jury, if you are satisfied that this boy did not understand the nature and the quality of his offence, you have to be satisfied by the evidence called on his behalf, and the onus of proof in this matter, and this matter only, is on the defendant who advances the story. You have to be satisfied first of all that there is something akin to disease of the mind.

Remember where his story starts with the cocaine. It starts with the statement that he found cocaine in his father's house . . . His father has told you that he has never had any cocaine in the house. The boy has made a statement that on the day of the assault at about four o'clock in the afternoon he took two heaped-up teaspoon-fuls of cocaine. Assuming that is right, what sort of cocaine was it? It is said that the substance he took was a brownish substance with dark specks in it. The evidence is that that is a sort of cocaine the gentlemen who told us about these things had never heard of. Two heaped-up teaspoonfuls would be a very considerable quantity, you may think, of this drug, and yet, at eight o'clock that night, this young man who, according to this theory, had been acting under an impulse, got into his master's car, drove some three or four miles, borrowed a mallet, and having come back with the mallet, and presumably therefore having arrived back at the Villa Madeira some time after half-past eight, waited two hours before he struck the blows which eventually ended fatally, somewhere about half-past ten, some time just before he got into bed with Mrs Rattenbury . . .

CASSWELL: What story is that?

THE JUDGE: He is talking of the story told by Mrs Rattenbury.

O'CONNOR: That is not the story told by Mrs Rattenbury.

CASSWELL : My lord, there is no evidence of Mrs Rattenbury's that the blow was struck later than nine o'clock, and the evidence of the prosecution is that when Miss Riggs went down there the blood was clotted as if it had been there some time. I hope my friend, if he is going to suggest to the jury that this took place at half-past ten . . .

CROOM-JOHNSON : I am not . . .

CASSWELL : . . . will at any rate put his finger upon the evidence upon which he bases that statement.

CROOM-JOHNSON : . . .

THE JUDGE : Go on, please, Mr Croom-Johnson.

CROOM-JOHNSON : Members of the jury, I am sure you understood me. I was putting the case to you on the assumption that you are to accept the story which has been advanced to you upon those points on behalf of the defendant Stoner. I am sure you quite understood I was not accepting any part of that story except those parts of it which we know of with regard to the mallet. The suggestion plainly, I submit to upon that evidence, was that the hurt had been done certainly later than half-past nine, because at half-past nine Mrs Rattenbury, according to her story, had gone to bed leaving Stoner somewhere about – I think she said she could not tell us where – and very soon afterwards, certainly not half-past ten, this man was in her bed, in her bedroom, telling her that he had done the injuries.

Having thus lamely excused his mistake of an hour in the time of the attack on Mr Rattenbury, and then covered it up, he continued :

All those things, in my submission to you, do suggest deliberation, if that story is true, and do not suggest an impulse brought on by a man being reduced into some sort of condition of excitement or overweening jealousy or the like, as the result of the evils which he suffers from being a cocaine addict.

The story which I submitted to you in opening the case, which it is my painful duty to submit to you as the truth, is that the mallet having been borrowed between eight and eight thirty, the blow was struck somewhere about nine o'clock, the time which gets into two of the lady's statements, although they are not statements, I agree, in which she said she did any particular act at that time . . .

The object of my observation when I was interrupted by my two learned friends, was to point out to you that if you accept the suggestions that are made on behalf of Stoner, they do appear to involve premeditation by him, carried out with premeditation over a fairly long time, some hours at the very least, and I suggest to you that you should reject those suggestions, just as I suggest to you that it is your duty in pursuance of the oaths you have taken, to reject the conclusion at which you are invited to arrive based on these hypotheses. I think I have said all that is necessary that I should say in the case.

I should like to wind up as I started: If you come to the conclusion that these facts are consistent and only consistent with the view that is put before you on behalf of the prosecution, that this was a crime committed by these two people helping one another with one common object, if you have no reasonable doubt, such a doubt as would induce you to act or refrain from acting in your ordinary every-day affairs, then it will be your duty in vindication of public justice to say so by your verdict. If, in pursuance of your oaths, you can still bring yourselves to the view that you are not satisfied, that the case has not been made out to our satisfaction, then it would be your duty, and possibly the pleasure of us all, for you to say that not being satisfied, your verdict is a verdict for the defendants.

At last it was the turn of Alma's counsel to speak in her defence. It must have been a relief to feel that she had a champion after having to endure Casswell's description of her as 'unbalanced, hysterical, and apt to fly into fits of excitement', the frequent references to her most intimate moments as 'adulterous intercourse', and the prosecutor's contemptuous attitude and sceptical treatment of her story 'of immorality and vice' which 'unfortunately' the supposedly pure-minded jury had to listen to in the painful discharge of their duties.

O'Connor's speech, however, was even more painful for her to endure. He seems to have assumed that the jury were morbidly obsessed with sex, and that he had to associate himself with their views in order to lead them round to the idea that Alma was not on trial for having had sexual relations, but for murder. This led him to say more unsavoury things about her than either of his learned colleagues at their most offensive. Possibly he thought the jury would be prejudiced against her because she had broken two rules of contemporary English morality, by having sexual relations with a servant, and by having sexual relations with a man a great deal younger than herself; though no stigma was attached to a man for having sexual relations with a woman a great deal younger than himself : but it would not be fair to blame the jury for the censorious attitude of the lawyers.

If it please your lordship, members of the jury, nobody would listen to the concluding remarks of my learned friend, or indeed to the tenor of the whole of his remarks, and noticed his conduct of the case, can doubt that he has maintained the tradition of British justice in the fairness with which he has presented the case against these two accused. . . . We are all assisting in our different capacities in the discharge of one of the highest functions of citizenship – the doing of justice.

By English law we do not allow, in criminal cases, evidence to be given of previous convictions of an accused person. Presumption of innocence is at the root of the whole of our legal system . . . A jury comes to its task on the assumption that there is nothing upon which the person's record can be questioned. But cases arise in which, through no fault of the prosecution, a person comes before you with a record and with a history which inspire you with revulsion. It is in those cases, perhaps, that the task of the jury is the most difficult of all. They have to separate in their minds the natural revulsion which they feel against behaviour which nobody would seek to condone or commend, to disassociate in their minds evidence of evil character and evil behaviour, of ill or damage done to other people – to divide all these prejudicial elements and features of the case from the crime of which that person is being arraigned. I want you, in your approach to this case, in your consideration of it after I have sat down, and after my lord has summed up to you, to begin, each and all of you, by making quite certain that you have purged your minds of any feeling that this woman should suffer because of the woman she has been. I am not here to cast one stone against that wretched boy whose position there in the dock may be due to folly and self-indulgence on her part, to which he fell a victim.

He said the jury must not imagine that the two defences had been arranged in consort, or were connected in any way: each defence was in its water-tight compartment.

He explained that they were not entitled to convict Alma even if they did not believe everything she said, or felt she was holding something back, perhaps to help the boy: if what she said had created in their minds a reasonable doubt that she was guilty, she was entitled to an acquittal.

This seemed to indicate that he knew of something which Alma had not divulged, but without giving any hint of what it might be, he continued:

With these general considerations in mind, let us now approach the case which is sought to be made out by the Crown . . . Mr Croom-Johnson has spoken to you of motive, and has suggested that Mr Rattenbury was in the way. Is there any foundation whatsoever for this suggestion? All the evidence is to the contrary. Mr and Mrs Rattenbury were leading the comfortable ordinary life, not very exciting perhaps, which you would expect from the disparity of ages. Is it suggested that this designing, self-indulgent woman – as the Crown wish to make her out to be – would exchange her comfortable middle-class surroundings with her car and villa and reasonably ample means, for life with Stoner on a pound a week? I venture to suggest that the case of motive is so impalpable and flimsy that you will desire to discard it out of hand.

Turning to the events of the fatal night, he described how Irene Riggs – whom the Crown put forward as their witness of the truth – came down to the drawing-room and found Mrs Rattenbury slipperless and prostrated with grief. Irene had last seen her when she had come into her room and talked cheerfully about the arrangements for the proposed trip to Bridport. At that time she was cool and collected :

If the case for the Crown is to be accepted, while she was talking to Riggs about the morrow's arrangements in this way, she knew that Rattenbury was bleeding to death in the room below. You have seen Mrs Rattenbury in the box. Can you credit her with such diabolical finesse, with such exact and careful preparations for her defence? We know that she did in fact, earlier in the evening, ring up Jenks and make arrangements for the visit on the following day. We know that she had put out Rattenbury's clothes, as it was her custom to do when they were going away. The suggestion of the Crown, of course, is that this was part of a premeditated scheme. Can you believe that possible? . . . If you believe Riggs, as the Crown asks you to do, when she says that when she came down to the drawing-room a few minutes after the bedroom conversation, Mrs Rattenbury was in the extremities of grief, and, as she described her, 'a changed woman'.

. . . Do you think that she could have possessed the cunning to remember to come downstairs slipperless so as to give the impression of haste? You remember how Riggs spoke of her solicitude for Rattenbury? About her impatience when the telephone messages to the doctor did not seem to go through fast enough? Must you come to the conclusion that this was all exquisite play acting? Is that hypothesis easier to accept than the simple story told by Mrs Rattenbury in the box? That hearing a cry she rushed downstairs and found her husband with blood streaming from his head. Again, the truth often emerges irresistibly through little details. Do you remember how she told you in the witness-box that 'I found his teeth on the floor and put them in so that he could speak.' Can you imagine a mind so cunning, so deceitful, so careful in the preparation of a defence as to invent an incident like that? Members of the jury, I suggest to you that upon the objective evidence produced by the Crown, no jury in the world could convict this woman.

But the Crown in this case is furnished with material which they think far deadlier than the objective evidence. They have the statements of Mrs Rattenbury herself and they invite you to say that upon these statements you are entitled to convict her.

He then took each of Alma's statements in turn, and showed that they became progressively more absurd as her drink-sodden condition blurred the outlines of her reason and left, outstanding and distinct, only the growing instinct to save her lover at all costs. He said that if the Crown was right in suggesting that Mrs Rattenbury had carefully prepared a defence, putting out her husband's clothes ready for the trip to Bridport, the conversation with Riggs, etc., how came it that none of it appeared in any of her statements? The first two were made when her mind was comparatively clear at 2 a.m., and they were entirely consistent with the story she told in the witness-box:

But it is when we come to the third and later statements that the Crown asks you to believe that these are confessions of guilt. She says to Bagwell at half-past two in the morning: 'I know who did it. I did it with a mallet. It is hidden. Ratz has lived too long. No, my lover did it. It's urine on the chair. I will give you ten pounds. No, I won't bribe you.' A rambling incoherent statement which cancels out. It is suggested that this is a confession. But if it is a confession, why does it not confess the truth? Why does she not say to the police, 'I will show you where the mallet is'? You will find, as the statements progress throughout the night, there is one strange lacuna: on no occasion does she tell the police where the mallet is hidden. Can you imagine any reason for this omission other than the fact that she didn't know? and as the night wore on, and her determination at all costs to take the blame and shield her lover takes shape in her fuddled brain, you can see that she is beginning to grasp the fact that she cannot successfully take the blame unless she can account for the whereabouts of the mallet. When she is being taken away to the police station, she hisses into Riggs' ear: 'You must find out where the mallet is.'

Members of the jury, I suggest that that final remark offers you the clearest and most cogent evidence that this woman was inventing a confession which she saw would be incomplete, and which she knew would never be convincing unless she could indicate where the weapon was hidden with which the act had been done.

Mr O'Connor described the suggestion that the crime was prearranged as a 'fantastic and absurd hypothesis'.

'Then there is progressive deterioration and absurdity in the statements made by her as the night wears on. There is progressive disorder of mind indicated by them; there are progressive frantic efforts to grasp the one link which will clinch her own guilt and clear her lover. That is the whereabouts of the mallet.

'There is the statement showing the developing cunning of the drunken woman she has now become, anxious to shield this boy. "I did it with a mallet," she said, as though a mallet were one of the everyday pieces of furniture you might pick up in a dining-room or a drawing-room!'

'It is said that these statements are this woman's confessions. Confessions! They are fragments snatched from the disordered mind of a woman sodden with drink and hysteria.'

Mr O'Connor referred to the statement beginning, 'About 9 p.m. on 24th March . . .' and asked: 'Do you think a woman in her state would begin a statement in that way? Would she not say, "Last night about nine. . . ."?'

. . . Mr O'Connor once more referred to the statement made by Mrs Rattenbury, and commented:

'I ask you to consider not only whether you would deprive a fellow citizen of life on that document but whether, indeed, you would feel justified in killing a cat.'

'I don't wish to say anything which will make the position of this wretched boy worse, but I ask you to contrast these vapourings in this woman's statement, these imaginative remarks, with what I suggest to you is true and clear, and bears the imprint of truth in every line of it – the statement of Stoner himself made after a few days, during which remorse had been tugging at his heartstrings, that he had let his mistress go to prison for a crime for which he was responsible.'

Mr O'Connor had been examining the statement made by Stoner, preparatory to reading it to the jury once more, when his junior counsel drew his attention to the notebook of a police officer. They had a whispered conversation lasting several minutes, and Mr Justice Humphrey broke the silence by saying :

'There is something which I noticed in that book, which may or may not have been noticed by the counsel. It was entirely new to me and caused me some surprise. I thought counsel on both sides ought to see it before I handed it down. I was looking at something quite different. Of course, that would not be admissible in evidence as a statement, but if you want to enquire into it, by all means finish your speech tonight and come back to it tomorrow morning. You might like to try to find out what the explanation is, and then get a witness in the box to-morrow morning.'

Mr O'Connor : I am very grateful to your lordship. I have not seen the exhibit.

Mr Justice Humphreys : I don't suppose anyone has noticed it before.

No further reference was made to this discovery, and the judge did not further enlighten the court. (*Daily Mail, 31st May 1935*)

O'Connor, resuming his speech, reminded the jury that Dr O'Donnell had told the police at 3.30 in the morning that Mrs Rattenbury was not fit to make a statement and that the Governor of Holloway Prison had reported that for some days after her reception there she was still suffering from the effects of the drug. And he maintained that neither upon the objective evidence, nor upon the statements of Mrs Rattenbury herself, had the Crown made out a case which could be acceptable to twelve reasonable men and women.

> The Crown say this was a premeditated crime. If this woman had the foresight and cunning to make the preparations of which you have heard on the fatal evening, is it conceivable that she should have been so clumsy as to bring home for the week-end her child who might have remained at school? Can you conceive that she would have ordered from Harrods for her lover, to be delivered on the Monday after the crime, those fatally incriminating tokens of her affection for Stoner? . . . it appears to me that throughout this case the Crown have been asking you to accept the most difficult hypothesis instead of the simple one.

All this added up to the conclusion that it was Stoner who was guilty, and Stoner only. He could no longer avoid saying so :

> Is it so hard to see where the truth lies here? Perhaps the most

horrible part of my task is, in the performance of my duty to Mrs Rattenbury, to have to call your attention to the facts which clearly indicate that Stoner conceived and executed this crime. But that duty must be discharged. Let us consider for a moment the facts which incriminate him.

Stoner, as you know, is still but a lad. His upbringing was simple, he had but few friends and no girl friends. He is flung, at the age of eighteen, into the vortex of illicit love. The evidence shows him to have been an unbalanced melodramatic boy, given to violent outbursts. The witnesses for the Crown have proved that on previous occasions he had assaulted Mrs Rattenbury. They have also proved that he used to go about with a toy dagger and with a toy revolver. An unbalanced, hysterical, melodramatic youth. Consider his first associations with passionate womanhood. The natural reactions of a jealous youth, possibly, I do not know, accentuated by drug taking. He is taken away from his work as a chauffeur, stays sumptuously in a west-end hotel for a week with his mistress, dressed in silk pyjamas from a west-end store, and then brought back to earth and to his drudging duties, and submitting to the orders of his mistress's husband.

If you were judging of moral responsibility in this case, your task might be a light one, for you cannot resist nausea and disgust at the way in which this middle-aged woman has ensnared and degraded this hapless youth. But that is not your task today.

Miss Tennyson Jesse thought O'Connor had a very clear notion of the mentality of his client, and that he was able to give full play to his sympathetic interpretation of that mentality because, unlike Casswell, he was not handicapped in his defence. She thought it was an effective speech, particularly when he went on :

I will say no more about what is past in Mrs Rattenbury's life. I would only say that if you may be tempted to feel that she has sinned, that her sin has been great and has involved others who would never otherwise have been involved, that you should ask yourselves whether you, or anybody of you, are prepared first to cast a stone.

She described the hush that descended upon the Court when he pleaded the deathless words of one of the greatest speeches for the defence ever uttered. He went on to add a sort of apology for Alma :

Perhaps also you may think that during that fatal night there were indications of belated nobility on Mrs Rattenbury's part in the way in which she sought to shield her lover, and in the indications of her anxiety at all hazards to take the blame. Too late, like Frankenstein, she had discovered that she had created a monster which she could not control. You may think of Mrs Rattenbury as a woman, self-indulgent and wilful, who by her own acts and folly had erected in this poor young man a Frankenstein of jealousy which she could not control.

I beg you, as I began, to discount your horror at her moral failure, and to remember that the worst misery which you could inflict upon this wretched youth would be to convict her of something for which he knows she is not responsible. You may, as moral men and women, as citizens, condemn her in your souls for the part she has played in raising this position. She will bear to her grave the brand of reprobation, and men and women will know how she has acted. That will be her sorrow and her disgrace so long as she lives. That is not your responsibility, that is hers. Mercifully, perhaps, you may say to yourselves: 'She has been punished enough. Wherever she walks she will be a figure of shame.'

That is not to say she is to be branded as a murderess, that her children are to go down as the children of a murderess; that justice is to be prostituted because you have been misled because of your hatred of the life she has been leading, because of thinking she has done something she has not done.

Weigh carefully all the evidence, bearing in mind all the considerations I have put before you, remembering that the Crown must prove its case unerringly to your satisfaction, and remembering that if you allow prejudice or moral turpitude to cloud your judgement and to blur the true issue, you will not be faithful to your oaths, but you will be debauching the law and degrading our conception of justice.

When O'Connor sat down, the judge referred to the notebook that had been previously mentioned. It belonged to Detective-Inspector Carter. It transpired that the judge had discovered in it an undisclosed statement made by Alma at 6.10 a.m. on the 25th March. He recalled Carter to the witness-box, and questioned him about it:

CARTER: This statement I have written in that book was made while Mrs Rattenbury was lying down, directly she woke up. I did not refer to it in evidence because, in my opinion she was not then in a normal condition, and I had not cautioned her.

THE JUDGE: Then, in your opinion, she was not in a condition to make a statement at 6.15? –At 6.10, no.

The significance of this find was that the two statements, the one made at 6.10 a.m. and the one she made at 8.15 a.m. after her bath, coffee, and walking about, were almost the same; from which it might be assumed that she was no more in a condition to make a statement at 8.15 than she had been at 6.15. This strengthened Alma's case, and weakened that of the detectives.

The court adjourned.

'MRS RATTENBURY AIMED THE BLOW' – CROWN COUNSEL. K.C. SAYS WOMAN WAS SHIELDING LOVER. REMORSE AT HIS HEARTSTRINGS. 'JEALOUSY CREATED BY A WOMAN'S FOLLY.' SODDEN WITH DRINK. VORTEX OF ILLICIT LOVE. STONER AS FRANKENSTEIN. WIFE'S ALLEGED STATEMENT. FRAGMENTS FROM A DISORDERED MIND.

CHAPTER ELEVEN

Casting the First Stone

On the last day of the trial, Friday 31st May, Stoner still sat unmoved in his corner of the dock, his eyes downcast. 'Mrs Rattenbury also,' Miss Tennyson Jesse said, 'was perfectly calm, but it was a frozen, and not an apathetic calm. Her physical aspect changed, without any movement on her part, in a curious manner. By Friday she looked twenty years older than she had on Monday. On the last day even her hands changed colour, and were a livid greenish white.' She was wearing the same short fur coat she had worn throughout the trial.

Sir Travers Humphreys was a supremely self-confident judge. He believed a British jury is always right in its decisions – 'when properly directed' – and his directions to the jury were always clear and precise. He believed himself to be perfectly fair, balanced, reasonable and humane – and to a great extent he was, but he was also imbued with some of the prejudices of the age in which his character had been formed, and with some of his own. He explained in his autobiography that as a result of twenty-five years in the Courts, (mostly for the prosecution), his experience of women had hardened into a principle: that in a case in which the question of sex might possibly account for a woman's evidence, it should not be accepted 'unless there is other evidence tending in the same direction.' He thought this rule should never be relaxed, 'even if in the witness-box she behaves like an angel and looks like a Madonna.'[1] It was obvious that Alma's magnetic influence on the opposite sex, (if any of it remained after her gruelling experiences of the past four days), was not going to help her with this stern, upright, methodical and unimaginative judge. He believed that punishment was necessary to prevent crime, and that in order to uphold the sanctity of life, capital punishment should be inflicted upon those who had taken it upon themselves to terminate the existence of a fellow human being.

He had evidently been displeased by Casswell's remarks to the jury on the significance of the recent successful appeal to the House of Lords in the case of *Rex v. Woolmington*, for the first important point he made in his summing up was that he considered matters of law were no concern of the jury – thus adding his contribution to the centuries-old controversy between the unrestricted authority of the law and the unrestricted right of the jury to come to their own decision. The right of the jury to decide on matters of law as well as on matters of fact had been maintained by successive juries in the face of threats and persecution until at last, in 1670, Lord Justice Vaughan, supporting Edward Bushel in his suit for false arrest against the Lord Mayor and the Recorder of the City of London, ruled that juries could not be punished for their decisions – thus leaving them free, in theory, to decide on matters of law as well as on matters of fact, for they could not be required to give reasons for their verdicts. This ruling was still accepted as good law and as in accordance with the public conscience. It was also considered to be one of the bulwarks of civil liberty against the possible despotic manipulation of the law.

This is what the judge, Sir Travers Humphreys, said :

Please remember this: all questions of facts are for you. The proper inference to be drawn from the facts is for you, and for you only; and while you will accept without question my direction to you upon the law, because that is my province, you will arrive at the facts upon your own interpretation of the facts. . .

Having repeated five or six times in a few sentences that they were judges of the facts, and that they were to accept without question his direction on matters of law, he proceeded to remind them of what Mr Croom-Johnson had said in his opening speech :

'We believe we shall be able to prove to you that Mr Rattenbury was murdered by somebody. We believe we shall be able to establish as against each of these persons jointly that they had the opportunity for committing that murder, that they had the motive for committing that murder and their conduct was such as to make it, as indeed the prosecution suggest, clear that the murder was the result of a joint agreement between them.' He said to you, each of these persons has made statements, each of them has made at one time or the other, statements that they were completely innocent. . . at other times a statement to the effect that he or she, as the case may be, alone was responsible for the injury and death of Mr Rattenbury.

Mr Croom-Johnson said to you, 'Under these circumstances, if
we prove that, we shall ask you to say that this is a case in which it
is established that the death, the murder of Mr Rattenbury, was the
result of the joint agreement of the two persons who are now being
tried together.' As a proposition of law that is undoubtedly correct,
for the law is this: if two persons agree together that a felony . . .
such as grievous bodily harm shall be committed upon somebody . . .
by one of them, and death is caused . . . then each of those persons
is equally guilty of murder. That is the law, and it matters not by
the hand of which of them the fatal blow was delivered, and it
matters not whether both of them were even present at the time
when the fatal blow was delivered.

He explained that a person who commits a crime is called a principal
in the first degree, a person who has agreed that a crime is to be
committed and is present when it is committed is called a principal in
the second degree, and a person who has inspired, conspired, counselled
or suggested a crime but is absent when it is committed is called an
accessory before the fact. They may all be tried together or separately.
In this case these two persons were charged singly, and jointly, with the
crime of murder:

Now, that is the law . . . as it relates to the case as it was opened.
You have since that day had before you a good deal of evidence,
indeed, some evidence, and not unimportant evidence, has been
given in this case which it is quite clear the prosecution were quite
unaware of, for at one period of this case it seemed that the two
accused were instructing their respective counsel by no means to help
each other, but to bring out facts which would be, which perhaps
were, damaging to the case of the other accused.

The judge was not the only one who had the impression that the
counsel for the defence were damaging each other's cause: Mrs
Kingham, accommodated now with a seat in the court-room, just to
the right of the entrance, had listened to them with increasing anxiety.
She had the feeling that they disliked each other, and it was fairly
obvious to her they had come to the conclusion that either Alma or
Stoner had committed the murder, not both of them; therefore the
best way for each to clear his own client was to blame the other. For
reasons of her own, she thought that if they had worked together and

made an appeal for the sympathy of the jury on behalf of the ill-starred lovers, both might have been saved.[2]

Miss Tennyson Jesse's opinion was that there was no case against Alma. She thought :

The woman who at first seemed so guilty, was seen to be undoubtedly innocent. This was not merely because there proved to be no evidence beyond her own drunken utterances, but because of her own attitude in the witness-box – it is deadly to the guilty, and it may save the innocent. In most criminal trials the pattern is set at the beginning and merely strengthens as the trial progresses. In the Rattenbury case the evidence which seemed so damning on the first day – completely altered in character; what had seemed to be undoubted fact proved to be an airy nothing and the whole complex pattern shifted and changed much as the pattern of sand changes when it is shaken, and, like sand, it slipped away between the fingers, leaving a residue of grains of truth very different from the pile that the prosecution had originally built up.[3]

That apparently was not the judge's opinion. He said :

You will remember facts were elicited from witnesses on behalf of Mrs Rattenbury as against Stoner, and *vice versa*, and it appeared, and apparently was so, that the prosecution were quite unaware of that evidence. We know that Miss Riggs had made a statement to Mrs Rattenbury's solicitor who is instructing Mr O'Connor, and apparently told that solicitor things which she had not thought necessary or proper to tell the police, and you may think that as the result of that evidence as a whole, the case that is made against these persons now – I do not mean by counsel, but as the evidence rather shapes itself – is rather a case in which the evidence points, whether it proves is quite another matter, to Stoner as being the person whose hand caused the injuries to Mr Rattenbury and that Mrs Rattenbury was a party to, but not an actual assailant of Mr Rattenbury – party to the crime but not an actual assailant. . . .

In order to understand this remark – because the evidence most certainly did not point to Alma being a party to the crime – it has to be borne in mind that there was a prejudice at the time, shared by the judge, that when a woman has a younger lover she dominates him. Miss Tennyson Jesse drew attention to this attitude and maintained, 'the actual truth is that there is no woman so under the dominion of her lover as the elderly mistress of a very much younger man.' The judge continued :

> . . . If that is so, let me tell you in a word exactly how the law stands . . . If it is proved to your satisfaction that Stoner attacked Mr Rattenbury, attacked him as he sat in his chair asleep or awake, without any sort or kind of justification – not in self-defence, or anything of that sort – but made an attack upon Mr Rattenbury, and delivered those three blows upon his head, which the doctors spoke of . . . if you come to the conclusion that that is proved, then, unless something else appears in the case, Stoner is guilty of murder and no other crime. If you come to the conclusion that it is proved that Mrs Rattenbury was present aiding and abetting Stoner in the commission of that crime, or that although she was absent, or may have been absent, at the time, yet she had counselled and procured, that is to say advised, agreed with, suggested to Stoner that he should commit that crime, then, as an accessory before the fact, she is equally guilty of that murder.
>
> Now, I have used the word 'proved' several times, and what is meant by that is this : you know, as you know many things which I am saying to you, and many things which counsel has said to you, you knew before you ever came into the jury-box; but you will understand, I know, that we all have certain duties to perform, and we have to perform them, even though at times it may seem to be a little unnecessary. It is my duty to tell you, and I do tell you, that in this as in every other criminal case proof must be given by the Crown of every material fact which is necessary to prove the crime which they have alleged. It is never for the accused person to establish his innocence : it is necessary for the Crown to prove his guilt, or the jury are obliged to say, 'The guilt is not proved, and therefore we say not guilty.'
>
> Not guilty in this country does not mean in the least that the person has established his innocence, not in the least. Sometimes, of course, it amounts to that. In the case, you may say of a person whose defence is, 'I never was near the place at all, and I call witnesses to show that I was a hundred miles away,' it may be said he has established his innocence. That is not the way we look at it. A verdict of not guilty means no more than that the prosecution have failed to establish the guilt of that person. . .

Next he talked of the words 'reasonable doubt' in the context 'the prosecutor must prove beyond reasonable doubt,' and commented that he thought the expression added nothing to the law as he had stated it. If they were not quite sure, then the case had not been proved. The accent on the word reasonable did not mean they could avoid what must always be a very unpleasant thing for a citizen to have to do – joining in a verdict of guilty on a capital charge. It did not mean they were entitled to conjure up fanciful doubts or say, 'After all, nobody saw this thing done, therefore we cannot say it was done,' or anything of that sort. If the evidence had shown them where the truth lay, they should act upon it :

That applies, of course, to the case of either of the accused. Although they have been indicted jointly and have been tried together – and I may say that the five days' experience which I have had of this case has satisfied me that I was right in ruling that they should be tried together as they were jointly indicted. Although they are being tried together, your verdicts must be separate in regard to each of them, because in law it may be that on such an indictment as this, one is proved guilty and the other is proved not guilty, or they may both be proved guilty, or neither may be proved guilty, but you must deliver a separate verdict in regard to each of them; and that verdict must be based solely on the evidence which is, as I direct you, evidence against that particular person; and for that reason we shall have a little later to deal separately with the case of Stoner and separately with the case of Mrs Rattenbury, because there are statements in this case which have been given in evidence, which are evidence against the person who made them and not evidence against the person who did not make them, and in whose presence they were not made. But there are, of course, first of all, a number of facts which are common to the case of both of them.

The first thing that one, I think, should have in his mind, perhaps, is this : who were the persons, what do we know about the persons, who were living at 5 Manor Road on that fatal Sunday, the 24th March last, 5 Manor Road, Bournemouth?

He reminded them that Rattenbury was a retired architect, aged sixty-seven, living apparently on his savings. He was, according to the evidence of Dr Simmons, well preserved and healthy, just under six feet tall, strong for his age. He was described by Dr O'Donnell as very charming, quiet, not at all of a violent nature; and by Miss Riggs as a man who seemed to enjoy himself thoroughly in his quiet way :

His widow has given us a less sympathetic picture of her late husband. She says that he was mean about money matters – that may, or may not be – and she says moreover that he was that very unpleasant character for which, I think, we have no suitable English expression, but which the French call *un mari complaisant*, a man who knew that his wife was committing adultery and had no objection to it. Not a nice character. That is said by Mrs Rattenbury, and it depends on her statement alone.

The judge seemed to imply here that Alma had called her husband 'not a nice character', but she had done nothing of the kind. It was the judge's own opinion that Rattenbury was 'that very unpleasant character' if he had, as it appeared, allowed Alma to lead her own life. Miss Tennyson Jesse again strongly dissented from his opinion. She wrote that 'a man who no longer leads a normal life with his wife, yet thinks of her, not as his property, but as a human being who belongs to herself, and has a right to a normal life is not necessarily despicable.'

Alma herself, the judge said, was described, principally by Dr O'Donnell, as being always very excited, unstable – that meant a little unbalanced – when in drink wildly excited, a woman of strong will, apparently of strong passions, liable to get very excitable and very bad tempered if she did not get her own way, and particularly when she was in drink; not a woman who habitually drank too much, but a woman who at times had drinking bouts when she did drink too much :

She says of herself that she was fond of her husband although not intimate with him, and she says she was devoted to her children of whom she had two, one thirteen years of age by her former husband – Mr Rattenbury was her third husband – and a little boy of six by Mr Rattenbury.

Members of the jury, it is not a pleasant thing to have to say anything about that woman's moral character, but even her own counsel addressing you yesterday said things about her which must have been very painful for her to hear, if, indeed, she has any moral understanding at all. But it is necessary, and I agree with Mr Croom-Johnson, and, indeed, it was not disputed, that it is necessary that you should form an opinion in your own minds of that woman's character, the sort of woman she is, from two points of view. She has given evidence. Of the three people concerned in this tragedy one is dead and can give no evidence, one has preferred to remain in the shelter of the dock and, although an admissible witness, has preferred not to give evidence; and so it is that as regards many of the matters in this case all that week – for my part I think that all the events of that week are of the greatest importance in this case – I mean the week beginning 18th March and ending on 24th March – the only person who has given evidence first hand about the events of that week is Mrs Rattenbury, and therefore it is essential that you should make up your minds whether she is a person whose evidence you believe. Whether you believe part of it or whether you reject the whole of it (he gave them only these two alternatives) that to some extent must depend upon the view you take of the sort of woman that she is. It is also necessary that you should do that for this reason : it is the case for the prosecution, as I understand, that this woman is a woman so lost to all sense of decency, so entirely without any morals, that she would stop at nothing to gain her ends, particularly her sexual gratification, and if that be true, then, say the prosecution, do you think that woman would stop at the killing of her husband, particularly if she had not to do it herself, if she were once satisfied that that would enable her to live the sort of life that she was living more comfortably or with less interference, or prospect of interference? And so it is that it seems to me necessary that you should for yourselves have in your minds a picture of that woman; and there is one incident in this case which you may think is sufficient to show you the sort of degradation to which this wretched woman has sunk.

You will remember that she gave evidence herself that she was committing adultery – she is an adulteress, of course – regularly in bed with her husband's servant in her bedroom, and in that bedroom in a little bed there was her child of six; and counsel asked her, 'Do you really mean that you chose that room when, if you wanted to gratify your passions, you could have gone into the man's room which was just along the passage, and done it there? Did you really choose the room where your child was asleep?' And you will remember that the woman, who was in the witness-box, seemed surprised that anyone should put such a question to her, and her answer was apparently given in perfect good faith, 'Why not? The little boy was asleep. He was a sound sleeper.' Well, there it is. That is the woman, a woman who, having ceased, as she says, to have the ordinary relations with her husband, chose as her paramour a boy of seventeen, almost young enough to be her son. She was then thirty-seven.

Brushing aside her explanation that she believed he was much older, which he thought unlikely as she had advertised for a boy between fourteen and eighteen, he dealt with what he called 'this orgy' in London :

> That is the woman – a woman who tells you that she deceived her husband. She says she had to in order to get money; she had to lie to him, and she lied to some purpose at the end of March because she got £250 out of him by saying that she wanted it for a serious operation which had to be performed on herself – quite untrue – and then spent a great deal of it upon this man in a different station of life from herself, buying him such things as silk pyjamas at three guineas a pair.
>
> Members of the jury, having heard her learned counsel, having regard to the facts of the case, it may be that you will say you cannot possibly feel any sympathy for that woman, you cannot have any feeling except disgust for her, but let me say this : that should not make you more ready to convict her of this crime; it should, if anything, make you less ready to accept evidence against her. If you think there can be any explanation consistent with her innocence of that crime, I know you will not let it prejudice you against her. So far as it is material evidence in the case you must use it, and if it is against her, if it shows that she is the sort of woman who might well have a motive to do this, then you must use it because that is admissible evidence; but beware that you do not convict her of this crime of which she is accused because she is an adulteress, and an adulteress, you may think, of the most unpleasant type. Now, that is Mrs Rattenbury.

Continuing his survey of the people who had been living in the Villa Madeira at the time of the tragedy, he said no one could fail to feel regret that at the age of eighteen Stoner was in the dock, but he too must be tried by the laws of the country : they had no more right to refuse to give effect to the evidence in his case through motives of pity than to refuse to give effect to the evidence in Mrs Rattenbury's case, which might be in her favour, because they thoroughly disliked her; 'but it is a pitiable thing,' he said, 'that that youth should have been brought to this pass, and I do not think I am putting it unfairly against even her when I say whatever your verdict may be in this case his position is due to the domination of that woman over him. ('This was the assumption,' Miss Tennyson Jesse commented, 'which hanged Edith Thompson.')

Miss Riggs, the judge described as doing her best, and rightly, to help the woman who had been kind to her. She admitted frankly that she didn't like Stoner who had rather taken her place she had had in the affections of her mistress – 'I am not, of course, talking of sexual matters.'

Whether, as suggested by Casswell, that had tinged her evidence was entirely for the jury to decide, but she was really a very important witness:

In this case, murder being charged, the first question you have to decide, obviously, is: are you satisfied that murder was committed by anybody? The cause of death in the case of the late Mr Rattenbury was given to you in the evidence of Mr Rooke, the surgeon, and he told you that there were three wounds upon his head. One was on the left side just above the left ear, an irregular wound with jagged edges, $3\frac{1}{2}$ inches long, and so severe a blow was it that the bone was driven into the brain, the bone of his skull, forming what the doctors call a depressed fracture of the skull. That by itself was quite sufficient to, and did, cause death eventually . . . That was the cause of death, and there was no other cause of death, and there was no indication either there, I mean, upon the body or in the room, of there being anything in the nature of a struggle at all, and the picture which is presented to you by the prosecution – and I have heard nothing to the contrary from the defence – is a picture of a harmless old gentleman sitting in his chair, perhaps asleep, perhaps just dozing, perhaps – we do not know – reading, and this violent attack with some heavy instrument three times repeated upon his head, which resulted in him dropping like a felled ox, covered with blood; and although everything was done that was possible, that was little, he died. He died at half-past eight on the morning of the 28th, that is, four days after.

He described the mallet, the blood and skin on it, and how it had been found next morning by a police officer:

You have felt the weight of it yourselves and you can judge whether you accept the evidence or not of the medical men who say that it is such a weapon as would be likely to cause the terrible injuries from which this gentleman suffered. The cause of death, then, was those injuries.

You must be satisfied before you convict anybody in the matter that those injuries from which this gentleman died were felonious injuries, that is to say, that the assailant not only wounded him, but wounded him intending to do grievous bodily harm. Members of the jury, you will decide the matter for yourselves. I can only say that, to me, it seems a waste of time to discuss the question of whether anybody could ever deliver three blows on the head of a sitting man of that nature without intending to do grievous bodily harm, and there is an end of it. I am not speaking now of the question whether the man was mad, or anything of that sort. I will not say a normal person, because normal people do not commit crimes of this sort; but, assuming he was a person in possession of his senses, can you conceive any circumstance in which a person could deliver blows of that kind without intending to kill a man or, at least, to do him serious bodily injury? If he did, then that constitutes the felonious wounding, and if from that felonious wounding Mr Rattenbury died (and the doctors say he did) then I say the crime of that person is murder.

He talked for a while about Alma and Stoner's visit to London, the money they had had and what they had spent it on, at Harrod's, etc., and then asked:

Do you believe that you have been told the whole truth about that visit to London by anybody? Here were these two people being absent from Mr Rattenbury and his home for four days. It is true that Mrs Rattenbury has said that he was a man who, although she had never told him, yet she believes suspected her relations with her chauffeur – or his chauffeur – and raised no objection. He was a mean man, she says, about money. Do you think, is it even suggested, that he was a man who would willingly find large sums of money for her to spend upon her lover? Do you believe that while they were in London the future was not discussed? What were they going to do when they got back? Could life go on in the same way? Would not something have to be done with, or to, Mr Rattenbury?

It was this assumption – that Alma wanted Rattenbury put out of the way – that Miss Tennyson Jesse considered was based on nothing but the prejudice of the judge, unwarranted by the evidence, and totally lacking in common sense. She commented :

Ill-balanced as she was, Mrs Rattenbury was a woman of the world. The last thing she would have wanted was to have married a chauffeur, twenty years younger than herself; she was – again to use a slang expression, but slang fits Mrs Rattenbury's career – 'sitting pretty.' She had a kind husband who allowed her to live her own life. She had a young and ardent lover who satisfied her emotionally and physically. She had two children to whom she was passionately devoted. She was being supported as extravagantly as she could have hoped for, all the circumstances considered. She was, as she rather pathetically said in evidence, 'happy then.' For her husband she had a maternal affection – it must be remembered that in all her loves Mrs Rattenbury was essentially maternal. She spoiled and protected Stoner; she adored her children; she comforted her husband; she tried to give Irene Riggs as good a life as possible; she was kind to every stranger who came within her gates. The one thing that would have been impossible to Mrs Rattenbury, amoral, casual, unbalanced, and passionate as she was, would have been to have taken part in harming another human being. Mrs Rattenbury, both as a humane woman and a completely amoral woman, did not desire her husband's death, and did not wish to marry her lover, and there is no evidence, and none was ever brought forward, that she had ever desired either of these things.

The judge – unaware that he was being criticised by this keenly observant and penetrating critic who had so much human understanding – continued :

Would he [Mr Rattenbury] not ask, 'What about my £250? How much did the operation cost you? . . . I hope you are better for it,' Or, if he was so callous and disinterested a husband that he would not be expected even to ask about the operation, at least, as a mean man would you not expect him, and would not they expect him – that is the point – to make some enquiries about the money?

. . . I want to remind you now of what she said happened when she got back. They got back on the 22nd, the Friday night, I think it would be. This is what she said. This was a question put to her, and her answer :

'Did you get back to the Villa Madeira on Friday night? –Yes, about half-past ten.

'With Stoner? –Yes.

'Was your husband in? –Yes, in bed.

'Did he ask anything' – that was her own counsel putting questions – 'Did he ask anything about what had been happening?' And the answer was '–No, he always was jolly late at night.'

Then she went on to describe how on the Saturday she went to the school to bring little John home, and in the afternoon she went with him to see his half-brother play football, and so forth, and she said on the Saturday evening –

'On what terms were you with your husband on the Saturday evening? –Quite all right.

'What did you do? –I think we played cards. I think it was just the same as any other night.'

Do you believe that? Do you believe that after that absence of four days Mr Rattenbury never asked a question as to what had happened in London? and if you do not believe it, if it seems to you to be utterly incredible, then, has Mrs Rattenbury told you in the witness-box the truth, the whole truth and nothing but the truth, or has she not?

Then he dealt with the events of the 24th – Miss Riggs saying she went out and didn't return until about a quarter-past ten, so that the only persons in the house, apart from the little boy, were Mr and Mrs Rattenbury, and Stoner who went to his grandparents at about eight, between eight and eight-thirty, and borrowed the mallet which they had seen:

He said that he wanted it to drive some tent pegs in. We know there was no tent; there was a sort of sun shelter which was used in summer, and it was not up then; and, said Mrs Rattenbury, there was no attempt to put it up then. It was 24th March, mind, not July or August. We know what use was made of that thing . . . he would get back, I suppose – it is three and a half miles – somewhere before a quarter to nine; it would not take him very long in the car. The case for the prosecution is that the injuries to Mr Rattenbury were occasioned some time between then and a quarter-past ten when Riggs returned. . . .

'On one occasion when she was out of the room, she saw Stoner looking over the bannisters, and she said, 'What is the matter; what are you coming out for?' And the answer was, 'Oh, nothing. I was just looking to see if the lights were out.'

'Then, she said, she returned to her room – if that was the first occasion – or she had again returned to her room for the second time; but on the occasion when she did go downstairs she was, for some reason or other – we cannot enquire further – a little troubled in her mind, a little apprehensive that something had happened, and she heard heavy breathing coming from some room . . . and for some reason, perhaps a little oddly, perhaps it was a little nervousness, having gone into Mr Rattenbury's bedroom and turned on the light and seen that he was not there, from which it would seem to follow that he was in the drawing-room, she did not go into the drawing-room at all, but she went upstairs to bed and left that heavy breathing apparently going on in the drawing-room . . .

He referred to Alma coming into her room and speaking of ordinary household matters, ordinary matters of conversation, and incidentally mentioning that she had arranged to go with her husband the next day to Bridport to stay with a gentleman named Jenks. He left it to the jury to decide whether it was a real arrangement meant to be carried out. She had, in fact, telephoned Mr Jenks.

'Then five or ten minutes after that,' said Miss Riggs, 'I heard someone coming downstairs hurriedly, and directly after that there was a call from Mrs Rattenbury which brought me out of my room. Instantly I rushed downstairs into the drawing-room and there was Mr Rattenbury in his chair injured,' – that one word is sufficient to describe it. Mrs Rattenbury was in pyjamas, 'in a very terrified state,' and I, said Miss Riggs, 'at once rushed to the telephone to call up Dr O'Donnell . . .'

She said that Mrs Rattenbury, when she came into her room, was a little excited, apparently excited about preparations for Monday. She did not look as if she knew of her husband being injured. She said the sound of the person going downstairs was the sound of someone hurrying, and it was almost directly after that that she heard the call from Mrs Rattenbury of 'Irene!' and then when she got downstairs, she said Mrs Rattenbury was in a different condition. She called out, amongst other things, 'Oh, poor Ratz! What has happened?'

. . . Then she speaks about doctors coming and going, and she says when the police arrived Mrs Rattenbury, who had been drinking steadily, was in a terrible state and she behaved like a drunken woman. That is all one can say. She tried to kiss the policeman, and behaved in that sort of way which was compatible with her being at that time in a drunken state as well as, perhaps, very upset,

And he accounted for Alma being very upset by the fact that there was a lot of blood about, and many people, particularly women, were very upset by the sight of blood.

He reminded the jury that Irene's feelings had been hurt when Alma and Stoner started sleeping together; and he recalled her description of the lovers' quarrels:

It would be expected, would it not, that they would quarrel, having regard to their relations? The sort of relations existing between them lacked the one thing which makes for ordinary peaceful happiness between married couples, and that is mutual respect, and without it, it is not unlikely that there would be quarrels between two people under such circumstances – and they did quarrel.

Nobody had suggested, he went on, that when Stoner threatened Alma it was a serious statement that he intended to kill her – a bit of play-acting, carrying a 'dagger' and an air pistol . . .

On Casswell's suggestions that Alma was addicted to drugs, he commented:

All that comes to absolutely nothing. It is only fair to this woman to say there is not a rag of evidence that she was ever addicted to drugs, and whether Stoner was, or whether he was not . . . there is certainly no evidence that he got the habit from her.

CHAPTER TWELVE

The 'Dominated Youth'

Having commented on the evidence which related to both the accused, the judge now dealt with one as distinct from the other, beginning with Stoner, 'because he seemed to be alluded to as a principal in the first degree':

You will remember with regard to Stoner that when he came down that night he was at once sent off for the doctor. He did not get the doctor – they probably crossed each other, the doctor coming in a taxi-cab. So Stoner returned to the house, and he made himself useful in various ways. Then he was sent off in the car to the nursing home . . . and there he waited. At 2.45 he was seen by Inspector Mills asleep in this car, in the driving-seat of this car. I do not know whether you can draw any inference of any sort or description from that fact. I suppose it is what five out of six chauffeurs would be found to be doing if they had been up for some hours at a quarter to three in the morning . . . Perhaps it was referred to upon that issue of his being under the influence of cocaine. We have heard something about that : there is no reason to think he was at all.

At this time there was no doubt of two things : there was not the smallest suspicion on the part of the police that he had anything to do with this murder, and he certainly did not volunteer anything to the police to that effect. No one who saw him suggests that he was in other than a perfectly ordinary condition; nobody noticed that he was either drowsy or excited or noisy or misbehaving himself in any way, or showing any emotion or anything else; he was just the ordinary, well-behaved servant, as far as people could judge . . .

At half-past three, on his return . . . Inspector Mills asked him this question : 'Have you seen any mallet about the house?' The answer

was, 'No, I have not seen any mallet at all,' which you may think
was quite untrue.

The next statement, he said, was to Detective-Inspector Carter who
had asked him, not in the least as a suspected person, to give him any
information he could.

This is what Stoner said. The copy is Exhibit 40. The original is
written down in the inspector's notebook. He said, 'I retired to my
bedroom about 8.5 p.m. on Sunday 24th March, 1935' – 8.5 p.m. –
you shall have this, members of the jury, if you like. Being in writing,
it can be given to you. You shall have copies of it, if you do not
mind. I would rather you did not have it in the original book. There
is a reason why. There are things in the book which are not evidence
in this case, and therefore I do not want you to see them . . . This
is what he said : 'I retired to my bedroom about 8.5 p.m. on Sunday
24th March, 1935, leaving Mr and Mrs Rattenbury and the boy
John in the drawing-room. About 10.30 p.m. I was aroused by Mrs
Rattenbury shouting to me to come down. I came down into the
drawing-room . . .' and then he talks about blood, and so forth. He
says, 'Mrs Rattenbury was crying and screaming and said to me,
'Help me to get Ratz into bed, he has been hurt . . .' Mrs Rattenbury
was sober, and as far as I know she had not been drinking. . .'

Then he passed to the statements alleged to have been made by Stoner
to Irene Riggs – she had asked him if his fingerprints would not be
on the mallet, and he had answered, 'No, I wore gloves.' And on the
morning of the 25th, or 26th, he had said to her, 'I suppose you know
who did it?' and she had replied, 'Well?' but she had said no more.

There it is – cryptic. Perhaps you can understand it. The next
statement in regard to Stoner also comes from Miss Riggs and comes
in the same circumstances, cross-examined on behalf of Mrs Rattenbury. She said, 'On Tuesday I asked Stoner why he did it,' – not
whether he did it, but why he did it, assuming therefore that he had
done it, and his answer was because he had seen, not heard, the
deceased Mr Rattenbury living with Mrs Rattenbury that afternoon.
That is my note. If counsel's note does not agree with it . . .
    o'connor : Your lordship is perfectly right.
    I thought so. First of all, you will remember a good deal was said
to you on behalf of Stoner about hallucinations. It was suggested

that he suffered from hallucinations – he is a cocaine addict, and the proof of it is he told somebody, 'I heard Mr and Mrs Rattenbury living together' – I understand that meant having connexion – 'that afternoon.' It was suggested that must have been a hallucination. The point of this is, 'I saw them.' Do you think that is a hallucination? . . . is it conceivable that he could have intended to convey to anybody, or thought himself that these two people, husband and wife, on a Sunday afternoon were performing the sexual act with a door open so that people could look in and see them, or in the drawing-room where people could come and look through the french windows? Is it conceivable? . . . The importance of the matter, of course, is that if you believe Miss Riggs, Stoner is there saying in terms that it was he who inflicted these injuries on Mr Rattenbury, because, in answer to a question which assumes that, the question which is 'Why did you do it?' he gives the reason why he had done it. There it is. That comes from Miss Riggs and not from Mrs Rattenbury.

The next statement, also to Miss Riggs, was made when Stoner was very drunk : 'Mrs Rattenbury is in jail and I have put her there, and I am going to see her tomorrow and give myself up.'

I think we may say that he did go – there is evidence that he did, I do not think it is disputed – to see Mrs Rattenbury next day. He did not give himself up . . .

O'CONNOR : I think perhaps your lordship made one very slight mistake there, if I may correct it at once.

THE JUDGE : Yes?

O'CONNOR : I do not think there is any evidence that Stoner did see Mrs Rattenbury in jail.

THE JUDGE : No, you are quite right. If there is the least dispute about it, I am glad to be corrected. Mr O'Connor is quite right. The evidence is that he said he was going to see her in London in prison. He, in fact, went to London, because it was on the train that he came back in from London that he was arrested. I think probably that is what happened. It may not be, he may not have seen her at all. Mr O'Connor is quite right.

Then there was Stoner's statement after his arrest to Police-Constable Gates, 'You know Mrs Rattenbury, don't you?' He was cautioned, but went on, 'When I did the job I believed he was asleep. I hit him and

then came upstairs and told Mrs Rattenbury. She rushed down
then . . .'

That statement was made in the absence of Mrs Rattenbury and
is not evidence against her, and not being evidence against her, it is
not evidence in her case; but it has been read to you by Mr O'Connor
in the defence of Mrs Rattenbury.

I am not troubling about the irregularity of the matter in the
least, although, strictly speaking, it is not evidence and Mr O'Connor
would have been very angry indeed if anybody had tried to use it
against his client. I am complaining that he read it to you, and,
although he read it for a different purpose, of course the importance
to Mrs Rattenbury is that Stoner was then saying, 'Mrs Rattenbury
had nothing to do with this affair.' Well, there it is. That is the case
against Stoner, with the exception of the evidence of Mrs Rattenbury
because, any evidence that is given at the trial on oath is evidence
for all purposes. So when Mrs Rattenbury went into the box, for
good or evil, what she said is admissible as evidence in the case as
a whole.

He recapitulated the evidence that Alma had given as regards Stoner –
that she hadn't noticed anything unusual about him when he got into
bed with her, but he became agitated and said, 'I'm in trouble about
something.' She asked him what, and he said 'I can't tell you.' She said,
'You must tell me,' and that went on backwards and forwards, till he
said, 'I've hurt Ratz:'

I do not follow that was the exact expression. It is not the man's
expression, it is the woman's expression, that he had hurt Ratz, and
he said that he had hit him on the head with a mallet which he
had hidden outside. She was asked, 'What did you do?' She said
'Nothing.' I think she added that her brain did not quite take it
in or something of that sort, but very soon she said, 'I heard Ratz
groaning and I at once went downstairs, and in the drawing-room
I saw my husband in the chair,' and so forth. That is her account
of how she got to know of this matter, and her account of what
she says her fellow-prisoner said to her on that night that he had
done.

I only pause for a moment to say: you will observe here, if her
evidence is regarded as of any value, that she does not suggest any
failure on the part of Stoner to remember what he had done, or any

indication of his being under the influence of any drug or anything of the sort.

Apparently he was making that statement to her. That is what she says. I left out something. I think she said that the first thing he said was, 'You won't be going to Bridport tomorrow, I have hurt Ratz.'

He turned to the arguments put forward by Casswell for Stoner's defence, and began by criticising the newspapers 'which seem to regard this sort of terrible tragedy as a godsend to them', for displaying posters announcing 'Stoner's counsel says he committed the crime.' He told the jury this was a mistake; all Casswell had meant was that he was not in a position to call evidence to contradict the prosecution's case that it was Stoner who struck the blow, and therefore he did not propose to address them on that part of the case. In a criminal case, when his client has pleaded not guilty, counsel is not in a position to make admissions on his behalf, and assuredly not in such a terribly important matter as that his client has actually done the thing for which he is being tried. They must pay no attention to it :

Mr Casswell said to you, in opening the defence of Stoner, that he had a difficult task, and that the solicitor instructing him had a difficult task to perform – you may well believe him – and he said to you that the first thing the solicitor did, having got Stoner's story, was to go and see a gentleman who lives in Bournemouth and practises there, Dr Weatherly. It was Dr Weatherly who, I will not say provided, but produced the evidence which formed the basis of the defence . . .

First of all, Mr Casswell says, quite rightly, the prosecution must prove not only that Stoner did deliver these blows, but that the wounding that he caused was felonious wounding, that is to say, that he intended to do grievous bodily harm at least, or else to kill. Mr Casswell says, 'I do not complain, I cannot contend, that you could have any possible doubt about that in the case of a person who was in full possession of his senses.' And, of course, that is so . . .

A man is presumed to intend the reasonable consequence of his act. Mr Casswell says, 'I invite you to say that Stoner was in such a condition at the time when he did it' – all this, of course, upon the assumption, which I am going to refer to again, that he is proved to have done it – 'was in such a state that he was incapable of forming that intention.'

He quoted a ruling by the Lord Chancellor to the effect that evidence of drunkenness, falling short of a proved incapacity in the accused to form the intent necessary to constitute the crime, and merely establishing that his mind was affected by drink so that he more readily gave way to some violent passion, does not rebut the presumption that a man intends the natural consequences of his acts :

In this case it is not said that Stoner was drunk, but it is suggested by learned counsel – I cannot say this was given in evidence by anybody . . . that you ought to say that he was incapable of forming that intent. That is based on the assumption, first of all, that he was what is called a cocaine addict . . . and, secondly, that he had taken a very large dose of it on that afternoon.

Here I have to point out to you something which you may think is the most important fact about that matter, and perhaps is conclusive; and that is that there is one human being who knows whether Stoner was in the habit of taking cocaine or whether he was not, and whether, if he took it, he took it frequently or once or twice or all the rest of it, and whether he took it on that afternoon, and that person is Stoner himself. Nobody suggests that he is insane; nobody suggests that he is suffering from the effects of any drug at all. He is an admissible and available witness, and if he wishes, or those who defend him wish, to prove that he is, or was, addicted to drugs, had ever taken cocaine, was then under the influence of cocaine, is there any witness on earth who can do it as well as Stoner? That is, as it seems to me in the circumstances of this case, a fact of the most profound significance : Stoner prefers not to give evidence. His learned counsel told you that he had decided not to call Stoner – indeed that was obvious, that it was upon his advice, you may think very good advice too, that Stoner did not give evidence, because I have no doubt you noticed, we all noticed, that when learned counsel called 'Mr Stoner', meaning the father, the son stepped out and actually left the dock, with the permission of the jailer, in order to give evidence. But there is the fact that the person who of all others could, if he desired, give you first-hand evidence on that subject has not done so.

Now where does this idea of cocaine come from? It seems to originate in a statement made by Mrs Rattenbury to Dr O'Donnell on a date which I have not in mind at the moment – somebody can supply me with it . . .

HAWKE : February, my lord.

THE JUDGE : . . . that Stoner, who had been to London had told her, first of all, that there was some kind of medicine that he had to take two or three times a year to make his head normal, whatever that may mean, and then he had told her that he was in the habit of taking cocaine. So she told Dr O'Donnell, and Dr O'Donnell saw Stoner . . . So far as one could judge, the doctor did not think the matter very serious because he just left it there. He said, 'I saw no sign that he was a person given to doping.' You know what that means. That is the evidence of Dr O'Donnell. I am not sure whether it was Dr O'Donnell or some other witness who said that Stoner told him that he had originally acquired this habit from having seen cocaine in his parents' house . . .

O'CONNOR : Dr O'Donnell, my lord.

THE JUDGE : Well, that seems to be quite untrue; if you believe the father's evidence, quite untrue.

He then considered the evidence given by the key witness for Stoner's defence, Dr Weatherly, whom he called, 'a man of whom nobody would believe for an instant who knew him that he would say anything in the witness-box which he did not thoroughly believe to be true,' and a gentleman who might be described as experienced because he had been practising for sixty-two years as a doctor and had specialised in mental cases. The evidence of the Dorchester Prison Doctor was that there was not the least reason from the young man's appearance, appetite or habit of regular sleep, to suppose that he was other than a perfectly healthy person . . .

But on the 8th April Dr Weatherly came. He said, 'I examined him. I found both pupils were dilated and they did not react to light, and that is consistent with cocaine taking. He was not mentally deficient, he was a bit backward because his education had been neglected. He was anaemic, he had a poor circulation, and I definitely concluded he was a cocaine addict.'

Why do you think that gentleman came to that conclusion? . . . He then said, 'He described the effect of cocaine which lasted some hours. He described the hallucinations as a rash under the skin which seemed to move about. That is typical of cocaine. If he took fairly large doses once a week I should expect that sort of result' – that is, that imaginary feeling under the skin – 'in three months . . .'

There is no one, I suppose, in the medical profession who knows better than this gentleman, Dr Weatherly, what in law amounts to insanity, and this was the most he could say, 'It is possible that the reasoning process may be inhibited.'

. . . that is the evidence. You will observe that it is very general. It shows that, first of all, this gentleman came to the conclusion that, partly from what he was told by Stoner and partly from what he observed himself, Stoner was a person who had been taking cocaine. Whether he would have come to that conclusion apart from what he was told by Stoner is certainly a different matter, and he says that if it was true that he was an addict, which, of course, means something more than taking cocaine once or twice, then it may be, he said, that it would probably cause exaltation and it might make him very depressed and violent tempered afterwards, and it might have a weakening effect on his reasoning and judgement.

Now, in all that do you find the slightest justification for saying that when Stoner, if he did, struck those three blows on the head of Mr Rattenbury he did not know what the effect was likely to be? That is the question. Can you, with every desire to do justice, with every desire to assist this young man if the law and the evidence permit it – can you say that there is anything in that evidence which would justify you in saying that, although he was perfectly sane – I am assuming for the moment he is sane : I will say a word about that – that he was at that time in such a condition that, although he knew what he was doing and knew he was battering the man's head in, he was incapable of forming . . . an intention to injure?

Stoner had also been seen, this time in Brixton Prison last Saturday, by another expert, Dr Grierson, the Senior Medical Officer there, who had said that the principal symptom of cocaine taking was 'oscillation of moods :' in a more detailed statement he had said, 'The effect of a dose on an addict would be very likely to be exaltation for perhaps two hours and then depression and morbid irritability with lack of appetite and insomnia.'

The whole of the evidence, members of the jury, definite evidence, medical evidence, is that this man never suffered from loss of appetite and never suffered from insomnia from the moment he was arrested up to the present time.

He remarked that counsel had got as near as he thought desirable to the all-important point in the section of the defence which was insanity, and had asked the doctor what might be the effect on the mind of an addict of a large dose. The answer was definite: 'Consciousness would be clear,'

by which I understand the doctor to mean the person would be perfectly conscious of what he was doing, but his power to weigh the pros and cons of the situation might be lessened, and an addict would be less likely than another to consider the consequences of an act. He also said – I do not know whether it is of any importance in this case – cocaine speedily results in sexual impotence.

He was then asked about something which perhaps you could judge as well as he could, whether regular and repeated connexion in the case of a boy beginning at seventeen, who had led a quiet and decent life from a boy up to then, might account, without any question of drugs, for his being pale and seeming tired, and so forth. You know the sort of life that this young man was leading, certainly new to him, this sort of excitement which you may imagine would result from his relations with this woman. Do you think you want to go further than that to explain that he looked ill and rather worried? Is it not rather to his credit that he should be worried?

He recalled that the first mention of Stoner having had a large dose of cocaine on the afternoon of 24th March apparently originated in a statement he had made to Dr Grierson in Brixton Prison:

He told Dr Grierson an astonishing story. He said that he had had two eggspoonfuls of this stuff which he called cocaine. Was it cocaine? He was asked to describe it, and he said it was a brown powder with black specks, and no doctor who has been called in this case has ever heard in his life of cocaine, which is a white crystal substance or powder, ever being mixed with any brown powder. The suggestion is that if it were mixed with a brown powder these detestable criminals who go about selling to people at high prices in order that they may make an illicit profit would cease to make a living because people would not buy it: they want 'snow' as they call it, they want something that they recognise as cocaine, or they would not buy it. Do you think it was cocaine at all that this young man had? If so, it is a remarkably bad description that he gave of it.

Finally he referred the jury to the evidence of the Home Office Analyst, Dr Roche Lynch, who had made a study of this and many other poisonous substances. He said there was one thing that was eminently characteristic of a drug addict: if the supplies of the drug for which he was craving were cut off he would be affected immediately and might become seriously ill. Stoner had had no drugs in prison and had been perfectly well.

. . . the members of the jury who are trying this case have only one piece of evidence called before them which gives the smallest indication that there ever was such a dose taken, and that is the evidence of Dr Grierson who says that the prisoner told him that. That is the whole evidence about it. . . . I have come to the conclusion, and it is my duty to deal with the matter, that there is no evidence, and I so direct you as a matter of law – no evidence upon which you can come to the conclusion in this case that the accused Stoner, if he was guilty of this crime, was insane at the time so as not to be responsible in law for his actions.

The law in regard to this matter is that – these are a few lines from a judgement of the Court of Criminal Appeal upon this very matter: 'The jury ought to be told in all cases that every man is presumed to be sane and to possess a sufficient degree of reason to be responsible for his crimes until the contrary be proved to their satisfaction, and that to establish a defence on the ground of insanity it must be clearly proved that at the time of the committing of the act the party accused was labouring under such a defect of reason from disease of mind as not to know the nature and quality of the act he was doing, or if he did know it that he did not know he was doing what was wrong.'

. . . if a man is so insane that he hits at somebody's head with an axe, believing that he is cutting down a tree, then he does not know what he is doing, but thinks he is cutting down a tree. . . . That is the law, and you will observe that there must be some evidence from which a jury can reasonably draw the conclusion, and it is not right that such an issue should even be left to the jury unless there is some evidence.

I have looked through this case with care. I cannot find a ray of evidence which would justify me in leaving to you the question whether it has been proved that this young man was suffering from such a defect of reason through disease of the mind that he did not know on this occasion what he was doing, and still less any evidence to suggest that he thought that what he was doing was a right and proper thing to do, that he did not know the difference between right

and wrong . . . Therefore I have to tell you that, so far as that
defence is concerned, you are bound to reject it upon my ruling.
That is all I desire to say with regard to Stoner.

He had said enough to make it quite clear that, as far as he was
concerned, there was no hope for Stoner. He turned to the evidence
as it affected Alma. He said he could deal shortly with her case, now
that he had dealt with the many important matters that affected her
in conjunction with her fellow-prisoner. The remaining matters which
affected her were merely her statements. The first was made that night
quite early to Dr O'Donnell, round about midnight :

At that time, it is right to say, she was, according to the evidence of
Dr O'Donnell, very excited and inclined to be intoxicated – she then
had a whisky and soda in her hand – and she said this : 'We had a
very happy evening,' that means she and her husband, 'We arranged
to go next day to the Jenks's, and Mr Rattenbury (her husband) was
pleased at the idea of the visit. He showed me a passage in a book
about suicide,' and then she tried to show the doctor the passage,
but he brushed it aside . . . It is curious that she referred to that
much later on, to his having shown her a passage in a book about
suicide, but that is all she said at the moment.
      She went on to say, 'I had gone to bed early and was wakened
by a cry or noise, I am not sure which.' She said, 'I came down at
once and found him lying back in his chair with a pool of blood
on the carpet,' and then she spoke of his teeth on the carpet. That
is her first account, and it appears to be a perfectly clear statement.
Whether she was or was not really under the influence of drink, or
to what extent, I do not know – you will judge of that – but it seems
to be a perfectly clear statement. Whether she was or was not really
under the influence of drink, or to what extent, I do not know –
you will judge – but it seems to be a clear connected account and
certainly does not indicate that she had the least idea when she came
down that her husband had been attacked by any particular person
or that she knew all about it, nor does it indicate that she had any
part in the matter or was in any way blameworthy.

The next statement was made to Bagwell, the first police officer on the
scene. At that time he had no grounds for suspecting anybody
particularly, but wanted information, which she quite readily gave –
she had been playing cards with her husband that evening until about

nine o'clock, and then she went to her bedroom, and at about half-past ten she heard a yell. She came down, sent for the doctor, and so forth. Bagwell described her as 'under the influence of drink':

I think I am right in saying that the next account was given to Inspector Mills. I think I said at one time we would enquire whether it was the same account heard by two people or whether it was not. It is not sufficiently important to trouble about, because it is in effect the same thing. Whether told to somebody else who gave exactly the same time, two o'clock, a few minutes after or before, or whether it is actually the same statement does not seem to matter.

Mills' account of it was this. He refers to the woman as having been drinking. He says her statement was, 'I was in bed,' – if you recollect, he did not hear the first part of it – 'I heard groaning, I came down, found my husband in the easy-chair. He was unconscious with blood flowing from his head . . .

He wished the jury to observe here that so far, up to two o'clock in the morning, she had been perfectly consistent in her statements, which amounted to this: 'I know nothing whatever about it. I cannot give you any assistance. I only know that I came down after a happy night with my husband, I came down and found him hit. That is all that I can tell you':

At half-past two, according to Bagwell, she made quite a different statement, one which you will have to deal with. She suddenly said to him, 'I know who did it,' and then he stopped her and cautioned her, because now she was altering from her position of a person who was giving ordinary information – she was saying something about herself which made it necessary that she should understand that she was not obliged to make any statement at all, and the caution is given in such terms that it is rather a kindly suggestion, 'I think that perhaps you had better not.' She, however, continued: 'I did it with a mallet. Ratz has lived too long. It is hidden,' – that is, the mallet – 'No, my lover did it.' Then she refers to the chair. She says, 'I would like to give you £10. No, I won't bribe you.'

Members of the jury, the question is not whether she now remembers having made that statement or whether she does not. It does not seem to me, except upon the question of credibility, that it matters whether you believe her when she says, 'I have forgotten the earlier statement.' The medical evidence is to the effect that she may well have forgotten, if she was given, as she was some time after this, morphia; but there is no reason to suppose she would forget what happened earlier in the evening. . . . The question is, first of all, did she say this, and, secondly, what inference do you draw from it if she said it? Do you draw the inference that it was a true statement made by a person who was telling the truth, or was it a wholly made by a person who was telling the truth, or was it a wholly imaginary statement made by some person who did not in the least know what she was talking about, or do you come to a conclusion somewhere half-way between the two?

Let us see what it was. 'I did it with a mallet.' If you accept what may be called, I think, the generally accepted evidence in this case, that was untrue. She had not done anything with a mallet, but she knew, according to her own story, who had done it with a mallet.

'Ratz has lived too long.' Does that indicate to you, if the woman knew what she was saying, that she was regretting her husband's death, or she could not help it coming out that she was glad?

'The mallet is hidden.' She might have known that in many ways. She says the only way she knew was that Stoner told her so.

Then there is the sudden outburst : 'No, I did not do it; my lover did it.' She said, 'If I said that, I said it because my lover had told me upstairs that he had done it.'

And then the idea of bribing the policeman and then saying she would not bribe him, you may think is an indication, of which I do not think there is any doubt at all, that by this time the woman was in a state – it is too strong to call it intoxication, but semi-toxication, not drunk in the police sense, which seems to mean hopelessly drunk, but suffering from alcohol to such an extent that it would be very unsafe to rely in the matter of accuracy upon anything she said. The babbling of a drunken person. . . .

You obviously cannot draw the inference that she is telling the truth, because there are two directly opposite things in it – they cannot both be true – 'I did it – No, my lover did it.' It is entirely a matter for you. That is the statement she made.

He said the next statement came from the evidence of Inspector Carter: O'Connor reminded him there was another one from the evidence of Inspector Mills :

I beg your pardon, yes, there is. It is very short. This is at half-past three and she is slightly worse than before – her condition – according to Mills. He said to her, 'Your husband is in a critical condition,' and her answer was, 'Will this be against me?' There is something of importance – 'Will this be against me?' I do not know that you can draw any inference from that one way or the other.

Then she was cautioned, and she made this statement: 'I did it. He gave me the book. He had lived too long. He said "Dear dear." I will tell you in the morning where the mallet is. Have you told the coroner yet?' She seems to have made two or three references to the coroner – curious. 'I shall make a better job of it next time. Irene doesn't know. I made a proper muddle of it. I thought I was strong enough.'

He asked whether they were satisfied that she said this, and if so, what inference did they draw from it? It was entirely a matter for them, but it was perfectly obvious that it was a muddled inconsistent statement from the mind of a person who seemed to have been drinking since twelve o'clock and was pretty far gone in drink.

He reminded them that when she was given a dose of morphia she immediately followed the doctor downstairs, and when she began to make a statement he said, 'You cannot take a statement from her now; I have just given her morphia and she is not in a fit state to do this.'

Then the next thing that happens is that Inspector Carter arrives . . . Apparently she sleeps until six o'clock in the morning, and then she wakes up, and as soon as she wakes up she makes a statement. When I say makes a statement, I mean she says something which the inspector writes down in his book. Then, she is still lying on her bed, apparently it is before the restoratives – if that word can be used in regard to them – the bath and the coffee, walking about, and so forth, had been applied. . . . The inspector said, 'I do not think it is fair to use it in evidence.' He made a mistake in not informing the Director of Public Prosecutions that that statement had been made by the accused, and that he had it in his notebook . . . But, as I say, I am not blaming the inspector. He thought he did it for the best. He thought, quite rightly, that no credence ought to be attached to what the woman said under those circumstances.

But when, two hours later, at a quarter-past eight, she was, as no doubt she was, or certainly appeared to be, better, he thought it fair to take a statement from her.

I do not think that anybody will say that that inspector did not honestly believe that the woman was in a condition to make a statement, and no doubt she was in a condition in this sense. You have

(*Left*) George Stoner

(*Below*) The crowd outside the Old Bailey after the verdict

(*Right*) Alma after the trial

(*Below*) Amidst loud booing Alma's taxi leaves the Old Bailey after the verdict

seen her signature. The evidence is that the statement was read by her, and read out to her. She could write perfectly well and she appeared to be right. She signed it, and I think you will agree that her signature there is quite as good as, if not better than, some of the signatures that one has seen of hers upon other documents . . .

Dr O'Donnell, who knows much more about these matters than a police officer, says he saw her . . . later in the day, and he says, 'I who know that I had given her half a grain of morphia, say to you on my responsibility as a medical man that it would not be safe to attach any importance to anything that woman said while under the influence of that drug, which I am satisfied as a medical man persisted up to and after 8.15 that night.' That is his evidence, and I am quite sure I am voicing the view you yourselves would form, that it seems to me that after that evidence it would be very unfair to form any conclusion against the woman on the ground of a statement made in those circumstances.

He was quite sure Dr O'Donnell's opinion would have been reinforced by the evidence of that distinguished public servant, Dr Morton, governor of the prison where she had been confined, but unfortunately he was far too ill to attend. He said in his report that for the first few days after her reception she had been suffering from some form of confusion of mind, the result of alcohol and, possibly, a large dose of morphia. In the interests of the accused, with everybody's agreement, the rule had been relaxed to allow this written report to be given in evidence: it was one of the documents which they were entitled to have and look at for themselves, and if they drew any inference from it, he could not say they were not entitled to. He reminded them of the evidence of Police-Constable Bright who had formed – 'and it was not remarkable that he did form' – the same opinion as his superior officer as to the lady's condition; and he noted that the statements she made under the influence of morphia were quite different from those she made when she had merely taken some whisky:

Before you return your verdict, I think it would be right in the interests of this woman that I should read to you quite shortly the evidence which she herself gave in Court, or my notes of it; it is not very long, and as we have now arrived at the ordinary hour of adjournment, I think the best course to pursue would be that I should reserve that until after you have had your lunch. You will necessarily, I think, take some time in considering this matter and discussing it among yourselves, and there is no reason why you should do that in the ordinary interval. Will you oblige me by not talking it over during lunch? Do not do that. Just talk about other things and then, when I have read to you Mrs Rattenbury's evidence, you will be free to discuss the whole matter.

The Court adjourned.

VILLA TRIAL AND 'DOMINATED YOUTH'. THE SUMMING UP. ORGY IN LONDON. JURY TOLD TO IGNORE QUASI-ADMISSION: 'STONER HAS NOT SAID IT' DECLARES JUDGE. JUDGE'S WARNING: 'YOU MAY FEEL NO SYMPATHY FOR MRS RATTENBURY, BUT BEWARE. DO NOT CONVICT HER BECAUSE SHE IS AN ADULTERESS.' 'YOU CANNOT POSSIBLY HAVE ANY FEELING BUT DISGUST FOR HER.' JUDGE: 'YOU CANNOT HAVE ANY FEELING BUT DISGUST FOR MRS RATTENBURY.' PARAMOUR A BOY OF 17. FEELING OF DISGUST. JUDGE'S 'REGRET' FOR STONER.

CHAPTER THIRTEEN

The Verdict

Casswell had pinned all his hopes of saving Stoner's life on persuading the jury to give a verdict of manslaughter instead of murder, but the judge in his summing up had not dwelt on this possible alternative. During the lunch interval Casswell evidently spoke to him about it, for as soon as the case was resumed he said :

> Members of the jury, I have been reminded, quite properly, that I did not say anything to you about what your duty would be if you came to the conclusion that although Stoner delivered those blows which killed Mr Rattenbury, he did so without intending to kill or to do grievous bodily harm. Perhaps I ought to have said to you – learned counsel was quite right, it is material – in saying that, under those circumstances Stoner would not be guiltless, but he would be guilty of the crime of manslaughter; because manslaughter consists in the crime of unlawfully killing a person, without any intention of killing him. Perhaps I ought to have said that to complete the law.

Then he gave a rapid résumé of Alma's evidence : he had noted what he considered to be the most significant of her answers but not the questions to which they referred : the result was what he called 'a sort of narrative'. She had not lived with her husband since the birth of their boy, John . . . their relations happy and cordial . . . quarrels, but not frequent quarrels. His talk of suicide . . . her black eye. 'He was not very generous' . . . she told him lies to get money. In September 1934 Stoner came as chauffeur-handyman . . . in November she became his mistress . . . husband had told her to live her own life, and, later, she told him she was doing so . . . tried to sever relations with Stoner because of difference in their ages . . . regularly had connection . . . that she never gave him money to buy drugs . . . asked Dr O'Donnell to see him . . . the trip to London – the 'orgy' – with Stoner . . . sleeping together at the hotel in fact. Then there was something about a man's watch, her father's watch that she lent to Stoner . . . the ring, she said, was for her . . .

On return, husband asked no questions . . . his talk of suicide . . . because of a book he was reading . . . tried to make him jolly . . . Mr Jenks and the projected trip to Bridport . . . bedroom door closed for a time . . . Stoner's jealousy . . .

The sort of narrative continued :

About half-past seven John went to bed. I then played cards with my husband. I let the dog out through the french window and then closed the window. I went to bed at 9.30 exactly. I kissed him good-night. I went upstairs to the lavatory and when I got back to my bedroom the dog was there.

The judge commented, that meant the husband must have been alive at the time, because he must have let the dog in and closed the window afterwards; but Dinah must have come in when Stoner entered by the french window with the mallet, for Rattenbury would not have let her in so soon. It could be opened from the outside, according to Stoner's statement, unless it was locked.

Then came Alma's conversation with Irene Riggs in the latter's bedroom, Stoner's confession when he joined Alma in bed, and how she rushed down and found Rattenbury injured.

Because of all the detailed evidence that had been given, he took the rest of it very shortly – her trying to make her husband speak . . . the vexed question of her intoxication, the injection of morphia and her apparent loss of memory . . . her various statements and her desire to protect Stoner. Finally :

Members of the jury, that is the evidence in this case. You will now be good enough to go to your room and consider your verdict. I have told you, and I repeat it, your duty is to the accused separately. If the prosecution have established to your satisfaction beyond reason-able doubt in the case of either of these persons that the charge of murder is made out, having regard to the direction upon law which I have given you, it will be your duty to say so by your verdict. If in the case of either of them, the evidence of the prosecu-tion fails to satisfy you of the guilt of the accused, do not find that person guilty merely because of suspicion, or for any other reason, but say by your verdict in regard to that person that the prosecution have failed to establish the case, by returning a verdict of not guilty. I know you can be trusted to do your duty. Mr Foreman, would you like any of the things that have been produced in this case, what I call the Exhibits, I mean statements, so far as they are in writing, the mallet, or anything else?

FOREMAN OF THE JURY : My lord, may we send out for them later?

THE JUDGE : Yes, send for anything you want. Just make it clear what you want.

The jury retired at 2.48 p.m.

The impression the judge left upon his hearers was not exactly that Alma was innocent, for he still clung to his two basic arbitrary assumptions – that she dominated Stoner and that being lovers they both wanted to get rid of the husband – but that the prosecution had not made out their case against her, though they had against Stoner.

It was nearing four o'clock when the jury filed silently in again for the last moment of the five day trial. They had been considering their verdict only fifty minutes. Barristers and members of the public who had been loitering in the corridors, thinking the jury's decision would take hours in such a complicated case, rushed quickly to their places.

Five minutes elapsed, and then :

A rat-tat on the outer door hushed the court. Four aldermen, bearing bouquets of anemones and carnations, bowed the judge in. Mr Justice Humphreys returned their greeting. He strode to his chair, his white gloves carried on the arm of his crimson robe, and beneath the white gloves a neatly folded square of black cloth – the black cap. (*Daily Express, 1st June 1935*)

Mrs Rattenbury, her still handsome face deathly pale and her dark eyes so hollow and expressionless that it was impossible to tell whether she could see the court in front of her or not, was helped into the dock by two wardresses, each firmly grasping an elbow. Young Stoner, his face as impassive, his movements as controlled as ever, took his stand calmly in the dock and appeared to brace himself for what he already seemed to know must surely come.

Briefly, as if to spare all he could to the woman and boy before him, the clerk of the court put his question to the jury : 'Gentlemen of the jury, do you find Alma Victoria Rattenbury guilty, or not guilty?' As briefly, as mercifully, came the answer, 'Not guilty.'

'Gentlemen of the jury, do you find George Percy Stoner guilty or not guilty? 'Guilty.'

At the fatal word, so quietly spoken, Mrs Rattenbury took a frightened step forward, thrust out her hands as if by gesture alone she could somehow negative what had been said. 'Oh no . . .' she cried, almost voicelessly, 'Oh . . . oh no. . . .' The wardresses grasped her and hurried her from the dock. Young Stoner was left standing there alone. (*Daily Mail, 1st June 1935*)

For a full minute Stoner stood there while the judge bowed his head over the court records, entering the sentence in a silence so still that the scratching of his pen could be heard.

Women wept in the public gallery. The two jurywomen, set and serious in countenance, averted their eyes as the judge's clerk spread open the square-foot of black cloth and placed it evenly over the white wig. (*Daily Express, 1st June 1935*)

After a brief pause, in which Stoner remained with downcast eyes, the judge addressed him in a voice betraying the compassion he has obviously felt for the boy throughout the trial. He had been found guilty, and 'the only sentence which this court knows' in such a case was death. Had he anything to say as to why that sentence should not be passed upon him?

'Nothing at all, sir.' It was the only time, from beginning to end, that Stoner had spoken.

. . . in a level voice that carried without emphasis across the deathly quiet of the court, the judge pronounced on young Stoner that most painful sentence that can ever be within the duty of one man to put upon another. There was a recommendation to mercy which, Stoner was told, would be forwarded to the proper quarter.

Brave as the boy had been throughout the trial, so uncannily brave that it had been scarcely possible to guess what resolution lay behind that outwardly calm face, he could not quite control his emotion at hearing the fatal words. His eyes dilated, staring at the judge in a last supreme effort of self-control, his hands stirred vaguely from his sides and grasped the edge of the dock, he swallowed painfully two or three times, and the knuckles of one hand began to tap with gentle monotony against the edge of the dock until the judge's voice had ceased. Then he turned abruptly towards the stairway to the cells and was gone. (*Daily Mail, 1st June 1935*)

Counsel asked permission for Stoner's father to see the boy before he left the court. The judge bent over, and said, 'Certainly.' Mr Stoner senior passed through the dock and went below also.'

Mrs Rattenbury's ordeal was not over. She was brought back to the dock to face a second indictment – the charge of being an accessory after the fact, 'knowing that Stoner had wounded Mr Rattenbury with intent to murder him'.

She seemed bewildered. Ashen and shaken she moved her lips but no words came. She turned in anxiety to the wardress. Then her solicitor spoke to her. . . . She made three efforts before she could repeat the words 'not guilty'.

Counsel for the Crown said he offered no evidence. The judge directed the jury to return a verdict of 'Not guilty'. (*Daily Express, 1st June, 1935*)

Her self-control gone, her eyes shadowed with exhaustion, and her white face smudged with tears, this woman whom the judge had described in his summing up as 'a woman so lost to all decency, so entirely without any moral sense that she would stop at nothing to gain her ends' hung limp and weeping in the strong grasp of the two wardresses who supported her. On their strength only – for her own had broken utterly – was she able to leave the dock and pass, what is ironically called 'a free woman', for the last time down the steps of the Old Bailey. (Margaret Lane in the *Daily Mail, 1st June 1935*)

The judge then charged the Sherriff of Hampshire to make arrangements for Stoner's execution, and exempted the jury from further service for the next five years.

Going along the corridor below the dock, Alma met Stoner face to face – his arms were being held tightly to his sides by two burly warders. She tried to speak to him but no sound passed her lips: he smiled at her and nodded as his escort hurried him away. For a quarter of an hour she stayed in one of the rooms beneath the courtroom in a state of collapse. A doctor was called, who gave her restoratives, and Irene Riggs brought her a beautiful bunch of flowers.

Thousands of people had congregated outside during the closing scenes of the trial, hoping to see her, and crowds thronged the entrance. When she was ready to leave, the main hall of the Old Bailey, giving access to all the courts, was cleared, so no one saw her as she hurried along supported from time to time by the two wardresses. Mrs Kingham was waiting in a taxi in Newgate Street: at a given signal it backed along to the Barristers' Entrance from which she was able to leave without hindrance though a small crowd booed and a woman angrily flourished her umbrella.

Stoner, manacled to a warder, was taken out in a Black Maria through the great wooden and iron-bound gates where scores of police had been stationed to prevent any demonstration. Then Stoner's father came out, supporting his mother. Questioned by reporters, he replied, 'What can I say now that this terrible blow has fallen? He is my only son . . . My boy seemed glad that the jury had found Mrs Rattenbury not guilty. He said to me, "I am content. They have set her free. Whatever happens to me does not matter." '

DRAMA OF VERDICT ON STONER. MRS RATTENBURY CRIES 'OH, NO!' REELED IN DOCK. COLLAPSED AFTER ACQUITTAL. SMUGGLED FROM OLD BAILEY. CROWDS SEE STONER LEAVE. 'I AM CONTENT' AFTER SENTENCE OF DEATH. 'THEY HAVE SET HER FREE. I DO NOT MATTER.'

TAXICAB FOR ONE : BLACK MARIA FOR THE OTHER. LAST SCENES AT THE OLD BAILEY.

Mrs Alma Victoria Rattenbury, aged thirty-eight, was acquitted of the murder of her husband at the Old Bailey yesterday.

George Percy Stoner, eighteen years old – less than half her age – whose position in the dock was due, in the words of the judge, to 'the domination of that woman', was condemned to be hanged for the murder.

These two had spent months of stormy passion in the closest intimacy at the Villa Madeira, Bournemouth, where the husband was found dying from head wounds on 24th March. . . . Yesterday at four o'clock both the passionate intimacy of the villa and the chilly association of the dock were alike ended as they separated for the last time – she for freedom, he for the death cell (*Daily Express, 1st June 1935*)

CHAPTER FOURTEEN

'Thank God for Peace at Last'

Mrs Kingham took Alma to the home of Rattenbury's nephew, the solicitor Keith Miller Jones, at No 4 Halton Place where afternoon tea had been made ready for them, but she found no peace there : a crowd, 'rather a hostile crowd', Mrs Kingham said, followed them and stood waiting outside. The solicitor, seeing Alma's distress, telephoned the police and had the street cleared, but a group of reporters still obstinately besieged the entrance to the building : next, alarmed by Alma's condition, he telephoned Dr Bathurst of Harley Street who came at once, examined her, and arranged to take her to the Cleveland Nursing Home in Bayswater.[1] On their way out he refused to tell the reporters where they were going, or to answer any questions. As he helped her into his car, one of them shouted : 'If you take her to Bournemouth, we'll follow you there !' At the nursing home she had a perfumed bath and was put to bed, utterly exhausted.

On the following morning she seemed to be better. She sent Irene to the shops – she had come early with an armful of roses – to buy her a pink *crêpe de chine* nightdress which she said she particularly wanted. Then they had a long talk, just like old times, but in the course of it Alma told her to make sure that there were pink flowers at her funeral and that she was to be dressed in pink in her coffin. Irene was alarmed, and reported their conversation to the matron who arranged for a specially trained nurse to be always in attendance.

Alma had a photograph of Stoner with her – she could hardly take her eyes off it. She wrote to him, and sent the letter to Pentonville Prison : then she read in the evening paper that he had been moved. She broke down, and sobbed, 'If I could have just one word with him, if I had just one look at his face again, he would understand. I must see him once again . . . Can't anything be done?' She wrote to her solicitor instructing him that no expense was to be spared in helping him. Her doctor sent a petition to the Home Office requesting that she be allowed to see Stoner for a short time, to save her reason, even if they were not allowed to speak. She confided to the matron that she intended to die at the same time as Stoner was hanged.

'From the first day she was here,' the matron said, 'Mrs Rattenbury at intervals tried to compose a song. She would repeat variations upon the same lines and hum or sing melodies, trying to put them to music. She tried many variations of the words, but they were all on the original theme, which was :

> We have lived together
> We too;
> We have loved together
> I and you;
> We'll together die
> You and I –
> We'll swing together.

On Monday, 3rd June, she was still talking, a little wildly, of suicide, of Stoner, and of leaving the home; but the matron, hoping that as her health and strength returned she would be better in her mind also, treated the matter lightly, gave her a facial massage, sent for a manicurist, and for a hairdresser who gave her a shampoo and a permanent wave. She began to look attractive again, and seemed much more cheerful. She smoked cigarettes incessantly. She sent out for back numbers of the newspapers containing reports of her trial which she lived through again and again, re-enacting its scenes with great animation – he said this and I said that and he looked so funny when he said it and it was wrong what I answered I should have said this . . .

At ten o'clock that night a friend who was visiting her came running down and told the matron that Alma was getting ready to leave. The matron went up and found she had almost finished packing. 'One glance at her face,' she said, 'showed me that nothing I or anyone else could say would prevent her from going if she wanted to. She was that kind of woman.' As she was a private patient, the matron had, of course, no authority to keep her there against her will, so Alma drove away in a private car with her friend who took her to the Elizabeth Fulcher Nursing Home in Devonshire Street where, presumably, the supervision was less strict.

On Tuesday morning she went out by herself and wandered about the streets. She returned at midday, borrowed two pounds and went out again at 3.30 p.m., saying she would be back at about nine. She went to Waterloo Station and took the familiar Bournemouth train with the intention, probably, of going to see her children: she alighted at Christchurch which was not far from Christopher's school, but instead of going there she walked a long way out into the meadows that were golden with buttercups. She found herself beside a backwater of the River Avon at a place called The Three Arches Bend, from the triple arched bridge that carries the main London railway line across it there. She sat down in the long grass and lit a cigarette. Soon she took a pencil from her handbag, and an old envelope and began to write:

Eight o'clock, and after so much walking I have got here. Oh, to see the swans and spring flowers, and to smell them. And how singular I should have chosen the spot Stoner said he nearly jumped out of the train once at. It was not intentional, my coming here. I tossed a coin, like Stoner always did, and it came down 'Christchurch'.

It is beautiful here. What a lovely world, really. It must be easier to be hanged than to do the job oneself, especially under these circumstances of being watched all the time. Pray God nothing stops me tonight. . . . God bless my children and look after them.

Then she thought for a little while, and wrote on another envelope:

I tried this morning to throw myself under a train at Ox.cir. [Oxford Circus.] Too many people about. Then a bus – still too many people about. One must be bold to do a thing like this. It is beautiful here, and I am alone. Thank God for peace at last.

The river was overgrown with water-lilies: yellow irises spread along the banks. A farm worker was crossing the meadow behind her to attend to some heifers. He climbed the railway embankment, started to cross the bridge and, while doing so, turned and looked back at Alma. He saw her stand up and make determinedly for the water's edge, arms swinging from the shoulders: he thought she was going to pick some flowers, but then he saw the blade of a knife in her clasped hand. This is his description of what happened next:

When she came to the water's edge she bent slightly into a crouching position and then toppled over into the water. I raced to the spot, but when I got there she was floating face upwards about five yards from the bank. I lowered myself over the side and reached out with my foot in her direction, but she was just too far for me to touch her. All this time she was staring fixedly at me with a terrible look in her eyes. I saw her coat lying on the bank and snatched it up and threw the other end into the water towards her, yelling out, 'Catch hold of this!' But as I said the words she moved her head further back as though trying to go into mid-stream, and as she did so, blood oozed up to the surface from a wound in her chest. . . . She turned her head and looked at me and uttered one long cry which sounded like 'Oh!'

As the man, William Mitchell, could not swim, he ran for help. Her body was recovered and taken to the Public Assistance Institution, Fair Mile House, in Christchurch.

MRS RATTENBURY STABBED AND DROWNED. ACQUITTED BUT SELF-CONDEMNED. DRAMATIC SEQUEL TO MURDER TRIAL. MYSTERY OF LAST HOURS. WHY ALMA RATTENBURY DIED. FULL FACTS PLACED BEFORE THE SUNDAY DISPATCH. HOW SHE PREPARED. PERMANENT WAVE; PERFUMED BATH. VISIT TO VILLA OF SORROW? LAST CIGARETTE IN FIELD OF BUTTERCUPS.

Casswell said, when he was told of her suicide, '. . . not unnaturally I assumed that it was a belated confession of guilt. But there was no such admission in the scraps of written thoughts and torn-off pages of a diary which she left behind her in her handbag.'

Mrs Rattenbury, who, as reported on Page One, was found stabbed and drowned, would have been forty-three next Saturday. . . .

Throughout the trial Mrs Rattenbury was a compelling figure who seemed to overshadow her young companion in the dock. . . . During the summing-up she seemed numbed, and was obviously crushed by the judge's severe remarks about her conduct. (*Evening News, 5th June 1935*)

The last tragic moments of the life of Mrs Alma Rattenbury have done something to mitigate, if not condone, her guilt in a human drama the terrible consequences of which could never conceivably have been foreseen. Writing in advance of inquest proceedings which appear likely to confirm the obvious explanation of her death, it is a reasonable assumption that she had found an escape from self-condemnation impossible. In this desperate plight Mrs Rattenbury is an object for the pity of the least forgiving. The more forgiving may be brought to the state of sympathy by the realisation that such inexplicable acts of human folly can only have an explanation in an abnormality beyond the control of their perpetrators. It cannot be made the excuse for crime, but it can be advanced in extenuation of it even in a case so notorious as that of Mrs Rattenbury. (*The Bournemouth Times and Directory, 5th June 1935*.

MRS RATTENBURY'S PRISON SONG. 'TO KEEP MY MIND SANE.'

The public conscience may have passed a harsh judgement upon Mrs Rattenbury, but the tragic circumstances of her death have softened the condemnation.

The *Sunday Graphic* therefore publishes the words and music of the prison song of 'Lozanne' (Mrs Rattenbury). From the prison she wrote that she 'kept repeating the extraordinary words over and over again to help keep my mind sane'.

The unhappy woman wrote this song from the fullness of her heart; the words convey her love for the tragic boy Stoner. She blames Fate for their meeting – 'By some mistake you filled my empty days.' But so long as she lived she knew that never could she put him out of her mind, try as she would.

This is one of the most poignant documents ever published. It appears in the *Sunday Graphic* exclusively.

> By some mistake my spirit held you dear,
> But now I wake in agony and fear,
> To fading hope and thought distressed and grey,
> With outstretched hand I put your face away.
>
> By some mistake you filled my empty days,
> But now I wake to face the parting ways.
> I see your smile, I hear the words you say,
> With no reply I hush your voice away.
>
> By some mistake, by some divine mistake,
> I dreamed awhile, but now I wake, I wake.
> Yet, dying, dream you kept my vision true,
> I seem to climb to heav'n in loving you.
>
> (*Sunday Graphic*, 9th June 1935)

When the news of her death was broken to Stoner in the condemned cell at Pentonville Prison, he broke down and wept.

It was a week to the very hour from the time she was acquitted at the Old Bailey that the inquest was opened in the old board-room of the Public Assistance Guardians in Fair Mile House, Christchurch. About a dozen members of the public attended, half of them women.

On a raised platform, under a wooden canopy, Mr Percy Ingoldby, the coroner of South Hampshire, sat without a jury, and although he called six witnesses and read extracts from the messages left by Mrs Rattenbury, he announced his verdict within twenty-nine minutes.

Mr Lewis Manning, Mrs Rattenbury's solicitor, was one of the first to arrive. Then came Dr William O'Donnell of Bournemouth, her doctor, and Miss Irene Riggs who for four years had been her friend and companion. . . .

Just before the court opened, a policeman carried in a bedraggled brown umbrella and a parcel containing some of Mrs Rattenbury's personal belongings. These, consisting of her reptile skin handbag, her fawn hat, a large box of cigarettes, and a paper bag containing the sheath of a dagger, were placed on the table in front of the coroner. There, also, were laid the letters which Mrs Rattenbury had written just before her death on odd scraps of paper and the backs of envelopes, and which were addressed to nobody in particular.

The members of the public scattered themselves round the room, sitting in the yellow armchairs used on other occasions by the members of the Public Assistance Committee, and, when these were filled, sitting on the tables.

When the coroner asked who was represented, Mr E. W. Marshall Harvey stated, 'I appear on behalf of George Percy Stoner to watch the proceedings.' Mr Manning said he represented Mrs Rattenbury's relatives. (*News of the World, 9th June 1935*)

The first witness was the doctor who had carried out the post-mortem examination. He said he had found on the body two old operations scars 'apparently as the result of appendicitis' – but they were more probably the scars of the wounds she received while serving as a nurse and stretcher bearer behind the front line in France. There were also six stab wounds on her chest :

Five of the wounds, went on the doctor, were in the upper part of the left breast, and all passed downwards and inwards. The left lung had been punctured in four places, and there were three wounds in the heart, one where the instrument had passed more than once, another where it had entered once, and a third which was a slight scratch. Death was due to the injuries which, he was of opinion, were self-inflicted. The woman must have died almost instantaneously, and was certainly dead before she entered the water.

One of the most pathetic figures at the inquest was Miss Irene Riggs who was in tears throughout the brief proceedings. Looking very pale and clutching the table while giving her evidence, she was the next witness called.

She wore a grey costume and a wide-brimmed straw-hat, and was obviously greatly distressed. Her shoulders shook with sobbing as she struggled through the oath, and the coroner remarked, 'Pull yourself together. I will not distress you more than necessary.'

Miss Riggs identified the body as that of Mrs Rattenbury, widow of Francis Mawson Rattenbury, retired architect who, until recently, had lived at the Villa Madeira, Bournemouth. She stated she had been Mrs Rattenbury's companion for the last four years, and last saw her at a London nursing home on 1st June.

Miss Riggs also identified the hand-writing on the letters as that of Mrs Rattenbury. Asked the latter's age, she replied that she thought it was thirty-seven. 'That is correct, sir,' remarked Mr Manning to the coroner. . . .

The coroner picked up one of the letters, saying he did not intend to read them all, only some extracts. The first, apparently written on 4th June, said:

I want to make it perfectly clear that no one is responsible for what actions I may take regarding my life. I quite made up my mind at Holloway to finish things, should Stoner . . . and it would only be a matter of time – and opportunity – and every day, night, and minute. is only prolonging the appalling agony of my mind. . . .

The next extract was from a letter written on 3rd June on the back of an envelope:

If I only thought it would help Stoner I would stay on, but it has been pointed out to me only too vividly that I cannot help him – and that is my death sentence.

The coroner then read the messages Alma had written in the meadow by the River Avon. A statement was taken from the matron of the Cleveland Nursing Home, and the proceedings abruptly ended. The coroner picked up a paper from the table in front of him and, reading from it, said:

My verdict is that Alma Victoria Rattenbury was found dead on 4th June in the River Avon in the Parish of Christchurch. The cause of death was haemorrhage from self-inflicted injuries by some sharp-pointed instrument held in her right hand. So I do say that the deceased, not being of sound mind, did kill herself.

At the conclusion of the inquest a burial order was handed by the coroner to the representative of a firm of London trustees who were executors under Mrs Rattenbury's will.

Mr Lewis Manning told the *News of the World* reporter that whatever people might say he was convinced there was much that was noble in Mrs Rattenbury's character. From the very beginning her one thought had been to protect the boy Stoner. When she realised he had been condemned to death, and that she could do nothing to save him, life meant nothing more to her. 'If ever I saw into a woman's soul I saw into Mrs Rattenbury's, and I am convinced, as I was from the start, that she had no hand in the murder.'

CHOSE DEATH BECAUSE SHE COULD NOT SAVE LOVER. THREE WOUNDS IN HEART. MRS RATTENBURY'S LAST LETTERS OF DESPAIR. 'MY DEATH SENTENCE.' 'APPALLING AGONY.' ANGUISHED CRY OF 'I CANNOT HELP STONER.'

Bournemouth, Saturday. – Within a few yards of the last resting-place of her murdered husband, Mrs Rattenbury was buried today in a grave lined with moss and pink rhododendrons. Although her friends had done their utmost to keep the time of the simple funeral a secret, hundreds of the general public were waiting in the cemetery at Wimborne Road an hour before the service was due to begin.

An attempt was made to put the time of the funeral forward an hour, but this was found to be impracticable as representatives of a London trust company, who are looking after Mrs Rattenbury's affairs, were unable to reach the cemetery until shortly before the time originally fixed.

The throngs of people increased in numbers and, ultimately, police were rushed to the scene to control a crowd of over 3,000, mainly women, who were trampling over the graves in their eagerness to reach vantage points.

A short private service, to which only the chief mourners were admitted, was held in the cemetery chapel, the doors of which were locked to keep out the great crowd which surrounded them and tried to enter.

Those following the coffin included Miss Irene Riggs, a stooping, sobbing figure, and a little niece. Mr Riggs is employed as a grave-digger at the cemetery.

Mr Keith Jones, a London solicitor, who is Mr Rattenbury's nephew, was also present. The service was conducted by the Rev W. Freeman of St Peter's Church, Bournemouth. Nine wreaths and many bunches of flowers, including blue irises, pink carnations, cornflowers, and roses, had been sent by the mourners. Only two of the wreaths bore inscriptions. One was from 'Kathleen and family', and the other read, 'With deepest sympathy from Auntie Florrie, British Columbia'. A lovely cushion wreath of pink carnations was among the anonymous tributes. One of Mrs Rattenbury's last wishes was for pink flowers. Not only were pink rhododendrons piled on the coffin, but her shroud and draperies were of pink. The coffin was of polished oak and bore a simple inscription – her name, and the words, 'Widow of Francis Mawson Rattenbury'.

Mingling with the tremendous crowd was a man securing signatures

RS. RATTENBURY'S PRISON SONG

Help Keep My Mind Sane"

"By some mistake . . . . I dreamed awhile,
"But now I wake, I wake.
"Yet dying, dream you kept my vision true."

The public conscience may have passed a harsh judgment upon Mrs. Rattenbury, but the tragic circumstances of her death have softened the condemnation.

The "Sunday Graphic" therefore publishes the words and music of the prison song of "Lozanne" (Mrs. Rattenbury). From prison she wrote that she "kept repeating the extraordinary words over and over again to help keep my mind sane."

The unhappy woman wrote this song from the fullness of her heart; the words convey her love for the tragic boy Stoner. She blames Fate for their meeting—"By some mistake you filled my empty days." But so long as she lived she knew that never could she put him out of her mind, try as she would.

This is one of the most poignant documents ever published. It appears in the SUNDAY GRAPHIC exclusively.

By some mistake my spirit held you, dear,
now I wake to agony and fear,
...ding hope and thought distressed and grey,
...outstretched hand I put your face away.

By some mistake you filled my empty days,
But now I wake to face the parting ways.
I see your smile, I hear the words you say,
With no reply I hush your voice away.

By some mistake, by some Divine mistake,
I dreamed awhile, but now I wake, I wake.
Yet, dying, dream you kept my vision true,
I seem to climb to heav'n in loving you.

The song written by Alma Rattenbury whilst in prison

(*Left*) A constable carries Alma's handbag in a parcel and her umbrella to the inquest
(*Right*) Mr William Mitchell and Mr Penry who gave evidence at Alma's inquest

Three Arches Bend, the scene of Alma's suicide

for the petition which is being organised for the reprieve of Stoner. Hundreds of women signed their names.

In contrast to the flower-strewn grave of his widow, Mr Rattenbury's grave near by bore a vase of daisies and antirrhinums. (*News of the World, 9th June 1935*)

Astonishing incidents took place today at Mrs Alma Victoria Rattenbury's grave in the Wimborne Road cemetery where unseemly scenes occurred at her funeral yesterday. Throughout the day there has been a constant procession of Whitsun holidaymakers. Crowds also flocked to the Villa Madeira, the Rattenbury's home in Manor Road, A few of the visitors to the graveside bore flowers and wreaths with sympathetic inscriptions. Others, however, openly proclaimed that they did not feel charitably towards Mrs Rattenbury, and argued with any one who differed from them.

A protest against this behaviour at the graveside was made to me today by Miss Irene Riggs, for four years the companion and close friend of Mrs Rattenbury. Miss Riggs also disclosed to me plans Mrs Rattenbury had made for the future before she took her own life. 'I would have stayed by her to the end, no matter what happened,' said Miss Riggs, 'I spent a long time with Mrs Rattenbury after the trial, and her distress was pitiful. In her more hopeful moments Mrs Rattenbury was determined to live the scandal down. We had planned to go somewhere far away until people had begun to forget. But she was always thinking of Stoner and of all the terrible things people were saying about herself. She was so sensitive to criticism. When I took her to the nursing home after the trial she told me that as long as she lived she would remember what the judge at the Old Bailey said about her. I think his words hurt her more than anything else. I did think, now that Mrs Rattenbury is dead, people who did not know her – how kind and generous and good to others she was – would be more charitable. Their evil tongues are pursuing her even in her grave. It was shocking to hear some of the things that were said at the funeral and again by the crowds at the graveside today. They say the most scandalous and untrue things about Mrs Rattenbury, and now about me as well. I simply cannot bear it any longer. I am going away where no one knows me so that I can get rest and peace. I am sorry now I was not able to stay with Mrs Rattenbury in the nursing home. Perhaps I might have been able to save her life, but I was too ill. My nerves have gone. I had no idea when Mrs Rattenbury told me what she would like to have done when she died that she had any thought of suicide in her mind. I am happy now to think I have been able to carry out her last wishes. I dressed her all in pink – the colour she loved – before she was buried and I saw that there were plenty of pink flowers at the funeral. She had a horror of white. I say in spite of everything and everybody that Mrs Rattenbury was a wonderful woman. No one knows what an agony it was for her to give the evidence she did at the trial. Few other women would have had such supreme courage.' (*Daily Express, 10th June 1935*)

QUARRELS OVER MRS RATTENBURY. AMAZING DAY AT HER GRAVESIDE. 'SHOCKING TO HEAR WHAT THEY SAID' –her companion. POLICE CALLED TO CONTROL CROWDS AT FUNERAL.

When the crowd had gone, Irene came back and left a message on the cushion wreath of pink carnations, 'All my love, darling – Irene'.

Thus another dark chapter closed in the biggest drama unfolded for many a long day. More astonishing, this story, than any of the kind where passion ends inevitably in tragedy. (*Daily Express, 6th June 1935*)

After the funeral the Villa Madeira was raided by souvenir hunters. At first their activities were more or less harmless, and mainly a matter of stealing plants or picking flowers from the garden, but on the night of 16th June some person or persons unknown forced an entry and stole a little wooden model house belonging to the boy John, private letters of Alma and her husband, two pipes, a signed photograph of Frank Titterton, and other small objects. On one occasion the owner of the villa, Mrs Price, found a party of four men, six women and numerous children sitting in the garden while an ice-cream vendor supplied them with refreshments. They said they had come specially from London to visit the scene of the crime. On another occasion she found two men and a woman actually in the house : the woman imagined that she saw splashes of blood on the ceiling and promptly fainted. Finally Mr and Mrs Price moved into the villa and announced that legal action would be taken against trespassers. What remained of the Rattenburys' effects was removed to the home of Irene's parents, and the books were sold to a dealer who got a good price for them – particularly those with blood on them.

Meanwhile the campaign for Stoner's reprieve had been gathering momentum. A committee of local residents had been formed to collect signatures – Stoner's father was present at the inaugural meeting – and to approve the grounds upon which an appeal should be based. They were agreed as follows :

Stoner is a boy.
He was subjected to undue influence.
He was a victim of drugs.

He was probably under their influence when the crime was committed.

He showed by his behaviour at the trial that he was capable of better things.

His execution, while strictly legal, benefits the community in no respect.

He might, if reprieved, turn out to be a respectable member of society, and be an asset to the state.

He was temporarily insane when the crime was committed, though not legally so.

He might have been the son of any one of us.

Petition forms were displayed at street corners in Bournemouth and Poole, in hotels and boarding-houses, shops and places of amusement. Motorists went round with petition posters on the windscreens and stopped in busy streets to canvass signatures. Many signatures were obtained from the crowds listening to the band in the gardens. The Mayor of Bournemouth was the first to sign the appeal. The MP for East Dorset, Mr G. R. Hall Caine, in whose constituency Stoner lived, wrote:

> I entirely agree that this is a matter in which the king's prerogative of mercy should be exercised, and I shall be pleased to do whatever is required of me in bringing the case officially to the notice of the Home Secretary.

Stoner's execution had been fixed for 18th June, but it was automatically postponed on 8th June when Casswell sent in notice of appeal: he had held it back as long as possible, hoping that he would be reprieved.

On the Home Secretary's desk there stood permanently a framed card listing the names of convicted murderers who had been sentenced to death and were awaiting execution: the date of each step of the procedure was recorded, and there was a blank column waiting for his decision as to reprieve or hanging. Sir John Simon, Home Secretary in the Baldwin Government, took his duties very seriously. He had had engraved on the frame of the card the following line from Juvenal: 'Nulla unquam de morte hominis cunctatio longa est.' (You can never hesitate too long before deciding that a man must die.)[2]

When the petition for Stoner's reprieve, bearing more than 320,000 signatures, was brought to him by Mr Hall Caine and Sir Henry Page Croft, MP for Bournemouth, he told them it would be improper for him to consider a reprieve while an appeal was pending.

On 10th June Casswell received from Stoner a letter giving, for the first time, his own account of what had happened at the Villa Madeira. In it he not only withdrew the suggestion that he had acted under the influence of cocaine, but he denied explicitly that he had had anything to do with the killing. He implied that Alma had killed her husband.

The appeal was heard on 24th June by Lord Chief Justice Hewart, Mr Justice Swift and Mr Justice Lawrence, while London sweltered in a heat wave and sandwichmen paraded outside carrying boards proclaiming, STONER MUST BE REPRIEVED. STOP THE LAW KILLING THIS BOY. END CAPITAL PUNISHMENT.

Stoner was brought in wearing the same grey suit he had worn at the trial. His weeks in prison in the expectation of death had taken their toll; his face looked strained and had lost its healthy tan. He appeared to take very little interest in what was being said but kept looking round the spacious courtroom, which was very full, as if to find someone he knew.

Mr Casswell repeated his arguments – that the two prisoners should have been tried separately since each had attempted to take the blame and that much of the evidence admitted against Stoner would have been inadmissible if he had been on trial by himself; that Mr Justice Humphreys had 'slurred over' the defence that Stoner was under cocaine on the day of the assault; and that Stoner had not gone into the witness-box because he did not wish to incriminate Mrs Rattenbury. He submitted that now her death had freed him from the necessity of silence, Stoner should be given an opportunity of putting his account before the three judges: therefore, under these special circumstances, he applied to call him as a witness:

The Lord Chief Justice has said, 'A separate trial should be granted always if there is the likelihood of miscarriage of justice . . . I submit that this case was one in which there was a likelihood of somebody being wrongfully convicted. If Mrs Rattenbury had been tried first there would no longer have been any need for chivalry by Stoner, nor would there have been any feeling by Stoner that anything he said would prejudice Mrs Rattenbury . . . There was very good reason why, even if he were innocent, he should not have to go into the witness-box in the court below. If he were innocent he would either have to commit perjury or give away the woman he loved.

The judges consulted together for two or three minutes. Then Stoner was required to stand, with a warder on each side of him, to hear judgement.

Lord Hewart, without even calling upon Croom-Johnson to reply to Casswell, said, 'There is no need to re-iterate the evidence in this sordid and squalid case. There is nothing at all in this appeal except that it arises out of a charge of murder. It is a mere waste of time.' To dispose of the argument that there should have been two separate trials, he said it was a well-established rule that the question of whether two or more prisoners should be tried separately or together was at the discretion of the judge at the trial. To dispose of Stoner's application to give evidence he quoted the decision of a former judge, Mr Justice Bray, to the effect that only in very special circumstances would the Court hear an appellant who had not given evidence at his trial. It appeared to him most cynical to desire that Stoner should now go into the witness-box to swear that which he was not prepared to swear while Mrs Rattenbury was alive :

The fact, if it be a fact, that a lad of good character has been corrupted by an abandoned woman old enough to be his mother raises no point of law, nor can it be employed as a ground of appeal in this Court.

The decision was, therefore, that the judge had been correct in trying the cases together, and that there were no grounds for suggesting he had ignored the defence of drug addiction which, in the opinion of the Court he had treated with almost excessive respect. The suggestion that Mr Justice Humphreys did not quite appreciate the evidence, Lord Hewart treated as merely frivolous – 'a man who is capable of believing that is capable of believing anything.' Stoner's appeal was dismissed.[3]

Stoner remained standing . . . while Lord Hewart delivered the judgement which occupied less than a quarter of an hour. The condemned lad, whose face was white when he rose from his seat, grew paler as Lord Hewart proceeded, and he did not appear to realise his appeal was over until a warder touched him on the shoulder. He appeared dazed. The warder took him by the arm as he turned to leave the dock. Stoner then disappeared behind the curtains which hide the door leading to the passage behind the court. (*Bournemouth Daily Echo, 24th June 1935*)

STONER DAZED BY HIS FATE. SCATHING JUDGEMENT BY LORD CHIEF JUSTICE. DEMONSTRATION OUTSIDE LAW COURTS.

On the following day Sir John Simon decided upon a reprieve and the death sentence was commuted to one of penal servitude for life. The Home Secretary is not called upon to give reasons for his decisions: he probably felt the tragedy had gone far enough, so perhaps Alma had helped Stoner by her death.

What are we to think of Stoner's belated plea of not guilty? This is the gist of his letter as given by Casswell:

He began by saying that I had been misled (presumably by the instructions which I had received as to the defence to be put forward) and that he had done so in order to help Mrs Rattenbury, with whom he was in love; that he would not have given the full story if she had lived.

'I will start off,' he wrote, 'by saying that I am perfectly innocent of the crime.' He referred to the fetching of the mallet for an innocent reason and said that on his return to the house he had put it in the coal-shed and then gone to bed. After about an hour he had woken up and judged that Mrs Rattenbury would then have gone to her room. He got up, and was looking over the bannisters, as Irene Riggs had said, as she emerged from her door. He was, in fact, looking to see whether the lights had been extinguished, because on occasions they had been left on. Then, having answered Irene's questions, he went into Mrs Rattenbury's room. He found her in bed, and she seemed to be 'terrified'. She said, 'Hear him!' At that moment he himself heard a loud groan. She got out of bed and ran downstairs. He immediately dressed, all but his coat and waistcoat, and followed her, because he realised that something was wrong. Downstairs in the drawing-room he found Mr Rattenbury in the armchair with severe head injuries. Then by accident he came across the mallet on the floor, and he kicked it behind the sofa. Apparently Irene had not noticed it and he didn't want her to see it; later on, when she had gone to telephone, he hid it in the garden. (The mallet was, in fact, discovered hidden behind some trellis work in the front garden.) He then described how they carried the old man into his bedroom and laid him on the bed, how he motored to the doctor's house and afterwards to the nursing-home. When he and the doctor arrived back at the house Mrs Rattenbury was under the influence of drink, the doctor gave her morphia and put her to bed, but as soon as he had gone she came down again. That time Stoner carried her upstairs and put her to bed. In the morning he made a statement to Inspector Carter. If he had known then that Mrs Rattenbury had made any statements he would have 'placed himself' in her position there and then. When she was arrested he was terribly upset. He did everything that he thought would provide sufficient evidence against himself: that is why he showed Miss Riggs where he had fetched the mallet from.[4]

Later on, Stoner gave Casswell a different explanation of why he had been leaning over the bannisters. It was, 'I was trying to see if the old man had gone to bed so that I could go into Alma's room as usual.'

At first glance this might seem a plausible enough story, but it disagrees totally with Alma's evidence, and with Irene Riggs's account of Alma's visit to her room during which she talked in a natural way that would have been impossible if she had just murdered her husband. The story of the mallet is unconvincing – the innocent reason for fetching it, given elsewhere, was to hammer in some small tent pegs which had been done on previous occasions with an axe, and the point had been made that the tent was not required in March. It seems highly improbable that Irene would not have noticed a large mallet lying on the drawing-room floor. Then, if Alma had committed the crime and was terrified, she would not have got out of bed and run downstairs: *he* would have run downstairs, without waiting to get dressed, when he realised something was wrong. But the main objection to the story is that nothing in Alma's character leads us to believe her capable of the crime. She had never displayed resentment towards her husband – except when she bit his arm, but that was a natural reflex action in response to a blow in the face. She seems, indeed, to have been remarkably devoid of resentment, whereas Stoner's violent jealousy had been apparent on a number of occasions. She had no reason to get rid of her husband, there was a friendly companionship between them, he was entirely complacent about her personal affairs, and he was the father of her son John whom she loved dearly: one of her greatest ambitions was for her children to be proud of her; and to brutally murder the father of one of them would hardly have furthered this end.

Casswell commented that he didn't know which of them to believe, Alma or Stoner, and he supposed the murder at the Villa Madeira would continue to be a mystery to the end. There does not appear to be any mystery about it. Stoner's final letter is exactly what he might have been expected to concoct when Alma was dead, and he cannot be blamed for this attempt to save his life.

One other piece of information has come to light. Mrs Kingham said in a recent interview that in Holloway Prison she asked Alma why Stoner had done it, and she replied he was angry because he had overheard Rattenbury telling her to make up to the man – presumably Mr Jenks at Bridport – who could arrange the finance for the projected block of flats, even expecting her to have an affair with him if necessary.[5] This perhaps explains O'Connor's hint that she had kept back something when giving evidence and his plea that this was not a reason to bring in a verdict against her – he may have feared the information had come out in the form of rumour and reached the ears of the jury, for it was a dangerous secret which, if divulged to the prosecution would have provided them with a motive applicable to both the accused, for the attack on Rattenbury. Lacking this information they had had to fall back on the general supposition, which the judge also adopted in his summing up, that lovers want to get rid of the husband. The motive that Stoner gave to Irene Riggs in response to her question – that he had seen the Rattenburys 'living together' that Sunday afternoon – is not less unsatisfactory, for he had complained to Alma that the door was closed, so he couldn't have seen anything, and there would have been no 'living together' with a six-year-old boy playing about the room.

Obviously Alma and Rattenbury had been alone together frequently with Stoner's knowledge, and he had never objected. There must have been some very strong reason for his anger on this occasion. It is hardly possible to doubt that Mrs Kingham gave a true account of what Alma told her : she knew nothing of Rattenbury and had no reason to invent anything. If Stoner believed, perhaps mistakenly from scraps of conversation imperfectly overheard, that Rattenbury intended to exploit Alma's well-known magnetic effect on men for commercial reasons, we can understand and sympathise with the desperate action he took to prevent her from going to Bridport. At last, forty-five years after the trial and Alma's death, we have a motive in which we can believe. We can also understand why Mrs Kingham thought that if O'Connor and Casswell instead of working against each other had put up a combined defence, both lovers might have been acquitted.

The trial of Alma Rattenbury shows the British legal system at its best and at its worst. At its best because her trial was admirably fair, and at its worst because the court was turned into a court of morals which pronounced a pitiless condemnation of a woman who was innocent of the crime for which she had been arrested but who had offended against the conventions existing at that time in England.

According to her staunch defender, Miss Tennyson Jesse, it was not only the law officers who cast a stone :

Most people in England [she wrote], especially women, seem easily able to feel superior to Mrs Rattenbury. She had had 'adulterous intercourse'; she had taken for her lover a boy young enough to be her son; and the boy was a servant. That out of this unpromising material she had created something that to her was beautiful and made her happy, was unforgivable to the people of England. Her life had been given back to her, but the whole world was too small a place, too bare of any sheltering rock, for her to find a refuge.

Her conclusion was that Alma had been so vilified and turned into a figure of shame that she knew it would be better for her children, whom she adored, if she died than if she lived : therefore, being a woman of immense courage – she died.

Postscript

The orphaned children became wards of the court. Christopher at first lived with his aunt, Mrs Kingham, in a Norfolk rectory, then, about a year later he was adopted by Alma's mother who, he told us, had been mellowed by two religious conversions. He joined her in Vancouver.

Keith Miller Jones assumed responsibility for John Rattenbury. When the Second World War loomed he was sent for safety to Alma's mother also. Meanwhile Christopher headed back to England where he joined the US Army (he had dual nationality). After the war he was discharged in the US. He remained there, married, and made a career for himself as a commercial artist. He said his parents' tragedy had a deep effect on him, but by the age of thirty or so he had got over it.

John followed in his father's footsteps: he has become a successful architect practising in the U.S.A. He too has come to terms with the tragedy, and both sons think of their parents with affection and respect.

Stoner served only seven years of his sentence. Then, in 1942 at the age of twenty-six, being a model prisoner, he was released, joined the forces and took part in the Normandy Landings. He survived the war, married, and settled down as a responsible citizen.

Alma's talented and eccentric second husband, Thomas Compton Pakenham, began to make a name for himself soon after she had left him. In 1929 he became music correspondent for the *New York Times* and was recognised as an authority on Wagner. He also published articles on the British Empire and on India. He co-authored a book called *Dreamers of Empire*. In 1933 he helped to found the magazine *Newsweek*. The *New York Times,* in his obituary, gives an interesting account of his later career: after World War II he returned to China and became a personal friend of Chiang Kai-Shek and his wife; he wanted to make a first-hand study of the charges of corruption levelled against Chiang's government. From China he went to Macao, and from there to Japan where he took charge of *Newsweek's* Pacific Bureau. In

234

Japan he became a very influential figure and a personal friend of the Emperor Hirohito and his brother, Prince Takamatsu. There was some trouble in 1948 – General Douglas MacArthur banned him from Japan because he had criticised the conduct of the occupation forces: this action caused great annoyance in Washington, and Pakenham was considered to be so important that MacArthur was persuaded to change his mind.

In 1950 he brought off his greatest coup. It is reported that in the secret negotiations for the 1951 Japanese Peace Treaty, it was Pakenham who arranged the rendezvous between John Foster Dulles and the future Prime Ministers Ichiro Hatojama and Tanzan Ishibashi. Both had been removed from public life by the occupation forces and it would have been highly embarrassing for both the Americans and the Japanese had the meetings been made public.

Pakenham taught the Prime Minister, Nobusuke Kishi, English, and he was on terms of close friendship with every succeeding prime minister of Japan from the end of the war to his death in 1957. He was married four times. After his divorce from Alma he married Sarah Furnam of South Carolina by whom he had twins, a boy and a girl. In 1954 he married the Japanese concert singer, Masea Inaha.

Rattenbury estimated that he lost 500,000 dollars through Government action. He had found it difficult to attract settlers to his land because of the war; and then in 1917 the Land Settlement Board was set up to make purchase easier for ex-servicemen: it was empowered to impose special taxes on unused lands if improvements were not carried out by a certain date. Rattenbury had either to sell at a loss or pay a heavy tax – from 1920 onwards his tax bill was 90,000 dollars a year. He therefore challenged the validity of the Land Settlement Act in general and the land tax specifically, maintaining that it was an indirect tax and therefore the provincial government had no power to impose it. The case went ultimately to the Supreme Court of Canada where the final decision, in November 1928, was that the land tax was within the competence of the provincial legislature and, moreover, that the Land Settlement Board could not be sued as it was a department of government. The Government might have done better to let Rattenbury, and others like him, get on with the job. They made a terrible mess of their scheme: only one third of the ex-servicemen who took advantage of it stayed on the land, and millions of dollars were lost in money advanced and not repaid.

In 1937, two years after his death, heavy legal costs and the expenses incurred through the children being wards of chancery had reduced his estate to about 28,000 dollars, to which must be added his house in Oak Bay, valued at 17,500 dollars. He left his money equally to Alma's two children, Christopher Pakenham and his own son, John Rattenbury. His two grown-up children contested the will and were awarded 125 dollars a month and 25 dollars a month respectively for one year.

Most of Rattenbury's buildings in Victoria have survived intact, and his court house in Vancouver is still an important landmark in the city centre: it is being converted into an art gallery. The fine private houses are still there, bought and sold now for very high prices: his own house, *Iechinihl,* has become a school. The interior, but not the exterior, of the Canadian Pacific Railway Terminal has been changed and now houses the Royal London Wax Museum. Renovation of the Crystal Gardens Amusement Centre is almost complete. The Empress Hotel and the Parliament Buildings have been modified, but not spoilt, and stand there today, Victoria's pride and joy, the most permanent memorial to his talent.

A detailed study of Rattenbury's career based on the newly discovered correspondence is being prepared by Professor Barrett.

Source Notes

Chapter Two

1. *Sunday Dispatch* 9th June 1935.
2. Raymond Massey, *When I was Young* Page 21 Robson Books 1977.
3. Press notices are from a printed collection in possession of the family.
4. Information provided by Caledon Dolling's brother Harry. For the Dolling family see Joseph Clayton, *Father Dolling, a Memoir*. London 1902, and Charles Osborne *The Life of Father Dolling*. London 1903.
5. *The Times* 31st August 1916 and the *Sunday Dispatch* 9th June 1935.
6. On the outbreak of the war The Scottish Women's Hospital Organisation, founded by Dr Elsi Inglis, offered two fully equipped hospitals to the War Office. They were refused because they were staffed entirely by women, including the doctors and surgeons. The French Government gratefully accepted them and they became part of the French Red Cross. They had 600 beds at Royaumont and 600 at Villers Cotterets (until it was overrun by the Germans in June 1918). By the end of the war they had provided twelve hospitals – in France, Belgium, Serbia, Russia, Corsica and Salonika. They won international acclaim for their devoted service. The staff, when not on duty, wore uniforms of hodden grey with Gordon tartan hatbands. See E. S. MacLaren, *A History of the Scottish Women's Hospitals*, London 1919, and Margot Laurence *Shadow of Swords*, London 1971.
7. Family correspondence.
8. Information provided by Christopher Pakenham, and see the Vancouver *News Herald* 20th April 1935.
9. This photograph is reproduced in the illustration facing page 32.
10. Information provided by Harry Dolling.

11. Information provided by Simona Pakenham, and see her *Pigtails and Pernod* MacMillan 1961.

12. *New York Times* 18th August 1957 and *Newsweek* 26th August 1957.

Chapter Three

1. Information supplied by Mrs K. Bentley Beauman, and see *The Original Visitation of Devon in 1620*, and *The History of Okehampton*, published in 1836.

2. *The Journal of the Royal Architectural Insitute of Canada*, April 1958, and *British Columbia from the Earliest Times to the Present*, Vol. III 1914. Derek Pethick, *Men of British Columbia*, 1975.

3. W. P. Morrell, *The Gold Rushes*, Adam and Charles Black 1940.

4. *Henderson's Gazetteer*, 1900.

5. A. C. Retallack. White Pass and Yukon Company representative.

6. Rattenbury family correspondence.

7. Some idea of the prejudice of the local inhabitants against Alma may be gleaned from Terry Reksten's *Rattenbury*, Sono Nis Press Victoria BC 1978, and see the *Sunday Dispatch*, 9th June 1935.

Chapter Four

1. 'Night Brings Me You'. Words by Edward Lockton, Music by Lozanne. By permission of EMI Publishing Ltd.

2. Letter communicated by Mrs Keith Jones.

3. *Daily Express* 1st June 1935.

4. 'Dark-Haired Marie'. Words by Edward Lockton, Music by Lozanne. By permission of EMI Publishing Ltd.

5. Eliot Crawshay-Williams, *Stay of Execution*. Jarrolds, London 1933.

Chapter Five

1. See Miss Tennyson Jesse's introduction to *The Trial of Alma Victoria Rattenbury and George Percy Stoner*. Notable British Trials series. William Hodge & Co. Ltd., Glasgow.

2. The *Daily Express* 1st June 1935.

3. 'By Some Mistake'. Words and Music by Lozanne.

4. Interview with Mrs Kingham, 26th Sept. 1978.

5. J. D. Casswell, QC *A Lance for Liberty*. Pages 99-118. George G. Harrap & Co. Ltd., 1961.

Chapter Six
1. Stanley Jackson, The Life and Cases of Mr Justice Humphries, 154N. Odhams Press Ltd., London.
2. Casswell page 109.
3. Casswell page 111.

Chapter Seven
1. Kingham interview.

Chapter Eight
1. Tennyson Jesse's introduction in *Notable British Trials* series.
2. Raymond Massey, *When I was Young* page 22, and correspondence.
3. Casswell, page 111.
4. Casswell, page 113.

Chapter Nine
1. Casswell, page 114.

Chapter Eleven
1. Travers Humphreys, *Criminal Days*, page 133. Hodder and Stoughton, 1946, by courtesy of Curtis Brown Ltd.
2. Kingham interview.
3. Tennyson Jesse's introduction in *Notable British Triflls* series.

Chapter Thirteen
1. For the judge's opinion of the verdict, see Travers Humphreys, *A Book of Trials*, pages 153-5. Heinemann 1953.

Chapter Fourteen
1. Interview with Keith Miller Jones, 6th June 1978.
2. Sir John Simon, *Retrospect*, pages 208-9, Hutchinson 1952.
3. Casswell, page 116.
4. Robert Jackson, *The Chief*, pages 284-5, and the *Bournemouth Daily Echo*, 24th June 1935.
5. Interview with Mrs Kingham, 26th September 1978.

Postscript
1. The *New York Times*, 18th August 1957. *Newsweek*, 26th August 1957.
2. The *Vancouver Provincial*, 21st July 1936.

Index